Cornwall
with Kids

William Gray

For Sally, Joseph and Eleanor
All photos by the author

It's a shore thing – surf at Sennen Cove and (previous page) cliff-top vigil at Polperro.

Cornwall is special. It gets hold of you like a big sandy hug, and won't let go. If you went there on holiday as a child, you'll be wanting to take your own children there. Cornwall stays with you for life. It epitomizes the childhood holiday idyll: tradition spiced with adventure; days on the beach that become days of discovery.

North Cornwall offers a frothy cocktail of Atlantic breakers, surf schools and beach cafés, sprinkled with legends of King Arthur at Tintagel Castle. You can sea kayak from rocky coves, hike to cliff-top lookouts or cycle the Camel Trail from Padstow to Bodmin – gateway to a wonderfully wild and woody side of Cornwall.

By contrast, South Cornwall is for messing about in boats and delving in to gardens. The sheltered estuaries of the Fal and Fowey are ideal for launching a canoe; Falmouth has boat trips galore and the shipshape National Maritime Museum, while St Austell is the gateway to leafy gems like the Eden Project and Heligan Gardens.

Undecided? Then go for West Cornwall where you'll find the best of both worlds – surf at Whitesand Bay, smugglers' coves on the Lizard Peninsula, fine art and fine food at St Ives, boat trips on the Helford River, plus the big attractions of Land's End and St Michael's Mount.

Award-winning writer and photographer **William Gray** is the author of Footprint's *Travel with Kids*, voted Guidebook of the Year 2008 by the British Guild of Travel Writers, as well as *Europe with Kids* and *Britain with Kids*.

Galloping through the gunnera, Trebah Gardens.

About the book

Just like an RNLI beach lifeguard *Cornwall with Kids* is good looking and useful to have around. It will happily grace a coffee table for winter evening perusal, just as it can slip into a coat pocket or the glovebox of your car for on-the-spot holiday reference (all entries for attractions, accommodation and places to eat have postcodes to help you find your way by Sat Nav). On this page you'll find background information on getting the most out of the book, plus some important safety information.

Beach safety

The 'FLAGS' code by the RNLI (rnli. org.uk/beachlifeguards) is a handy checklist for staying safe at the beach:
F Find the red and yellow flags and swim between them.
L Look at the safety signs.
A Ask a lifeguard for advice.
G Get a friend to swim with you.
S Stick your hand in the air and shout for help if you get into difficulty. See also page 185.

Family rates

Unless otherwise specified, family rates quoted in *Cornwall with Kids* are for two adults and two children. If you have more than two children it's always worth checking if there are special deals for larger families. Similarly, some attractions have rates specifically for single-parent families.

Members' perks

Throughout *Cornwall with Kids*, look out for nature reserves, gardens and historical sites that are free to members of English Heritage, the National Trust or the Royal Society for the Protection of Birds (RSPB). Family membership of these charities represents excellent value for money when travelling in Cornwall, and also helps to support conservation work. **English Heritage** T0870-333 1182, english-heritage.org.uk. Annual adult membership costs £43, including up to six children (under 19). **The National Trust** T0844-800 1895, nationaltrust.org.uk. Annual family membership is £82 (two adults and their children under 18, free for under fives), while a direct debit rate of £61.50 is available for the first year's membership. For single-parent families, membership costs £62 or £46.50 by direct debit. **The RSPB** T01767-693680, rspb. org.uk. For family membership (two adults and all children under 19) you can choose how much to give, although £5 per month is suggested.

Blue Flag awards

Please note that these awards (given to beaches with outstanding water quality) are given for one season only and are subject to change. For details of current Blue Flag beaches, visit blueflag.org.uk.

Tourist Boards

The official website of the Cornwall Tourist Board can be found at visitcornwall.com. Details for local tourist boards are given in the Grown-ups' section, see page 183. You can also find information about visiting Cornwall at enjoyengland.com, while a good starting point for overseas visitors is visitbritain.co.uk.

Symbol Key

Beaches

🌊 Blue flag award
🍴 Café/pub/restaurant
🏖 Beach shop
🏖 Deckchairs
⛱ Beach huts
🏄 Water sports
🎡 Amusement arcade
➕ Lifeguards (summer)
🚻 Toilets nearby
🅿 Car park nearby
❗ Warning!

Campsites

🅰 Tents
🚐 Caravans
🏪 Shop
🎠 Playground
🌳 Picnic area
♿ Disabled facilities
🐕 Dogs welcome
🏔 Walk to beach
⚡ Electric hook-up
🚾 Family bathroom
👶 Baby care area
🚲 Bike hire
🥤 Café/takeaway van
🔥 Campfires permitted

It is up to parents to assess whether the information given in *Cornwall with Kids* is suitable or appropriate for their children. While the author and publisher have made every effort to ensure accuracy with subjects such as activities, places to stay and food, they cannot be held responsible for any loss, injury or illness resulting from advice or information given in this book.

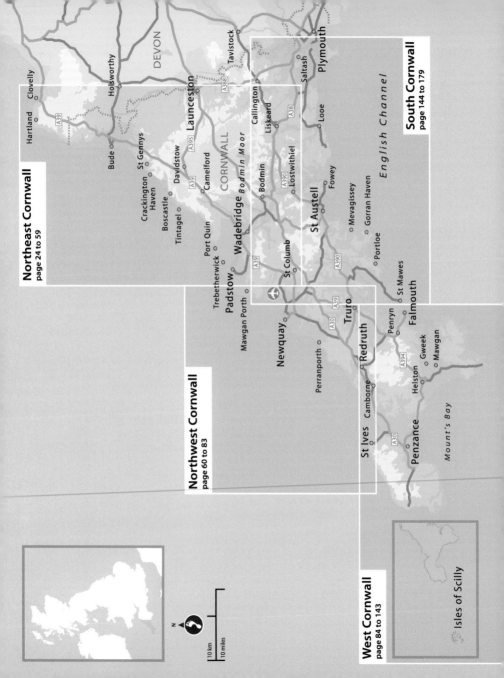

Northeast Cornwall
page 24 to 59

Northwest Cornwall
page 60 to 83

West Cornwall
page 84 to 143

South Cornwall
page 144 to 179

DEVON

CORNWALL

Bodmin Moor

English Channel

Mount's Bay

Isles of Scilly

Hartland
Clovelly
Bude
Holsworthy
A39
St Gennys
Crackington Haven
Boscastle
Tintagel
Davidstow
Camelford
Launceston
A395
A39
A388
Tavistock
Saltash
Plymouth
Callington
Liskeard
A38
Looe
Port Quin
Trebetherwick
Padstow
Wadebridge
Camelford
Bodmin
A390
Lostwithiel
Fowey
St Columb
A39
Mawgan Porth
Newquay
A30
A39
Truro
A390
St Austell
Mevagissey
Gorran Haven
Portloe
St Mawes
Penryn
Falmouth
Perranporth
Redruth
A394
Gweek
Mawgan
Camborne
Helston
St Ives
A30
Penzance

N

10 km
10 miles

Contents

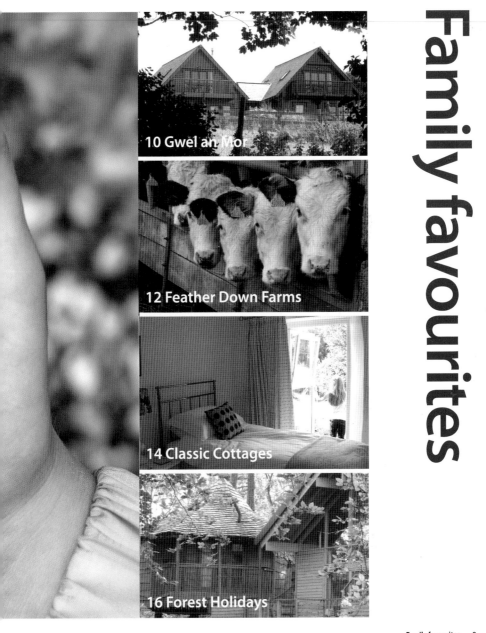

10 Gwel an Mor

12 Feather Down Farms

14 Classic Cottages

16 Forest Holidays

Family favourites

Gwel an Mor

Cornish for 'view of the sea', Gwel an Mor certainly gets a good eyeful of the Atlantic, its 60 timber lodges occupying a grandstand position above Portreath on the north coast. Fling open the doors to your balcony and you can gaze dreamily at the serene blue horizon and hear the swish of surf.

Some say location is everything, but that's not how they see it at Gwel an Mor. Sea views are almost a happy coincidence at this luxurious resort where quality accommodation, great facilities and friendly, helpful staff have set it on course to becoming one of Cornwall's holiday hotspots.

Granted, the two- or three-bedroom lodges have been designed upside down (living rooms upstairs to make the most of those views), but don't overlook the hot tub on the deck, the cosy wood-burning stove or flat-screen television.

It's stylish rather than rustic – a theme that continues through the landscaped grounds (where kids will quickly find the putting green and adventure play area), the Clubhouse with its swimming pool and the Wellbeing Spa.

When not self-catering, you can dine at the superb Terrace Restaurant which uses ingredients that are almost exclusively Cornish. Local knowledge also shines through at Gwel an Mor's reception where staff provide a tailormade booking service for whatever activities take your fancy – from surfing to horse riding.

If there's just one thing you do while staying here, however, make sure it's a walking safari with Gary Zammit, the wildlife ranger at Gwel an Mor's adjacent Feadon Farm. Cornwall's Dr Doolittle, he'll have your kids' eyes on stalks as he reveals slow worms, slugs and sparrowhawks in the woods and meadows below Gwel an Mor. You'll go pond dipping, rock-pooling, badger watching and – best of all – get to meet Gary's rescued foxes and fly his barn owl, Sly, and Harris hawk, Harry.

Portreath, TR16 4PE, T01209-842354, gwelanmor.com.
Year round. Lowenna Lodge £399-1439/wk,
Tregea Lodge £499-1779/wk, VIP lodges £559-2499/wk.

Feather Down Farms

Safari chic with wellies on, Feather Down Farm tents lead the herd when it comes to luxury camping. Lift the flap on these canvas creations and you step into a snug den complete with wood stove, oil lanterns, three bedrooms (including a secret cubbyhole for kids) and everything you need for a relaxing farmstay – including a flush toilet and kitchen sink.

A working dairy farm near Penzance, Boswarthen is the only Feather Down Farm location in Cornwall – its six tents enjoying glorious views towards Mount's Bay. Like all Feather Down Farms, there's an outdoor clay oven for baking potatoes or pizzas, and an honesty shop stocked with local produce. Boswarthen Farm also has a rustic, outdoor hot tub, a farm trail, maize maze and the option of renting a private chicken coop.

A typical day starts with children hurrying outside in pyjamas and wellies to collect chicken eggs, while you grind fresh coffee beans and clunk the kettle on top of the stove. Breakfast is always late – it will take the kids at least an hour to check on the pygmy goats, Freddie and Tiny Tim, and to help Farmer Nicholls feed the calves. With your car parked out of sight (and mind) in the farmyard, and with no electricity to bring radio, television or computer games crashing into your consciousness, time at Boswarthen Farm ebbs and flows to a calming, rural rhythm.

Later in the day, you might plan a picnic or cycle ride, play hide and seek, walk the goats, watch swallows flitting to and from their nests in an old barn or set off on a pilgrimage to St Michael's Mount or the Tate Gallery in St Ives. Some of Cornwall's most beautiful beaches, like Porthcurno and Whitesand Bay, are also nearby.

At meal times, cooking becomes a family affair and a chance to indulge in the often-neglected pleasures of a good old chat, while bedtime stories are infused with the magical glow of candlelight.

T 01420-80804, featherdown.co.uk. Apr-Nov. £395-825/wk, £275-575/weekend, £195-525/midweek (Mon-Fri).

Classic Cottages

They're not the only cottage agents in Cornwall, but Classic have a rare knack of finding those 'X-Factor' properties with all the star qualities that discerning families look for – great location, beautifully furnished, child-friendly inside and out, plus that extra little touch – a sunny terrace or a path to the beach perhaps – that ensures everyone gives it an emphatic 'yes'. In short, they are the kind of cottages you hate to leave.

Classic Cottages have specialized in the West Country holiday cottage business for over 30 years, so they've had time to build an impressive portfolio of properties (over 530 in Cornwall alone). Take your pick from stone cottages in Mousehole and Coverack, waterside apartments in Falmouth and Newquay, houses overlooking St Ives Bay and the Fowey Estuary, character barns tucked away in the Cornish countryside and farms with sweeping views of Bodmin Moor.

The collection shown here is a mere taster. Occupying the ground floor of an immaculate barn conversion near St Just, two-bedroom Lower Wesley's Barn (photos 1 and 2, £315-708/wk) has an open-plan living room, kitchen and dining area that opens onto a sun-drenched patio (with table tennis tucked away in an outbuilding).

In Sennen Cove, the New-England-style Atlantic House (photo 3, £546-1449/wk, see also page 106) accommodates seven and has a bespoke kitchen and raised garden with views across the sea towards Cape Cornwall.

Sleeping six, Penally Cottage (main photo and photo 4, £441-1113/wk, see also page 44) overlooks Boscastle Harbour and is the perfect retreat for a smuggler's cove-style holiday.

Combining coast and country, Trewane Barn (photos 5 and 6, £462-1176/wk) is hidden away in a wooded valley just three miles from Port Isaac. With room for five, it has a gorgeous walled garden.

Leslie House, Lady St, Helston, TR13 8NA, T01326-555555, classic.co.uk. Year round. Mon-Fri 0900-2000, Sat 0930-1700, Sun 1100-1600.

Forest Holidays

A partnership between the Forestry Commisson and the Camping & Caravanning Club, you'd expect Forest Holidays to know a thing or two about running campsites in beautiful woodland locations. But its select group of cabin sites, including Deer Park, near Liskeard, might come as a surprise.

Branching out into cabin holidays has come as easily to Forest Holidays as falling off a log. Not only has it infused this secluded patch of Cornish forest with home comforts, but it has done so in such a way as to preserve the elemental thrill of sleeping deep in the woods. You'll hear tawny owls hooting – but from the comfort of your deck, a wood stove glowing in the lounge behind you. And chances are, your best sightings of woodpeckers will be in the treetops directly above your open-air hot tub.

Each cabin is carefully sited so that you feel an intimate part of the woodland – and many have the added bonus of overlooking a lake (you can almost feed the ducks without leaving your bed). Double-storey windows flood open-plan living areas with tree-dappled sunlight. Kitchens come with all the mod cons; most cabins have barbecues, flatscreen TVs and DVD players, while a few have an en-suite treehouse attached by an adventurer's bridge. You'll even find a Wii games console in Golden Oak cabins, but don't fret – children get ample opportunity to live in the real world thanks to ranger-led activities that include bat watching and forest survival skills. You can book them at the Forest Retreat, an information hub at the heart of each site, where you can also buy local food and arrange activities such as mountain biking, fishing, sailing and pony trekking. Don't miss the duck race – a great way to meet the lively, fun staff at Deer Park before racing yellow bath ducks along a stream through the woods.

T0845-130 8223, forestholidays.co.uk. Year round. Cabins include Evergreen (sleeping 4-6) £225-913/wk, Silver Birch (sleeping 4) £345-1238, Golden Oak (sleeping 6) £474-1699 or sleeping 8 with attached treehouse £672-2407. Midweek and weekend breaks from £127.

Dig for glory
Make the perfect sandcastle

1 Location is crucial. Site your castle near a stream so it's easy to divert water into the moat. Also, make sure the sand is neither too dry nor too sticky.

2 A moat without a boat is no fun at all. Create a harbour on one side of your castle, using a piece of driftwood as a gate. Periodic dredging will be required.

3 Using a spade, carve steps and terraces on the flanks of the castle. Add pebbles and shells for windows and seagull feathers for medieval banners.

4 Don't overlook your outer defences. At least one tide-restraining wall will be required outside your moat. This should feature crenellations or 'dribble sand' towers.

5 Main access should always be via a bridge with pebble parapets (or a drawbridge using flat driftwood). Cobbles make ideal stepping stones across the moat.

6 Special features can include jetties to outlying towers and lighthouses, or tunnels scooped by hand through sturdy bastions of the main castle.

Beach games

Beach bowling Using a bucket and spade, make 10 sand skittles arranged in a triangle and take turns in bowling a ball at them.

Frisbee golf You'll need a big sandy beach at low tide for this one. Mark out as large a circle as you dare and dig a shallow, frisbee-sized hole in the middle of it. Throw the frisbee from the circle and see how many 'shots' you take to get it in the hole. Move around the circle until you've completed nine holes, taking a few steps inside or outside the circle to lower or raise the par for each hole.

Rapid runners Many Cornish beaches have a shallow stream flowing across them at low tide. Buy model boats (or build your own from picnic containers or strandline debris) and race them through the rapids. First one to reach the sea wins.

Boredom busters

Car bingo Give players a sheet of paper and ask them to write down 25 different numbers between one and 99. The person in the front passenger seat calls out the last one or two digits from the licence plates of passing cars. The winner is the first to cross off all their numbers and shout "Bingo!"

Licence to thrill Make up phrases based on the letters of licence plates. For example, 234 IFS 00 could be 'Ice-cream for Sally', 'Ian fancies Susan' or 'I feel sick!'

Buzz words Pick a word, then turn on the radio or play a story CD and try to be the first to shout "buzz" when the word is mentioned.

Good read
10 great children's books set in Cornwall

Early years

Cat on the Hill
by *Michael Foreman* (Andersen Press)
A simple, but poetic, season-by-season account of the life of a stray cat in St Ives.

Dolphin Boy
by *Michael Morpurgo* (Andersen Press)
A close bond between a boy and a dolphin brings life and energy back to a Cornish village.

The Mousehole Cat
by *Antonia Barber* (Walker Books)
The classic tale of fisherman Tom and his faithful cat Mowzer. Take a copy with you to the fishing village of Mousehole, near Penzance, where the adventure is set. See page 90.

The Sand Horse
by *Ann Turnbull* (Andersen Press)
One windy summer day, an artist makes a beautiful sand sculpture of a horse at St Ives. It's much admired by everyone on the beach, but as they leave at the end of the day, the Sand Horse hears the surf calling to him and he longs to join the white horses.

The Seashore
(Usborne Spotters Guides)
Essential reference book for all rock-pool detectives (of any age) with colour illustrations and short descriptions of 200 seashore species.

Shanti The Wandering Dog of Sennen and the Land's End
by *Janeta Hevizi* (Cornish Cove Publishing)
A free-spirited dog called Shanti goes walkabout around Sennen, exploring the village, the beach and the cliffs around Land's End. Follow Shanti's trail if you're planning to visit Sennen yourself.

Ages 6-12

The Wreck of the Zanzibar
by *Michael Morpurgo* (Egmont books)
It is 1907 in the Scilly Isles and a time of extreme hardship. Laura Perryman's diary tells of a violent storm and the unexpected harvest that it brings. A tale of high emotion and dramatic events in which Laura traces her family's history from present to past and back again.

The True Story of Bilbo the Surf Lifeguard Dog
by *Janeta Hevizi and Steve Jmo* (Cornish Cove Publishing)
Get to know adorable Bilbo, a 14-stone chocolate Newfoundland, who became the world's first qualified surf lifeguard dog at Sennen Cove.

Teens

Rebecca
by *Daphne du Maurier* (Virago)
A classic tale of love, jealousy and intrigue, set in the fictional stately home of Manderley on the south Cornish coast.

How to be a surfer
by *C Nelson, D Taylor & Z Sandler* (Puffin)
Step-by-step guide to catching your first wave and the surfing bug!

Super surfer

You can't go to Cornwall and not try surfing – even if it's just mucking about with a bodyboard. A proper surf lesson, though, is not only fantastic fun, but you'll gain a real sense of achievement standing up and riding waves like a proper little dude (even if it is only for a few seconds before you wipe out!). Instructors will also teach you about the beach flag system, how to avoid dangerous situations and even how to fall off safely.

10 more things you've got to try on holiday

Fly a kite Low tide on a big sandy beach is best.
Catch a crab Try your luck off the harbour wall.
Take a boat trip Fish for mackerel or search for seals.
Look for treasure Scour the strandline for mermaids' purses, cuttlefish bones, shells and feathers.
Go rock-pooling Compulsory! See the guide opposite.
Become an ice cream expert There are lots of local ones to try, like Roskilly's, Kelly's and Callestick.
Plan a picnic Stock up on local goodies from a farm shop and set off for the sand dunes.
Go snurfkling Paddle a surf board with a mask and snorkel and see what lies beneath.
Hold back the tide Build a massive sandy wall and see how long it takes the sea to knock it down.
Visit a lifeboat station Check out the cool gear and don't forget to drop some coins in the donation box.

Snazzy snorkeller

Follow these steps to happy, safe and leak-proof snorkelling: Get gear that fits properly (hold the mask up to your face and breathe in through your nose – it should stick to your face) • Rub some spit on the inside of the glass to stop it misting over • Start in calm, shallow water and make sure you're happy with everything before swimming out of your depth • If water seeps into your mask, tread water and pull the lower edge of the mask away from your face to allow it to drain out • Check every few minutes to make sure you haven't drifted too far from shore • Be sun smart – wear a wetsuit and lots of sunblock.

Cool kayaker

Sit-on kayaks are all the rage in Cornwall. They're easy to paddle and great fun for messing about in calm, shallow seas or exploring sheltered estuaries on the south coast. You can hire them at several locations or, better still, join a guided kayaking trip. Remember to keep safe by always wearing a lifejacket (and helmet if it's choppy) and staying close to shore.

Seaside safari

Join an organized rock-pool ramble or set off on your own, equipped with a good guidebook, such as *Seashore* (Dorling Kindersley, 2008). Remember to check tide times to ensure that you do not become trapped by the rising tide. Wear shoes with good grip, take care to disturb animals and plants as little as possible – particularly when looking under rocks – and leave creatures where you find them. Find out more about the Seashore Code from the Marine Conservation Society (mcsuk.org).

Common blenny or shanny.

Barnacle rock pool/harbour

Beadlet anemone rocky shore/rock pool

Blue-rayed limpet rock pool

Brown shrimp sandy shore/rock pool

Common cockle sandy shore

Common blenny or shanny rock pool

Common goby sandy shore/rock pool

Common limpet rock pool/harbour

Common mussel rock pool/harbour

Common periwinkle rock pool

Common ragworm sandy shore

Common starfish rocky shore

Dog whelk rock pool

Flat periwinkle rock pool

Green sea urchin rock pool

Hermit crab rock pool

Painted top shell rock pool

Razor shell sandy shore

Rock goby rock pool

Shore crab rock pool/harbour

Snakelocks anemone rock pool

Velvet swimming crab rock pool/harbour

Common limpet.

Flat periwinkle.

Dog whelk.

Painted top shell.

Common periwinkle.

Common mussel.

Think twice before bringing shells home with you – they may look empty, but are often home to other animals. This old whelk shell, for example, is not only covered in barnacles, but is also inhabited by a large hermit crab. Why not make a digital collection of shells using the close-up mode found on many digital compact cameras.

Contents

Silver surfing – Trebarwith
Strand near Tintagel.

North Cornwall

Main photo: On the trail of King Arthur – doorway to Tintagel Castle. Opposite from top: The net result at Port Quin, a coasteering cliffhanger and the Rock–Padstow ferry.

Northeast Cornwall

From tales of King Arthur and the Beast of Bodmin to Bude's surf beaches and Stein's fish & chips, northeast Cornwall is the stuff of legends. You won't find mightier sea cliffs anywhere in the county, while A-list attractions like Tintagel, Boscastle and the Camel Trail are not to be missed.

Heading south from the Devon border on the A39 Atlantic Highway, you'll barely last four miles before **Bude** lures you to the coast. You can almost hear the rattle of spades on buckets as you approach Summerleaze, Bude's big family beach with its seawater pool and miles of sand.

Instead of rejoining the Atlantic Highway, continue south past the surf beach at **Widemouth Bay**, following coastal lanes to **Crackington Haven** – a rollercoaster ride along the rugged backs of Cornwall's highest sea cliffs (reaching 224 m). You won't find another decent sandy beach until **Trebarwith**, south of Tintagel. Instead there are some spectacular, if thigh-twanging, clifftop walks, and two of Cornwall's most enduring and engaging highlights – the definitive smugglers' hideout that is **Boscastle** (lovingly restored after the floods of 2004) and the mysterious ruins of **Tintagel Castle**, legendary birthplace of King Arthur. Both will have your kids wide-eyed with wonder, whether they're creeping into Merlin's Cave or clambering above Boscastle's axe-stroke harbour.

Another glorious stretch of coast, Tintagel Head to Pentire Point extends south in a wide bite of undulating cliffs studded with fishing villages like **Port Gaverne**, **Port Isaac** and **Port Quin**. At **Polzeath**, surfers get another crack at the white stuff, then it's all plain sailing in the sheltered waters of the Camel Estuary, where a ferry shuttles back and forth between **Rock** and **Padstow**. Cornwall's gastronomic capital ever since Rick Stein opened a restaurant here in the 1970s, Padstow is also the perfect spot to burn calories on the **Camel Trail** – a superb 18-mile cycling and walking trail to the edge of **Bodmin Moor**.

Often overlooked, but easily accessible from the coast, the moors have everything from woodland walks and watersports centres to standing stones and steam trains.

Here to there

For the purposes of this book, Northeast Cornwall covers the county's Atlantic shoreline from the Devon border to Padstow, including beaches like Daymer Bay and Rock in the Camel Estuary. For Trevose Head and attractions south of Padstow (such as Crealy Great Adventure Park), refer to the Northwest Cornwall chapter (see page 60). Inland, coverage extends to Launceston and Bodmin Moor, although many attractions in this region are just as accessible from South Cornwall (see page 148).

Bude – Padstow

N

5 km
5 miles

You must

❶ Track down the legend of King Arthur at Tintagel Castle.

❷ Get goosebumps at Boscastle's Museum of Witchcraft.

❸ Catch a wave at Summerleaze Beach, Bude.

❹ Jump off a cliff while coasteering at Port Quin.

❺ Cycle the Camel Trail between Padstow and Wadebridge.

❻ Conquer the Cheesewring Tor on Bodmin Moor.

❼ Watch the otters being fed at Tamar Otter Park.

❽ Ride the ferry from Padstow to Rock and walk to Polzeath Bay.

❾ Watch the surf roll in at glorious Trebarwith Strand.

❿ Munch Stein's fish and chips beside the harbour at Padstow.

From top left: cottage at Port Quin, flotsam sculpture at Trebarwith Strand, tea room in Port Isaac, Port Gaverne at low tide, beach gear for sale at Crackington Haven, Tintagel Head, strandline treasures on a door in Bude.

Out & about Northeast Cornwall

Fun & free

Track down a legend

You have to pay to visit Tintagel Castle (see page 40), legendary birthplace of King Arthur (and it's money well spent). On Tintagel's Fore Street, **King Arthur's Great Halls** (T01840-770526, kingarthursgreathalls. com), with its round tables, granite thrones and 72 stained glass windows depicting the Arthurian legend, also charges a small admission fee (£8 family). However, there are many other locations in northeast Cornwall where you can follow in King Arthur's footsteps for free. The waterfall at **St Nectan's Glen** between Tintagel and Boscastle, for example, is said to be the site where the mighty monarch was blessed before undertaking his quest for the Holy Grail. Just to the south is **Slaughterbridge**, where some believe Arthur was fatally wounded by Mordred in the Battle of Camlann. Just to the south, **Camelford** has been linked to Camelot, while Bodmin Moor has several Arthurian sites, including **Dozmary Pool** where Excalibur was returned to the mysterious Lady of the Lake.

Befriend a blenny

Top spots for rock-pooling along Cornwall's northeast coast include Crackington Haven, Port Isaac and Port Quin. If you're feeling slightly more adventurous, however, set off for **Lundy Bay**, a secluded rocky cove just to the west of Port Quin. To reach it, turn right off the B3314 between St Minver and Trelights, following the lane for a short distance until you reach a small parking area on the left. Alternatively, follow Bishop's Hill Road out of Polzeath. A short path crosses fields to the coast. Bear right and take the upper path to Lundy Hole, a spectacular sea arch, beyond which a trail descends into Lundy Bay. Be aware that the bay fills with water at high tide, so you will have to plan your rock-pooling expedition with the help of tide tables.

Fly a kite

Judging by its popularity with windsurfers and kitesurfers, **Daymer Bay**, just inside the Camel Estuary, is a good bet for flying a kite. Also try big, breezy beaches like **Widemouth** and **Summerleaze**.

> **❝❞** We moved to Cornwall from London in 2002. Our search for new surf breaks led us to discover lots of secret spots, but for reliability of surf and great facilities you can't beat Godrevy and Gwithian. In the summer you can still find peace and quiet, just off the beaten track. Perranuthnoe never gets too crowded. If it's raining we take our six-year-old to Jungle Barn at Paradise Park. If it's sunny we love the walk from Perranuthnoe to Marazion, ending up for lunch at Ben's Cornish Kitchen. The best thing about living here is how much is totally free. You can have a day on the beach with your family, sunbathing, making sandcastles and surfing world-class waves, and not spend a penny.

Ed le Froy
Global Boarders Surf School,
T01736-711404,
globalboarders.com.

Visit Trevathan Farm Shop

Why? As well as all the scrummy local food on sale, there's loads of outdoor space for kids to run around and let off steam. Football goals, ride-on tractors (coin operated), sand pit, swings, climbing frame and a speedy zip wire should keep most kids occupied for an hour or two – and there are also goats, rabbits and wallabies to pet. See page 45 for contact details, opening times and information on farm shop produce and restaurant menu.

Check out the events listings in the free *Coast Lines* newspaper or at the Boscastle Visitor Centre. Many of the rock pool rambles, beachcombing walks and treasure hunts are free or have a nominal charge.

Peruse Port Isaac

North Cornwall's favourite poster pin-up, Port Isaac (portisaac. org.uk; see also page 33) is well worth a morning or afternoon amble. Walking towards the village from the clifftop car park, you join the top of Fore Street where the Old School (now a hotel) was closed in 1978 for fear of the playground slipping into the sea. Continue down the hill, pausing to browse in Boathouse Stores. The low wall here offers a good vantage point over the harbour. Where the road bends right at the bakery, continue straight on into Temple Bar and what locals call Squeeze Belly Alley (for reasons that will become clear). Turn right into Dolphin Street and right again into Middle Street to reach the harbour. There's a lifeboat station here, as well as a small aquarium next to the fish market. Follow the lane up Roscarrock Hill to join the coast path, which hugs the cliffs all the way to Port Quin.

Catch crabs

There are some great spots to dangle a crab line along Cornwall's northeast coast. Padstow and Port Isaac are probably the best – you can stake out a patch of harbour wall (taking care of steep drops and slippery, seaweed-covered steps) and try scrounging some fish scraps from local fishermen to use as bait. You could even ask ice-cream sellers for empty plastic tubs – ideal for storing your crabs in. A net is useful for holding under your line as you haul crabs in (there are always one or two crafty nippers which let go of the bait just as you're about to swing them ashore). You can buy a crab line (with either hooks or a mesh bag that you stuff with bait). Alternatively, you could make one for practically nothing. Just get some old string, weight it with a pebble or two, tie a hook-shaped piece of wire to the end and hey presto – you've just saved yourself a few pounds. Shore crabs will dominate your catch but, with luck, you might be able to hook a red-eyed velvet swimming crab. Take care – they're much more feisty than shore crabs. Hold one by the back of its carapace and you should be able to spot three distinguishing features – red eyes, paddle-shaped back legs for swimming and soft, fuzzy carapace. Remember not to let the water in your bucket overheat in the sun, and always carefully return your crabs to where you caught them.

Cross the footbridge over to the left side of the famous dog-leg harbour and you are suddenly faced with dramatic vistas of sea cliffs, surging waves and wild Meachard Island. At low tide you can witness the Devil's Bellows blowhole at the base of the cliffs near the harbour entrance. Seals are often seen here too.

Explore Boscastle

This fascinating north coast village made headlines during the devastating floods of 2004. It's sobering to stand in the newly renovated visitor centre (where a sign at ceiling level marks the extent of the floodwaters) and watch video footage of cars and campervans being swept downstream. There are also displays on geology and wildlife, as well as children's brass-rubbing activities and a giftshop. Nearby, you'll find a National Trust shop and the spooky Museum of Witchcraft (see page 41), while the village centre has craft shops, galleries, a bakery, cafés and restaurants. However, don't get too waylaid in browsing Boscastle's tourist traps. To fully appreciate the village's dramatic setting you need to hike the short, but fairly steep, footpath up to the coastguard lookout. Start by crossing the footbridge over to

the left side of the famous dog-leg harbour, beyond which you are suddenly faced with dramatic vistas of sea cliffs, surging waves and wild Meachard Island. At low tide you can witness the Devil's Bellows blowhole at the base of the cliffs near the harbour entrance. Seals are often seen here too. Continue along the path, skirting a deep cleft where fulmars nest on narrow ledges, until you reach the lookout. Volunteers man this lonely outpost 365 days a year and you may well be invited inside the hut for a brief squint through powerful binoculars. On a clear day you can make out the buildings on distant Lundy Island. Another lovely walk follows the opposite side of Boscastle, past the little row of whitewashed cottages, to the vertiginous Pennally Point – a strictly hand-held adventure if you have young children!

Out & about Northeast Cornwall

Best beaches

The beaches described here are found east to west, from the Devon border to Padstow. For Trevose Head, see page 66.

Duckpool
🌊 P 🚻 ‼

Hemmed in by cliffs and raked by strong currents, Cornwall's far-north beaches are wild and rugged. Forget Stanbury Mouth a few miles south of the Devon border – it has no facilities, tricky access and dangerous swimming. Further south, Duckpool is more inviting. Nuzzled beneath the dramatic headland of Steeple Point, it's a sandy cove with rocky reefs at low tide (don't forget your shrimping nets). Surfers will find a fairly decent beach break, but remember to stay well clear of the rocks, particularly at the northern end of the cove.

Sandy Mouth
🌊 🏄 ⛱ ➕ 🚻 P 🚻 ‼

As with Duckpool, above, you need to take extra care at Sandy Mouth. Not only are the cliffs unstable, but there are strong undercurrents and a real danger of getting cut off by the tide. On the plus side, there's a lifeguard service during summer and a great little café/shop in the National Trust car park, selling drinks, snacks and beach gear, and renting out wetsuits and bodyboards for £5 per day. The

beach itself is a stunner: pebbles strewn with flotsam at high tide and then, as the tide ebbs, a broad swathe of golden sand and wave-smoothed reefs of rock pockmarked with pools. It's a good option for escaping the busier beaches near Bude and the surf can be just as good. Be wary of fierce riptides though.

Northcott Mouth
🌊 🏄 ➕ 🚻 P 🚻 ‼

A sandy precursor to the 'Bondi beauties' of Bude just to the south, Northcott Mouth actually merges with Crooklets at low tide. It's a great beach for strandline-roaming (tide tables to hand) and you can also reach it by following the coast path from Bude. Although the surf is consistently good at Northcott Mouth, the huge beach break is prone to rip tides.

Crooklets
🌊 🏄 ➕ 🚻 P

One of Bude's main beaches and home to Britain's first life-saving club (founded in 1953), Crooklets often has superb surf with breakers pounding a wide expanse of firm sand. Just don't expect to have it all to yourself.

Summerleaze
🌊 🏄 🏄 ⛱ 🚻 ➕ 🚻 P

Bude's spectacular downtown beach, Summerleaze has all bases covered. Sea too rough? Opt instead for the large saltwater pool scooped from

the base of the cliffs. It overflows into shallow sandy lagoons that are quick to warm under the sun. Then it's just a short sprint across hard, rippled sand to a stretch of lifeguard-patrolled surf. There's no shortage of surfing schools, if you feel like tackling the big stuff, but the beach is so wide and flat that even young children can have fun riding bodyboards in the frothy remnants of spent breakers. Higher up the beach, the sand gets softer, rucking up into dunes by the main beach car park and RNLI shop. To the north, Summerleaze blends with Crooklets; to the south it wraps around the harbour where the remaining mile or so of Bude Canal (dug in 1823) delves inland. Here you'll find Bude's gentlest waters, with rowing boats for hire, cafés, craft shops, Bude Castle (see page 41) and a lovely, grassy canal-side walk – the perfect way to get the sand off your feet.

Widemouth Bay
🌊 🏄 ⛱ ➕ 🚻 P

South of Bude, Widemouth Bay has over a mile of sand and promises fine surfing for beginners to pros. There's a surf school and board hire here, plus rock pools at low tide.

Crackington Haven
🌊 🏄 ⛱ ➕ 🚻 P

A dramatic beach snug between 130-m-high headlands with

cliffs striped black and white like humbug mints, Crackington Haven has a mixture of shingle, rock and sand. A stream flows across the pebbles, spreading out across darkish sand at low tide, when the time is ripe for building dams or rock-pooling. The Bude–Wadebrige bus calls here and there are also two excellent cafés (see page 46), one of which hires out westuits and surf boards from £9 per day.

Bossiney Haven

Park in Bossiney, near Tintagel, then follow the footpath to steep steps leading down to this sandy cove, wedged in a narrow cleft in the cliffs. You'll be wasting your time at high tide when there is little or no beach. Locals claim Bossiney is a good spot for mussel collecting.

Trebarwith Strand

With no sand at high tide, beach-goers stake out the flat rocks at Trebarwith waiting for the tide to ebb. Families with young children might find getting across the rocks tricky (wetsuit booties are recommended), but once you're on the beach at low tide, Trebarwith is a gem with plenty of sand, excellent surf, rock pools and natural paddling pools. Right behind the beach there's a cluster of beach shops, cafés (see page 46) and a surf shop

Top: Sandy Mouth at high tide. Above left: kayaks at Port Gaverne. Above right: Summerleaze.

with wetsuits and bodyboards for hire. After a long surfing session, bundle the kids up in towels and stop by the Shop in the Strand Café for freshly made doughnuts dunked in steaming hot chocolate. Holiday heaven!

Port Gaverne

Pilchard-fishing smacks and two-masted luggers laden with coal, lime and salt jostled for space in this haven during the mid-19th century. Nowadays, you'll still find a handful of fishing boats hauled up on the

pebbles, but it's the prospect of sea kayaking that draws many visitors to this sheltered cove. Along with Port Quin, it's one of the best paddling spots on the north coast (see page 36 for operators). Rock-pooling is also rewarding at Port Gaverne and, although the beach is narrow, you still get a fair wedge of (wet) sand at low tide.

Port Isaac

You can park on the beach at Port Isaac, but it's far easier (and less prone to tides!) to leave your car in the large cliff-top car park. The cutesy harbour town is only a 10-minute walk from here, and the views across the bay to Tintagel Head are glorious. Strolling down through the narrow lanes, you'll pass numerous gift shops and cafés (see pages 45-47) before reaching the harbour – cluttered with fishing boats and lobster pots and the site of a small fish market and aquarium. As you'd expect from a busy fishing village, the beach is strewn with ropes and crab shells. It's weedy and whiffy, but fun to explore – particularly if you follow the concrete walkway on the right-hand side of the beach where there are some large rock pools.

Port Quin

A few houses, a small National Trust car park, a tiny snack shack and that's about it. Port Quin may be small on facilities but it's big on adventure. A sheltered rocky inlet west of Port Isaac, this is an excellent location for sea kayaking, snorkelling or coasteering (see opposite). There's not much of a beach at high tide (try crabbing off the slipway) but, as the sea ebbs, you'll find rock pools shimmering with green and purple snakelocks anemones.

Polzeath

Cool Cornwall's surf central,

Left: Mighty surf at Polzeath. Right: Mere ripples at Daymer Bay.

Polzeath squirms with neoprene during the height of summer when wetsuited bodies take to the sea in such numbers it can resemble a crowded seal colony. This superb family beach is so popular that part of it has long been commandeered as a car park. Everything crowds in on the beach: cars, surf shacks, snack bars – even ice cream vans drive out across the bay! There are good surf breaks along the beach, with waves for all abilities. If the sea gets too crowded, try New Polzeath on the northeast side of the bay. Alternatively, swap surf board for frisbee – there's usually plenty of unclaimed sand in the middle of the bay at low tide. You can also follow the coast path north to rugged Pentire Point, a good vantage point for spotting seabirds and marine wildlife.

Daymer Bay

Sheltered from the surf that pummels Polzeath a mile or so to the north, sandy Daymer Bay is an ideal spot for young children to go paddling. Low tide exposes acres of beautifully

rippled (but hard) sandflats that will test the backs and spades of sandcastle-builders – or form a challenging wicket for beach cricket. Rock-poolers, meanwhile, should check out the north side of the bay. The tide sweeps in fast at Daymer Bay, so be prepared to beat a hasty retreat to the softer sand and dunes above the high-water mark. If it's windy, bring a kite or watch the windsurfers and kitesurfers tacking back and forth across the Camel Estuary.

Rock Beach

A long sandy beach stretching from Porthilly Cove to Daymer Bay on the east side of the Camel Estuary, Rock is linked to Padstow (see pages 48-51) by a landing-craft-style passenger ferry (return tickets around £3 adult, £1 child). Depending on the tide, you land either on the slipway at Padstow Harbour or on Lower Beach just to the north of the town. Rock Beach is a popular spot for sailing and windsurfing, and there's a lovely coastal walk north to Daymer Bay and Polzeath (see above).

Action stations

Boat trips
See also Cornish Rock Tors, page 36, and Padstow, page 48.

Orcades II
Port Isaac Harbour, T01208-880716, carn-awn.co.uk/orcades. Call for rates. Sightseeing and mackerel fishing.

Winnie the Pooh
Port Isaac Harbour, T01208-880421, 1-hr mackerel fishing £12, 2-hr wildlife safari £20.

Canoeing
Atlantic Pursuits
20 Priestacott Park, Kilkhampton, Bude, EX23 9TH, T01288-321765, atlanticpursuits.co.uk. Half-day £20, full day £40.
Paddle a three- or four-seater Canadian canoe along Bude Canal's 'Jungle Run'. Surfing and bodyboarding are also available.

Coasteering
Cornish Coast Adventures
Scarrabine Farm, Port Quin PL29 3ST, T01208-880280, cornishcoastadventures.com. Coasteering and sea kayaking £30 (minimum age 8, under 14s must be accompanied by adult). Family fun session (2 hrs) £25.
Throw caution (and yourself) to the wind and sea on a three-hour coastal romp, leaping from ledges, swimming into sea caves, spinning in whirlpools and generally behaving like a crazed mermaid. Relax – you're

Leap of faith – coasteering at Port Quin.

in safe hands. CCA's coasteering trips are led by beach lifeguards or lifeboat crew members and are suitable for complete beginners. You'll be kitted out with wetsuits, helmets and lifejackets on the slipway at Port Quin before taking the plunge and entering 'seal mode'. Sea kayaking trips (on two-person sit-on kayaks) are also available, nosing about the inlets and sea caves at Port Quin and, if conditions allow, venturing along the coast in search of deserted coves, seals and basking sharks. Flop overboard for a cooling swim or have a go at fishing by trawling a mackerel line behind your kayak or pulling up one of CCA's lobster pots.

Cycling
See page 38 for the Camel Trail.

Goss Moor Cycle Hire
Screech Owl Sanctuary (see page 76), nr Indian Queens, T01726-861545, screechowlsanctuary.co.uk. Adult bike £10/day, child's bike £8/day, trailer £10/day, tag-a-long £8/day.
Most people experience Goss Moor as a 60-mph blur from the A30 just before they reach Indian Queens. But this 480-hectare National Nature Reserve is crying out for more leisurely exploration by bicycle. An easy, relatively flat seven-mile circular trail winds its way around a widlife-rich patchwork of heathland and scrub that, according to legend, was once a hunting ground for King Arthur.

Horse riding
Efford Down Riding Stable
Efford Down Farm, Vicarage Rd, Bude, EX23 8LT, T01288-354244, efforddown.co.uk. Easter-Oct Mon-Fri, plus weekends during school holidays. Rides from £22 or £20 for groups of 4 or more.
There's a horse or pony for everyone at Efford Down – from a diminutive Shetland to a 16-hand Shire cross. Escorted riding takes place on the farm with fantastic views along the coast.

Out & about Northeast Cornwall

Gooseham Barton Farm

Morwenstow, Bude, EX23 9PG, T01288-331204, gooseham-barton. com. Rides from £22/hr.

Hacks of up to three hours are available for experienced riders, while novices can join hour-long walks with children taken on a leading rein for safety.

Tredole Farm

Trevalga, Boscastle, PL35 0ED, T01840-250495. Call for rates.

Family groups and all abilities for beginners' lessons or romantic sunset canters along the coast.

Multi activity
Cornish Rock Tors

Polzeath, PL27 6SS, T07791-534884, cornishrocktors.com. Coasteering £30 (minimum age 10), rock climbing £60, sea kayaking £25 (minimum age 8), Sea Safaris £40 adult, £30 child.

As well as three-hour coasteering and sea kayaking tours, Cornish Rock offers full-day rock-climbing trips (for all abilities) and two-hour boat trips on the *Mor Cannow*. Operating from Rock, this high-speed RIB can whisk you to The Rumps (via Pentire Head), to Gulland Rock (a nursery ground for seals) or to Tintagel, via seabird cities and the cathedral-like caves of Cartway Cove.

Outdoor Adventure

Widemouth Bay, Bude, EX23 0DF, T01288-362900, outdooradventure. co.uk. Adventure family holidays, mid Jul-late Aug, 7-day from £615 adult, £509 child (8-14); 5-day from £459 adult, £369 child.

With the added bonus of a wild cliff-top setting, this residential centre offers family holidays packed with pursuits, such as surfing, bodyboarding, kayaking, Canadian canoeing, archery, climbing, abseiling, windsurfing, coasteering, orienteering and coastal traversing (boulder-hopping along rocky shores).

Shoreline Extreme Pursuits

Crooklets Beach, Bude, EX23 8NE, T01288-354039, shorelineactivities. co.uk. Year round half-day kayaking, surfing, rock climbing and abseiling sessions £23.50; canoeing £16 or £32/canoe (up to 4 people); archery £20. Minimum age for sea kayaking 12.

A one-stop shop for adrenaline junkies with introductory sessions and qualification courses in a range of activities. Most can be tailored to all abilities, except surf kayaking where you need some paddling experience – perhaps from one of Shoreline's more gentle sojourns on the Bude Canal. Also on offer are beach ecology safaris where you can expect another, albeit milder, adrenalin rush if you spot the elusive Celtic sea slug, *Onchidella celtica*.

Tamar Lakes Watersports

Kilkhampton, Bude, EX23 9SB, T01288-321712, swlaketrust.org.uk. Pedalo £12/hr, kayak £10/hr, Canadian canoe £16/hr, windsurfer £14/hr, Pico sailing dinghy £16/hr; call for details of RYA courses, taster sessions, Junior Club (8-16) and 5-day multi-activity Cadet Week (8-16).

The antithesis to Bude's surf scene, the calm waters of Upper Tamar Lake are perfect for learning to sail or windsurf. For camping, see page 42.

Sea kayaking
Camel Canoe & Kayaks

Trenant, Wadebridge, PL27 6HB, T01208-895151, ccak.co.uk. Double sit-on kayaks and canoes £35/day, guided trips from £25.

Sales, hire, tuition and guided kayaking tours on the Camel Estuary and beyond.

Cornish Coast Adventures
See page 35.

Surfing
See opposite.

Waterskiing
Camel Ski School

The Pontoon, Rock, PL27 6LQ, T01208-862727, camelskischool. com. £25/15-min session, £48/30-min lesson; banana boat rides £8/person (minimum 4 people).

Learn how to waterski or wakeboard on the calm waters of the Camel Estuary – or go for a bit of 'Costa del Cornwall' with a high-speed banana boat ride.

Surf schools

Animal Surf Academy
Wavehunters UK, 6 Fore St, Port Isaac, PL29 3RB, T0870-242 2856, wavehunters.co.uk. £25/2½-hr lesson at Polzeath. Also runs Kids' Surf Club, rock pool safaris, eco-coasteering and 'snurfkling' (snorkelling from a surf board when it's flat calm).

Atlantic Pursuits
Bude, T01288-321765, atlanticpursuits.co.uk. £20/2-hr lesson, £40/day (2 lessons). Also offers bodyboarding, kayaking and canoeing.

Big Blue Surf School
Mead Farm Cottage, Welcombe, Devon, EX39 6HQ, T01288-331764, bigbluesurfschool.co.uk. Operates from Summerleaze, Bude. £25/2½- to 3-hr lesson, £45/day (2 lessons), £80/weekend (4 lessons).

BSX Surfing Centre
Adventure International, Belle Vue, Bude, EX23 8JP, T0870-777 5111, budesurfingexperience.co.uk. £25/2½-hr lesson.

Harlyn Surf School
23 Grenville Rd, Padstow, PL28 8EX, T01841-533076, harlynsurfschool.co.uk. £35/2-hr lesson, £115/fast track course (4 lessons) on Harlyn Beach (see page 66). Also offers stand up paddleboarding and sit-on-top kayak hire.

Outdoor Adventure
Atlantic Court, Widemouth Bay, Bude, EX23 0DF, T01288-362900, outdooradventure.co.uk. £25/2½-hr lesson, £45/day (2 lessons). Also runs family holidays and multi-activity weekends (see opposite).

Padstow Surf School
Trevone Bay, T01841-533382, padstowsurfschool.co.uk. Operates from beaches in the Padstow area. £25/2½-hr lesson.

Raven Surf School
32 Seawell Rd, Poughill, Bude, EX23 8PD (or EX23 0AW for beach location), T01288-353693, ravensurf.co.uk. £25/2½-hr lesson, £45/day (2 lessons).

Shoreline Extreme Pursuits
Crooklets Beach, Bude, EX23 8NE, T01288-354039, shorelineactivities. co.uk. Operates from Summerleaze or Crooklets. £23.50/2½-hr lesson. Also offers sea kayaking, canoeing, rock climbing and other activities (see opposite).

Surf's Up Surf School
21 Trenant Close, Polzeath, PL27 6SW, T01208-862003, surfsupsurfschool.com. £25/2½-hr lesson, £14/1½-hr taster lesson (for kids aged 7 and under).

Trebarwith Surf School
Trebarwith, T07528-436760, surftrebarwith.co.uk. £25/2-hr lesson.

Waves Surf School
St Merryn, Padstow, PL28 8NW, T01841-521230, wavessurfschool. co.uk. £30/2-hr lesson, £60/day (2 lessons) on Harlyn or Constantine Beach (see page 66).

Don't miss The Camel Trail

Cornwall's most popular cycling adventure, the 18-mile Camel Trail links Padstow, Wadebridge, Bodmin and Wenfordbridge via a largely traffic-free route that follows an old railway track alongside the River Camel.

The trail is divided into three main sections: Padstow to Wadebridge, five miles, flat all the way; Wadebridge to Bodmin, six miles, with a small climb to Bodmin; and, finally, the slightly more challenging seven-mile sector between Bodmin and Wenfordbridge. You could also try a circular route to Rock and catch the ferry back to Padstow.

Allow 45 minutes each way for the estuary-side pedal between Padstow and Wadebridge. You can hire bikes at either town (see box right). This often busy section (used by walkers and birdwatchers as well as cyclists) follows the south bank of the estuary, crossing the old iron bridge over Little Petherick Creek and ducking under the A39 bypass before reaching Wadebridge. Stop en route for a picnic or encourage tired legs with the promise of Granny Wobbly's fudge in Wadebridge or ice cream at Stein's Deli if you're Padstow-bound.

Intrepid cyclists can push on past Wadebridge to Bodmin, where the Camel Trail delves into beautiful riverside woodland. For refreshments, stop at the Camel Valley Vineyard or Camel Trail Tea Gardens near Nanstallon or make for the picnic tables at Grogley Halt, where there's access to the river. Look out for a steam train at Boscarne Junction, the western terminus of the Bodmin and Wenford Railway (see page 57).

From Dunmere (near Bodmin), the Camel Trail loops north towards Poley's Bridge and Wenfordbridge. This is the quietest section of the trail, climbing gently through beech woodland with views of the river below. There is a seasonal tea room at Tresarrett, while the Blisland Inn makes a worthwhile one-mile detour off the trail.

Bike hire

Bike Smart
Eddystone Rd, Wadebridge, PL27 7AL, T01208-814545, bikesmart.eu. Daily from 0900.

Bridge Bike Hire
Wadebridge, PL27 7AL, T01208-813050, bridgebikehire.co.uk. Daily 0900-1700.

Padstow Cycle Hire
South Quay, Padstow, PL28 8BL, T01841-533533, padstowcyclehire.com. Daily 0900-1700, plus evening hire mid July-end Aug.

Trail Bike Hire
South Quay, Padstow, PL28 8BL, T01841-532594, trailbikehire.co.uk. Daily 0900-1800.

For all of the above, expect to pay: Adult bike £9-14, adult tricycle £10-12, tandem £18-24, child seat £1-3, bike and tag-a-long £14-18, trailer £6-7, dog trailer £6, junior 24-in bike £6-8, junior 20-in bike £5-6, junior 16-in bike £4-5. Helmets, locks, pump, toolkit and map supplied free of charge.

Watch the birdies

A nutrient-rich medley of sandbanks, mudflats and salt marsh makes the Camel Estuary a favourite spot for a wide variety of birds. Cycle the stretch of the Camel Trail between Padstow and Wadebridge at low tide for your best chance of sighting common waders like the little egret, curlew, heron and oystercatcher. During summer, shelduck young venture out onto the mudflats and occasionally fall prey to marauding peregrines. If you're really lucky, you might spot an osprey, spoonbill, or glossy ibis. Mute swans nest at several locations on the estuary, while kingfishers are more frequently seen further upriver.

Encourage tired legs with the promise of Granny Wobbly's fudge in Wadebridge or ice cream at Stein's Deli if you're Padstow-bound.

No need to get the hump – the section of the Camel Trail between Padstow and Wadebridge promises effortless cycling on a level track.

Out & about Northeast Cornwall

For the Bodmin and Launceston area, see pages 52-59.

Cornish Birds of Prey Centre
Nr St Columb Major. See page 76.

Crealy Great Adventure Park
Nr Tredinnick. See page 74.

Screech Owl Sanctuary
Nr Indian Queens. See page 76.

Tintagel Castle
Tintagel, PL34 0HE, T01840-770328, english-heritage.org.uk. Year-round daily from 1000. £4.90 adult, £2.50 child (5-15), £12.30 family. Like St Michael's Mount (see page 102), a large part of Tintagel's appeal lies in its location – perched on surf-scoured cliffs where the only access is by a long flight of uneven steps and a dramatic footbridge. In fact, at Tintagel you won't find much of a castle at all. Crumbling walls are all that remain of the 13th-century fort. It's what Tintagel could have been, however, that puts a spring in the step of all who venture here.

The discovery of the inscribed sixth-century Artognou Stone fuelled tantalizing speculation that Tintagel was the birthplace of King Arthur – a great excuse for the riveting myths and legends recounted during summer by a local storyteller. You can also

delve into Tintagel's mysterious past at the excellent little visitor centre where a short film, *Searching for King Arthur*, turns "the forensic eye of archaeology on Arthur's bond with Tintagel".

Sorry kids, but the evidence is pretty scratchy. What you will find, having scaled the steps onto Tintagel Head, are the remains of a medieval castle built by Richard, Earl of Cornwall, between 1233 and 36 – some 500 years after the supposed reign of King Arthur.

None of this, however, detracts from the thrill of exploring the network of skeletal walls clinging to the clifftop or venturing inside Merlin's Cave (reached from the cove below). Interpretation boards reconstruct what life was like at Tintagel, while free quiz sheets challenge children to devise the best way to lay seige to the castle. There's also a beach café (see page 46) and a giftshop selling Arthurian nick-nacks, Callestick Farm ice cream and other local goodies.

Looking across the cove to Tintagel Castle, with Merlin's Cave at the base of the cliff.
Above left: Exploring the ruins.

🌊 Walk this way

Park in the free car park at St Materiana's Church (signposted from Tintagel village to Glebe Cliff), from where it's a fabulous 10-minute cliff-top walk to Tintagel Castle – by far the best way to appreciate the natural spectacle of the Atlantic-gnawed headland rearing 80 m above the sea.

About half a mile inland, Tintagel village will make short work of pocket money thanks to Merlin's Gifts, Granny Wobbly's Ice Cream Parlour and other irresistible temptations. Try to find time for the Old Post Office (see right) – a medieval yeoman farmhouse with a slate roof that 'heaves and rolls' like the sea. It's delightfully dingy and atmospheric inside.

It's what Tintagel could have been that puts a spring in the step of all who venture here.

More family favourites

Bude Castle Heritage Centre
Bude, EX23 8LG, T01288-357300, bude-stratton.gov.uk. Year round daily 1000-1700. £3.50 adult, £2.50 child (5-15), £10 family.

Small but captivating, this quirky museum covers everything from the geology of north Cornwall and the making of Bude Canal to shipwrecks, Civil War costumes and the inventions of 'forgotten genius' Sir Goldsworthy Gurney.

Museum of Witchcraft
The Harbour, Boscastle, PL35 0HD, T01840-250111, museumofwitchcraft.com. Easter-Hallowe'en Mon-Sat 1030-1800, Sun 1130-1800. £3 adult, £2 child.

Get face to face with 'horrible history', wise up on witchcraft and curses, peruse torture instruments (used for extracting confessions from witches) and meet Harry the tarred head.

The Old Post Office
Fore St, Tintagel, PL34 0DB, T01840-770024, nationaltrust.org.uk. Feb-Nov daily from 1100. £3 adult, £1.50 child (5-17), £7.50 family. See Tintagel Castle, left.

Trevigue Wildlife Conservation
Trevigue, Crackington Haven, EX23 0LQ, T01840-230730, wild-trevigue.co.uk. Call for details.

Join a guided walk or 4WD farm tour to learn how modern agriculture can co-exist with wildlife. Learn about shipwrecks and smuggling at Strangles Beach, watch badgers and bats and search for dormice.

Rain check

Cinemas
Cinedrome
Lanadwell St, Padstow, T01841-532344.

Rebel
Treskinnick Cross, Bude, T01288-361442.

Regal
The Platt, Wadebridge, T01208-812791.

Indoor play & amusements
Harlequinns Leisure
Stucley Rd, Bude EX23 8AR, T01288-355366, harlequinns.com. Weekends and school holidays daily 0930-2300. Huge indoor play zone, ten-pin bowling, café.

Kids' Kingdom
Colliford Lake Park, see page 57.

Porteath Bee Centre
See page 45.

Indoor swimming pools
Budehaven Leisure Centre
Stratton Rd, Bude, EX23 8AW, T01288-353714.

Camelford Leisure Centre
Sportsmans Rd, Camelford, PL32 9UE, T01840-213188.

Dragon Leisure Centre
Lostwithiel Rd, Bodmin, PL31 1DE, T01208-75715.

Phoenix Leisure Centre
Coronation Park, Launceston, PL15 9DQ, T01566-772551.

Splash Leisure Pool
Stucley Rd, Bude, EX23 8AR, T01288-356191.

Wadebridge Leisure Centre
Bodieve Rd, Wadebridge, PL27 6BU, T01208-814980.

Museums
North Cornwall Museum
The Cleave, Camelford, T01840-212954. Apr-Sep Mon-Sat 1000-1700. Showcase for the old days, with exhibits on farming, wagon-making and other trades.

Wonder Years Toy Experience
27 Queen St, Bude, T01288-359979, wonder-years.co.uk. Year round, daily 1000-1700. £2 adult, £1.50 child, £6 family. Toys galore from the '60s-80s.

Sleeping Northeast Cornwall

Cornish Coasts

Middle Penlean, Poundstock, EX23 0EE, T01288-361380, cornishcoasts. co.uk. Apr-Oct. £12-14/pitch, plus £3-4 extra adult, £2-3 extra child.

Quiet site with terraced pitches overlooking Widemouth Bay.

Lower Pennycrocker Farm

Nr Boscastle, PL35 0BY, T01840-250257, pennycrocker.com. Easter-Oct. £5 adult, £3 child.

This small family-run campsite (with 40 pitches sheltered by wildlife-rich hedgerows) is located on a dairy farm, so no shortage of fresh eggs or milk.

Southwinds

Polzeath, PL27 6QU, T01208-862215, polzeathcamping.co.uk. Apr-Oct. £20-40/pitch (4 adults, children under 14 free).

Half a mile from the sea, Southwinds offers a peaceful (families and couples only) alternative to its sister site, Tristram, which is perched right above Polzeath's beach.

Upper Tamar Lake

Kilkhampton, Bude, EX23 9SB, T01288-321712, swlakestrust.org.uk. £6 adult, £3 child (5-14), £14 family.

This slightly sloping site runs right down to the lake with its beach, pedaloes and watersports centre (see page 36).

Wooda Farm Park

Poughill, nr Bude, EX23 9HJ, T01288-352069, wooda.co.uk. Apr-Oct. £12-29/pitch (2 adults), plus £3.50-5 extra adult, £2-4 extra child (3-15). A holiday park with a rural twist, Wooda Farm has tractor rides, woodland walks, fishing, golf, archery and a mini-menagerie of chickens, goats and lambs. Some of the pitches on this well kept site have views of the coastline at Bude. There's a well-stocked shop and a bar serving home-cooked food. Facilities are top-notch – there are even private family bathrooms for hire.

Wooda Farm.

Go glamping

Belle Tents (Owls Gate, Davidstow, Camelford, PL32 9XY, T01840-261556 belletentscamping.co.uk) adds comfort, style and a touch of theatre to camping with its stripy-topped belle tents – each one lavished with beds, duvets and furniture. Campfires add to the atmosphere and there's also a fully equipped kitchen tent.

Feel the sea breeze at Southwinds, near Polzeath.

Pirate play at Sandymouth.

Holiday parks

Bossiney Bay
Nr Tintagel, PL34 0AY, T01626-855240, haulfryn.co.uk.
Smart country lodges and luxury cottages with hot tubs.

Hentervene Holiday Park
Crackington Haven, EX23 0LF, T01840-230365, hentervene.co.uk.
Peaceful park with lodges and caravans for hire.

Juliot's Well Holiday Park
Camelford, PL32 9RF, T01840-213302, juliotswell.com.
Rural setting with heated pool.

Little Bodieve Holiday Park
Wadebridge, PL27 6EG, T01208-812323, littlebodieve.co.uk.
Friendly family park with lots of facilities; close to Camel Trail.

St Minver Holiday Park
Nr Rock, PL27 6RR, T0871-641 2040, parkdeanengland.co.uk.
Beautiful parkland setting, quality lodges and caravans, heated indoor pool and free kids' club.

Sandymouth Holiday Park
Nr Bude, EX23 9HW, T01288-352563, sandymouthbay.co.uk.
Coastal views, excellent facilities; located up a steepish lane from Sandymouth Bay.

Widemouth Holiday Village
Bude, EX23 0DJ, T01288-361437, widemouthbayholidayvillage. co.uk. Well-equipped bungalows overlooking the bay; indoor pool.

Cornish Tipi Holidays

Tregeare, Pendoggett, St Kew, PL30 3LW, T01208-880781, cornishtipiholidays.co.uk. Apr-Oct. From £410-820/wk, plus £50 per person (age 3+) to cover fuel etc. Tipis have popped up all over Britain, but not only was this the first site to add a touch of 'pow-wow' to camping holidays, it is arguably still the best. That probably has something to do with the setting – a 16-acre woodland surrounding a spring-fed quarry lake where kids can play real-life *Swallows and Amazons*: swimming, fishing, boating or simply watching the dragonflies whizz past. Then there's the tipi experience itself – ducking inside to flop on cosy rugs and rolling on to your back to gaze up at the 18-ft high cone of canvas and locally sourced poles, lashed together with twine and hessian and daubed with authentic Native American designs. There are 40 tipis here, sleeping up to 10 and arranged either in village fields (complete with totem poles) or tucked away in private clearings. Each one comes with its own cooking fire and woodpile. There's a gas stove for back-up (plus flush toilets and hot showers at either end of the site), but essentially this is no-frills, back-to-nature camping where, in the absence of electricity, tipis take on a warm, magical lantern glow at night. A friendly warden that lives on site will be able to point you in the direction of Port Isaac (10 minutes' drive away) and other north-coast highlights.

Sleeping Northeast Cornwall

Cottages

Eastcliffe
Port Isaac, Pl29 3RN, T01208-841808, portisaaccottage.com. £300-850/wk.
Two-bedroom cottage with a sun terrace overlooking the harbour at Port Isaac.

Gooseham Barton Cottages
Gooseham, Morwenstow, nr Bude, EX23 9PG, T01288-331204, gooseham-barton.com. Cottages (sleeping 4-7) £215-595/wk, farmhouse (sleeping 8-10) £440-1040.
Cosy cottages with inglenook fireplaces and wood-burning stoves on a 50-acre farm with its own horse-riding stable.

The Olde House
Chapel Amble, Wadebridge, PL27 6EN, T01208-813219, theoldehouse.co.uk. £375-1350/wk.
Wide choice of lovingly restored cottages (sleeping 2-8) on a 500-

acre working farm with indoor pool and play barn, adventure playground, farm trail, tennis courts and pets corner.

Penally Cottage
Boscastle, available from Classic Cottages, T01326-555555, classic.co.uk. £441-1113/wk.
Sleeping six, Penally is the first in a row of fishermen's cottages perched above Boscastle Harbour. Traditional features like wooden shutters and window seats haven't been compromised by a slick makeover, which includes a useful utility/shower room for post-beach wash-downs.

Trevathan Farm
St Endellion, nr Port Isaac, PL29 3TT, T01208-880164, trevathanfarm.com. 2- and 3-bedroom cottages £260-1080/wk, 4-bedroom cottage £480-1470.
Well-equipped cottages on a working farm just three miles from the sea. Lambs, bunnies and other cuddlies for the kids.

Wooldown Farm Cottages
Marhamchurch, nr Bude, EX23 0HP, T01288-361216, wooldown.co.uk. Call for rates.
Although half of the properties on this immaculate complex are luxury escapes for adults only, that leaves four family-friendly self-catering cottages sleeping up to eight. All come with stylish features like spa baths and four-poster beds.

Penally Cottage.

Port Isaac.

Best of the rest

Forda Lodges
Nr Kilkhampton, EX23 9RZ, T01288-321413, forda.co.uk. £375-1200/wk.
Ten Scandinavian-style lodges in a tranquil woodland setting with fishing lakes and indoor pool.

Hengar Manor Country Park
St Tudy, PL30 3PL, T01208-850382, hengarmanor.co.uk. Lodges £230-1800/wk, bungalows £195-770/wk, villas £240-1420/wk.
Wide range of accommodation, including smart, open-plan lodges, in 35 acres of landscaped gardens, woodland and lakes. Facilities include crazy golf, kids' club, adventure playground and indoor leisure complex.

Ivyleaf Combe Lodges
Stratton, Bude, EX23 9LD, T01288-321323, ivyleafcombe.com. Lodges (sleeping up to 6) £425-1025/wk.
Timber lodges, some with hot tubs, snug in a wooded valley.

Cottage agents
See also page 186.

Cornish Horizons
T01841-533331, cornishhorizons.co.uk.
Cottages in and around Padstow, Wadebridge and Newquay.

Harbour Holidays
T01841-533402, harbourholidays.co.uk.
130 properties in Padstow area.

Padstow Cottage Company
T01841-532633, padstowcottagecompany.co.uk.
Select group of 23 cottages.

Eating Northeast Cornwall

Carruan Farm

Polzeath, PL27 6QU, T01208-869584, carruan.co.uk. Daily 0730-2030, later on family barbecue nights. Free entry to play areas and animal shed.
Around 1000 Poll Dorset ewes and 25 beef suckler cows – that's the mainstay of Mike and Clare Parnell's farm but, like so many farmers, they've also diversified into tourism with tractor tours and play areas etc. The Parnells stand out from the herd, however, with their superb Farmhouse Kitchen which serves breakfasts (including a Young Farmer's Breakfast of sausage, hash brown, baked beans and egg for £3.95), light lunches, cream teas and dinners (mains £8.50-12.95), including Sunday roasts. Best of all are the family barbecues and hog roasts (Jul-Sep from 1730), when special events like sheep racing, storytelling, farm olympics, sheepdog trials and bird of prey handling are run alongside a feast of lamb chops, burgers, steaks, veggie kebabs and home-made puddings.

Market days

Bude Farmers' Market
Parkhouse Centre,
second Friday 1000-1300.
Launceston Farmers' Market
St Mary's Hall, Friday 0830-1400.
Wadebridge Country Market
Town Hall, Thursday 0745-1200.

Dennis Knight

Fish Cellars, Port Isaac, PL29 3RB, T01208-880498. Mon-Sat 0930-1300, 1400-1700.
With daily catches landed straight into the cellars by the slipway, fish simply doesn't come any fresher. You'll also find Just Shellfish here.

Ice cream

Decadent and delicious, Treleavens (treleavens.co.uk) has an ice cream shop in Tintagel, while Helsett Farm in Boscastle churns out its own organic ice creams and sorbets.

Porteath Bee Centre

St Minver, nr Polzeath, PL27 6RA, T01208-863718, porteathbeecentre. co.uk. Easter-Oct.
Try hive-fresh honey in fudge, jams, ice cream or dripping from the end of a spoon. And, as if that wasn't a sweet enough temptation, this busy little centre has a Living Honey Bee Exhibition (where you can peer at beehives housed in glass-fronted cabinets), a Winnie the Pooh shop, a tea room serving light lunches and cream teas and a chance for children to make their own beeswax rolled honeycomb candles (£1).

St Kew Harvest Farm Shop

St Kew Highway, PL30 3EF, T01208-841818. Year round daily 1000-1800 (1700 in winter, 1600 on Sun).
Vegetables are picked daily from the field next to this organic farm shop, which uses

Pick your own at Trevathan.

composted seaweed to enrich the soil. You can also buy fresh baked bread and cakes, smoked bacon from Truro and free-range chicken from Bude.

Trevathan Farm Shop

St Endellion, nr Port Isaac (on B3314), T01208-880164, trevathanfarm.com. Year round daily from 1000.
The pick of the bunch when it comes to North Cornwall's farm shops, Trevathan almost warrants a day out in its own right. For starters there is a pick-your-own (raspberries, strawberries, blackcurrants etc) and a shop crammed with local produce, including home-made quiches, jams and chutneys, farm-fresh bacon, sausages and steak, Treleavens ice cream and Cornish blue cheese. You could easily buy everything you need for a beach barbecue at nearby Port Quin or Port Gaverne – trouble is, Trevathan also has a restaurant with a tempting array of dishes, from Sunday roasts to crab salads. The home-baked cakes (£2.75/slice) are a meal in themselves. Outside, there's a picnic area, playground, ride-on tractors, a wicked zip slide and a collection of rabbits, goats and wallabies (see also page 28).

Eating Northeast Cornwall

Quick & simple

Cabin Café

Crackington Haven, EX23 0JG
T01840-230238. Summer daily.
Colourful and trendy, the Cabin
Café sells Kelly's and Callestick
ice cream and smoothies, plus
pasties (from £2.95), freshly
baked cakes, paninis, toasties,
salads and cream teas. There's
a surf shop downstairs offering
wetsuits and boards for hire.
Haven Café (across the car park)
has fresh crab sandwiches,
cream teas and tasty dishes like
oak-roasted chicken.

Life's a Beach

Summerleaze Beach, Bude, EX23
8HN, T01288-355222, lifesabeach.
info. Dinner from 1900, ice cream
parlour and café open during the day.
The daytime menu here features
freshly baked baguettes and
bruschettas from £4, burgers
from £4.50, salads from £6.50,
plus various other snacks such
as cheesy nachos (£5) and shell-
on prawns (£7.50). It's during
the evening, however, that this
café/bistro really gets its creative
juices flowing. Main courses are

Fish & chips

Port Isaac's **Takeaway** (T01208-
880281) fries cod and haddock
fresh from village fishermen. Also
recommended are **Barny's Fish &
Chip Restaurant** (Wadebridge),
**The Port and Starboard Café Fish
& Chip Shop** (Indian Queens) and
Peck Fish & Chips (Camelford).

changed weekly, but typically
include local sirloin steak
(£16.50) and sublime seafood
dishes like prosciutto-wrapped
halibut with Cornish asparagus
and creamy mash (£17.50).

Nicki B's Deli & Bakery

Fore St, Port Issac, PL29 3RB,
T01208-880099.
Freshly made coffee, pasties,
cakes and local produce. The
Pea Pod, also in Port Isaac, is a
small deli offering pies, cakes,
sandwiches and baguettes
– just the job for picnic supplies.

Pilchard Cellar Café

National Trust Visitor Ctr, Boscastle,
T01840-250353, nationaltrust.org.uk.
Apr-Nov daily 1030-1700; Dec-Mar
daily 1100-1600.
Occupying a former pilchard
cellar where fish were packed
in salt, this busy café adjoins
the National Trust shop near
Boscastle's slipway. It serves
good-value snacks, with soup
and roll £3.75, sandwiches £3.25,
pasties from £1.75 and cakes
from £1.50. You can also pick up
children's picnic boxes for £2.95
or order a small-appetite soup
and roll for £2. They are heavily
into recycling here, so tea comes
in cardboard cups and scones
are served on paper plates. If
you want a more refined cream
tea, head to the quaint Harbour
Light Tea Gardens opposite.

The Strand Café

Beach Rd, Trebarwith, PL34 0HB,

Trebarwith's beachside café.

T01840-779109, thestrandcafe.co.uk.
Easter-Sep 1000-1800.
Just yards from the stunning
beach at Trebarwith, The Strand
Café has a menu packed with
bacon rolls, crab sandwiches,
salads, ciabattas, soups, burgers,
chips and cream teas – to eat
in or take away. Across the
road is the more basic Shop in
the Strand Café, where surfers
queue up for pasties followed
by fresh doughnuts (£1.50 for 4)
dunked in creamy hot chocolate.

Tintagel Beach Café

Tintagel Castle, T01840-772101,
english-heritage.org.uk.
Daily 1000-1730.
Located just above the cove
at Tintagel Castle, this popular
café has a small terrace with
views of King Arthur's legendary
stronghold. Standard café fare,
including sandwiches, soup,
baguettes, cakes, cream teas,
pasties and jacket potatoes, are
all available, along with local
specials such as crab linguine
(£7.50) and beer-battered Port
Isaac cod and chips with home-
made tartare sauce (£7.10).
Kids' meals (£3.95) include fish
goujons and shepherd's pie.
Work off the calories with a
jaunt on the coast path 2¼

miles to Trebarwith or 4½ miles to Boscastle. The café sells children's picnic boxes for £3.50.

The Waterfront Café Bar

Beach Rd, Polzeath, PL27 6SP, T01208-869655, thewaterfrontcornwall.co.uk. Summer daily 0900-2300.
This excellent beach café has a great selection of seafood – the platters and tapas are perfect for a family free-for-all and there's also a kids' menu. Dishes range in price from £6.95 to £16.95 and include everything from crab sandwiches and home-made burgers to prawn and mango kebabs and oven-baked seabass. The café's terrace (overlooking Polzeath's beach) can seat up to 90 people, but it's still worth making a booking in summer.

Also recommended
Antie Avice's Pasty Shop

St Kew Highway (next to Costcutter supermarket and garage).
Handy spot (just off the A39) to pick up a decent pasty.

Blue Tomato Café

Ferry Point, Rock, PL27 6LD, T01208-863841. Also at Port Isaac.
Bright and breezy café with excellent burgers. Food tends to be on the pricey side though.

King Arthur's Arms

Fore St, Tintagel, T01840-770831, kingarthursarms.co.uk.
Family-friendly pub opposite the National Trust's Old Post Office.

Posh nosh

Elements Hotel Bistro

Marine Drive, Bude, EX23 0LZ, T01288-352386, elements-life.co.uk/bistro. Mon-Sat from 1700.
Using locally sourced ingredients from Bude fishing boats and Cornish farmers, Elements prepares simple yet sophisticated food in a stunning location overlooking Widemouth Bay. Pick a window seat (or sit out on the terrace) and enjoy main courses such as turbot fillet with cucumber and crab risotto (£20) and 28-day hung sirloin steak (£18), followed by warm berry crumble and clotted cream (£5). Children's mains cost £7.

The Mill House Inn

Trebarwith, PL34 OHD, T01840-770200, themillhouseinn.co.uk. Daily.
Excellent gastropub with fancy dishes like shellfish, chorizo and runner bean bouillabaisse with pan roasted monkfish tail (£16.95). The bar menu (with kids' options) has more basic, cheaper meals, such as fishcakes or bangers and mash.

Salt Water Café Bistro

Tristram Cliff, Polzeath, PL27 6TE, T01208-862333. Daily from 1145, children's menu served until 1900.
With a prime spot overlooking Polzeath Bay, friendly service and excellent food, the Salt Water Café Bistro has established itself among Cornwall's culinary

elite. You won't taste better fish and chips anywhere, while more sophisticated seafood dishes, like the platter of smoked salmon, mackerel, pilchards and potted Newlyn Harbour crab, are always beautifully presented. The steaks and vegetarian mezze are also delicious.

Seven Bays Bistro

St Merryn, nr Padstow, T01841-521560, sevenbaysbistro.co.uk. Mon-Sat (plus Sun during school holidays) from 1830.
Seven Bays cooks up classic seafood dishes like fish pie, scallops and baked sea bass, as well as more daring concoctions with a Mediterranean twist. The pizzas (from £4.95) are excellent.

The Slipway Hotel

The Harbour Front, Port Isaac, PL29 3RH, T01208-880264, portisaachotel.com.
As you'd expect with Port Isaac's fish cellars practically next door, the Slipway's menus are dominated by seafood. For dinner in the atmospheric oak-beamed restaurant, try fillets of sea bass served with a crayfish tail and strawberry salsa (£16.25). The lunch menu, served alfresco on the terrace, includes sandwiches and jacket potatoes, as well as the signature dish, Doom Bar haddock and chips (£9.75). For something fishy but a bit different, try the fresh seafood pancake topped with Tintagel cheddar cheese (£9.45).

Let's go to...

Padstow

This is not just fish and chips. This is a succulent fillet of cod gently fried in a thin, crispy coating of beef dripping and served with hand-cut potato chips, a wedge of lemon and home-made tartare sauce. This is Stein's Fish & Chips...

Will you taste the difference? Quite possibly. Rick Stein has liberally seasoned Padstow with his gastronomic flare, transforming a pilchard port at the mouth of the Camel Estuary into a mecca for foodies. As well as a posh chippie, the celebrity chef's culinary empire includes three restaurants, a deli and a patisserie. Cafés, bistros, bakers, fudge shops and ice cream parlours have turned the knot of streets around the harbour into the most concentrated source of calories (and pasty-toting tourists) in Cornwall.

There's more to Padstein than food though. Look beyond the batter and you'll find a charming old fishing port, historic buildings, great crabbing, an estuary teeming with wildlife and beaches that are more golden than one of Stein's hand-crafted chips.

Get your bearings

Padstow's quayside car parks fill up quickly, but there are two great ways to arrive here without driving. The **Black Tor Ferry** (T01841-532239, padstow-harbour.co.uk, daily from 0800, return fares £3 adult, £1 child) shuttles back and forth across the estuary to Rock (see page 34), while the **Camel Trail** (see page 38) connects Padstow with Wadebridge – a five-mile cycle ride (or walk) that you can use to compensate for your inevitable pasty binge. If you do drive to Padstow during peak season, use the park and ride.

Located on the north side of the harbour, the **Padstow Tourist Information Centre** (Red Brick Building, North Quay, PL28 8AF, T01841-533449, padstowlive.com) is chock-a-block with leaflets, while the nearby Harbour Shop is a handy place to buy beach gear or crab lines. The safest spot for crabbing is on the harbour slipway.

Walk north out of town to sandy estuary beaches (or catch the ferry to Rock and hike to Daymer or even Polzeath, see page 34). To hire bikes for the Camel Trail, walk to South Quay,

Nip to the lobster hatchery

National Lobster Hatchery
South Quay, Padstow, PL28 8BL, T01841-533877,
nationallobsterhatchery.co.uk. Daily from 1000.
£3 adult, £1.50 child (5-17), £7 family.

This quirky quayside attraction at the head of the Camel Trail is good for nippers of both the curly-haired and crustacean variety. Lobsters are hatched and reared here before being released into the wild to replenish stocks around Cornwall. You can peer through portholes into the high-tech laboratory where planktonic lobster larvae swirl about inside giant glass cylinders, and tiny juveniles squat in ice-cube size containers. It takes up to seven years for them to reach maturity – if given the chance, lobsters can live for 100 years and grow to nearly 2 m in length! Dai the Claw is already halfway there. He's one of the hatchery's resident lobsters, inhabiting a small display of immaculate tanks, along with Charlie the albino lobster, Thermidor the orange-coloured lobster (a one-in-10-million occurrence), Sennen the spider crab, Gordon the edible crab and a trio of sponge crabs called Sponge Bob, Sponge Bill and Sponge Bert. Crustaceans have never seemed so cuddly and your children may never want to eat seafood again (parents, meanwhile, will be drooling over the recipe suggestion – grilled lobster with pernod and olive oil dressing – that's been sneaked into the display). Don't miss the rock-pool tank where domed glass provides a magnified view of blennies, crabs and anemones. There's also a small craft table with puzzles and colouring sheets, some fun interpretation boards about lobster life cycles and marine conservation, plus a chance to adopt a lobster – a snip at just £1.50.

Stein's Fish & Chips
South Quay, Padstow, T01841-532700, rickstein.com.
Daily 1200-1430, 1700-2000.

You can eat in or take away at Stein's, but be prepared to queue. Cod and chips costs £7.95 in the restaurant or £6.55 in a box; children's cod chunks and chips cost £6 eat-in, £4.50 takeaway. Is it worth it? You could save by not splurging on the home-made tartare sauce (55p/pot). The lemon wedge and, if you're lucky, a sprig of parsley, are complimentary. Portions are a bit measly, but the flavour really does set it apart. The batter is thin and doesn't hit your stomach like a depth charge; the fish is fresh and moist, and the chips, of course, are proper spuds and not too soggy. Other seafood on offer includes hake, monkfish, tiger prawns and scallops.

where you will also find the **National Lobster Hatchery** (see box opposite). The Elizabethan manor and deer park at **Prideaux Place** (Padstow, PL28 8RP, T01841-532411, prideauxplace.co.uk, Easter-Oct Sun-Thu from 1230) is a short walk from the harbour along Duke Street, Cross Street and Fentonluna Lane.

Retreat to a beach
When Padstow's busy harbour gets too much,

Local celebrity – Dai the Claw.

Let's go to... Padstow

escape the crowds by taking a low-tide stroll along the pristine sandy beaches that fringe the mouth of the Camel Estuary. To reach **St George's Cove** allow around 20 minutes to walk from the quay, past the war memorial to the ruined Napoleonic fortifications at Gun Point where, at low tide, St George's extends to **Harbour Cove** and **Hawker's Cove**. Quite tricky to find, Hawker's Cove is just beyond the Old Lifeboat Station – a secluded, sandy haven for a picnic.

Crabbing in Padstow harbour.

Take to the water

An old favourite for summer cruises out of Padstow, the 200-passenger **Jubilee Queen** (T07836-798457, padstowboattrips.com, Easter-Oct, check boards around harbour for rates and departures) explores offshore islands and potters upriver to Wadebridge on a high evening tide. Mackerel fishing boats include the **Celtic Warrior** (T01841-532639) and **Emma Kate** (T07970 595244), while **Padstow Speedboats** (T0781-111 3380, padstowboattrips.com, Easter-Oct daily, £5) offers 15-minute flits around the Camel Estuary. **Padstow Sealife Safaris** (T01841-521613, padstowsealifesafaris.co.uk, £35 adult, £25 child) runs two-hour tours in search of seals, dolphins, seabirds and basking sharks. See page 36 for details of the **Camel Ski School**. Padstow's nearest surf beaches are at Polzeath (see page 34) and Trevose Head (see page 66). See page 37 for surf schools.

Canvas & cottages

Close to the start of the Camel Trail and overlooking the estuary, **Dennis Cove Camping** (Padstow, PL28 8DR, T01841-532349, denniscove. co.uk, Apr-Sep, from around £13-17/pitch) is a small, sheltered campsite within easy walking or cycling distance of Padstow. For a more solid roof over your head, the **Padstow Cottage Company** (T01841-532633, padstowcottagecompany.co.uk) has a superb portfolio of over 20 cottages in and around the town, including Harbour's Reach – a four-bedroom cottage just 20 m from the harbour.

Grab a bite

The ultimate Padstow snack – a hot, flaky (and award-winning) Cornish pasty fresh from the **Chough Bakery** (The Strand, PL28 8AJ, T01841-532835, thechoughbakery.co.uk, Mon-Fri 1000-1700, Sat 1000-1400) – is best nibbled while dangling your legs over the quayside.

A fun, informal diner offering simple, tasty food for breakfast, lunch and supper, **Custard** (The Strand, PL28 8AJ, T01841-532565, custarddiner. com, daily 0900-1500, 1900-2130) serves delicious crab sandwiches (£8) and other local dishes, or you could just nip in for an egg and bacon butty (£5).

Padstow's best pizzas can be found at **Rojano's** (Mill Square, PL28 8AE, T01841-532796, rojanos. co.uk), while sweet options in the harbour area include **Roskilly's Ice Cream**, **The Fudge Shop** and **Stein's Patisserie**. If you just want to pick up a sandwich for a picnic, pop into **Simply Sandwiches** or **Doorsteps Sandwich Shop**.

Heading out of town, **Padstow Farm Shop** (Trethellick Farm, PL28 8HJ, T01841-533060, padstowfarmshop.co.uk, Tue-Sat 1000-1600) sells locally reared meat, Cornish cheeses, seasonal vegetables, honey, jams, chutneys and ice cream.

In nearby St Merryn, **Fryer Tucks** (T01841-520724) is a popular chippie, while **Seven Bays Bistro** (T01841-521560, sevenbaysbistro.co.uk) offers fresh Cornish cuisine with a Mediterranean zing – local seafood with spaghetti and a cream and white wine sauce, for example, costs from around £12.95. Pizzas, meanwhile, start at £4.95.

SCALLOPS
£1 EACH

GRADE 'A'
MUSSELS
(ST AUSTELL)
£5.0?

HAKE
FILLET £13.?0/

Stein's Deli
South Quay, Padstow, T01841-532700, rickstein.com.
Mon-Sat 1000-1700, Sun 1000-1600.
A gastronomic Aladdin's Cave, Stein's Deli is a feast for
the eyes, with fresh seafood and seasonal fruit and
vegetables arranged on counters like natural works
of art. There is also a good range of local meat (try
the lamb and mint sausages on your barbecue), lots
of preserves, a cookshop and a selection of luxury
Treleaven's ice cream for around £1.60 a scoop. Of
course, anyone with a genuine sweet tooth should
make for Stein's Patisserie on Lanadwell Street where
the shelves are packed with cakes and pastries. For a sit-
down treat, visit Stein's Café or The Seafood Restaurant.
See page 49 for Stein's Fish & Chips.

HADDOCK £15.12/kg
FILLET

COD
?ILL£?.66

FARMED
SEABASS
£23.79/kg

Off the beaten track

Bodmin Moor

You can have too much of a good thing in Cornwall, so when you feel 'surfed out' or just yearn for a beach-free day that doesn't resort to an expensive family attraction, head inland to Bodmin Moor for walks, woods and wonderful views. You can go sailing on one of the moor's reservoirs or cycle the Camel Trail from Bodmin. The town's other attractions include a steam railway and historic jail, while the splendid manor house of Lanhydrock is nearby.

Get your bearings

Remember Bodmin Moor? It was that hilly bit with the wind turbines and speed cameras that slowed you down on the A30 as you rushed to get to your seaside bolthole. It's the one part of Cornwall that most visitors see, but few ever explore. That's a shame because, not only is this a wild and beautiful place, but it's easily accessed – not only from the bisecting A30, but also from the A390/ A38 (linking Callington, Liskeard and Bodmin) and the A39 (running between Bude and Wadebridge).

If you don't fancy venturing straight onto the moors, pop into the visitor centre in Bodmin's 19th-century Shire Hall for information on walks. This is also where you'll find the dastardly **Courtoom Experience** (join the jury in a Victorian murder trial) and **Town Museum** (Easter-Sep Mon-Fri 1030-1630, Sat 1030-1430, free) – an ideal combo for a rainy afternoon. Bodmin Library has storytelling and activities for under-fives every Wednesday at 1400, while the Dragon Leisure Centre (see page 41) has a heated indoor pool.

Walk in the woods

Signposted from the A38 between Bodmin and Liskeard, **Cardinham Woods** is managed by the Forestry Commission (T01392-834233, forestry.gov. uk). Four waymarked trails weave through a woodland of oak, rowan, alder, willow and beech, including the two-mile,

Remember Bodmin Moor? It was that hilly bit with the wind turbines and speed cameras that slowed you down on the A30 as you rushed to get to your seaside bolthole.

Rock fan – the granite tors of the Cheesewrings are a magnet to adventurous children.

Off the beaten track Bodmin Moor

45-minute bike- and buggy-friendly Lady Vale Walk that follows a stream frequented by dippers and kingfishers. You might also spot buzzards spiralling above the treetops or glimpse a deer tiptoeing through the undergrowth.

Wheal Glynn Walk (1 mile, 45 mins) involves a short strenuous climb from Lady Vale Bridge to a long-abandoned lead and silver mine where you can still spot the old engine house and chimney stack amongst the trees. Lidcutt Valley Walk (3½ miles, 2 hrs) is a long loop leading off the Lady Vale walk, with a picnic area at Scotch Pine, while the moderately strenuous Callywith Wood Walk (2½ miles, 1½ hrs) skirts a wildlife research area where dormice are being studied.

There is a picnic area and playground near the car park (£2/day) or you could treat yourself to a cream tea at Woods Café. Summer events include bushcraft, wildlife detectives, fireside tales and bat-watching nights from around £6 child (free for accompanying adults).

Further east on the southern flanks of Bodmin Moor, **Golitha Falls National Nature Reserve** (T0300-060 6000, naturalengland.org.uk) is another shady woodland retreat that's popular with walkers. Several trails (including a buggy-friendly one) probe a steep-sided valley where the River Fowey tumbles and froths between ferns, fallen logs and moss-covered boulders – a hideout for woodland pixies if ever there was one.

Head for the hills

There are numerous walks on Bodmin Moor, but one of the most engaging for children is the 2½-mile **Cheesewring Trail**, which starts and finishes at the car park in Minions (signed 'The Hurlers').

To begin with, the easy path weaves across springy moorland pockmarked with tea-coloured pools and roamed by wind-tussled sheep and cattle. You'll soon reach a ring of standing stones with the higgledy-piggledy outcrop of Cheesewring Tor visible ahead. It's a short

Seven cottages in converted 18th century farmhouse and outbuildings. Heated indoor swimming pool with paddling pool perfect for babies and toddlers (open all year). Games room and play barn equipped for children of all ages. Country location with superb views to Dartmoor and only one mile from Launceston town centre, historic capital of Cornwall with all conveniences. Easy access to North Coast beaches and coastal villages, South Coast beaches and fishing ports, Bodmin Moor and Dartmoor. Cottages are well equipped and have VisitBritain 4-star rating. Pets Welcome.

See you soon! Simon & Clare

Bamham Farm Cottages

Simon & Clare Hirsh
Bamham Farm Cottages
Higher Bamham
Launceston
Cornwall, PL15 9LD

PS. for more information, contact:
Tel: 01566 772141, www.bamhamfarm.co.uk,
Email: simon@bamhamfarm.co.uk

Top: Plain sailing at Siblyback Lake; steaming along on the Bodmin & Wenford Railway; pretending to fly at Cheesewring Tor. Middle: The calm oasis of Lanhydrock. Bottom: Cardinham Woods, standing stones at The Hurlers and a view from Bodmin Moor across the Tamar Valley.

scramble through bracken before the impressive scale of these giant 'stone hamburgers' becomes clear. Adventurous kids will be bounding all over them, scrambling up their chiselled flanks and even reaching the top of one or two of the more accessible ones – arms spread wide, pretending to fly in the breeze. It's great fun, accessible, not too arduous, the views are tremendous and there's even a bit of geological and historical intrigue thrown in for good measure.

In Minions there's a tea room, shop and toilet, plus the Cheesewring Hotel – Cornwall's loftiest inn. Hurlers Halt offers B&B and self-catering, plus hot meals and cream teas.

Another high point for the kids, **Helman Tor** (Cornwall Wildlife Trust, T01872-273939, cornwallwildlifetrust.org.uk) was once a Neolithic hill fort and has far-reaching views towards Bodmin Moor's high-point, Brown Willy (417 m).

Alternatively, make a beeline for **Bodmin Beacon**, a great spot to fly a kite in the shadow of the 44-m-tall obelisk raised in memory of Sir Walter Raleigh Gilbert, a distinguished officer of the British East India Company.

Get afloat

Siblyback Lake (Common Moor, PL14 6ER, T01579-346522, swlakestrust.org.uk) has a wide range of activities on offer. You can hire kayaks, Canadian canoes, windsurfers

and rowing boats for £10-16/hour, enrol on a two-day sailing course (from £145) or try three different sports on a Wet 'n' Active Day (£45 for children aged 8 and over).

If that all sounds too energetic, Siblyback is also a lovely spot for a picnic with views across the lake and surrounding hills (legions of ducks will greet you as you step out of your car so don't forget to take bread). Other facilities include a playground, tea room, shop and campsite (see below).

Pitch your tent

The meadow campsite at **Siblyback Lake** (see above for contact details) is open April to October and has pitches for around £6 adult, £3 child (5-14) and £14 family.

Set on a 200-acre organic farm, the sheltered campsite at **South Penquite Farm** (Blisland, nr Bodmin, PL30 4LH, T01208-850491, southpenquite. co.uk, May-Oct, camping £6 adult, £3 child (5-16), yurts £220-360/wk) has solar-powered showers, family bathrooms and a children's play area. For a Mongolian twist try one of the four yurts (sleeping up to 6). Each has a wood-burning stove, rugs, futons and a roof light for star-gazing. Farm-made lamb burgers and sausages are available for your campfire barbecues, while a lovely farm walk takes you to a Bronze Age settlement and wildlife-rich ancient woodland.

Siblyback Lake.

Cosy up in a cottage

One of the best set-ups for families, **Bamham Farm Cottages** (Higher Bamham, Launceston, PL15 9LD, T01566-772141, bamhamfarm.co.uk. £295-1395/wk, see advert on page 54) is an attractive farm complex with seven cottages (sleeping 4-8), a large indoor heated swimming pool, games room and play barn.

Another sound choice, **Glynn Barton Cottages** (Cardinham, PL30 4AX, T01208-821104, glynnbarton.co.uk, £595-1985/wk for a 2-bedroom cottage) are a collection of beautifully restored 18th-century properties with light, contemporary interiors and lots of family-friendly features – from farm animals and softplay barn to farm shop and indoor swimming pool.

Also try **Coombe Mill** (St Breward, PL30 4LZ, T01208-850344, coombemill.com) and **Mount Pleasant Farm** (nr Bodmin, PL30 4EX, T01208-821342, mountpleasantcottages.co.uk).

Refuelling

Collect picnic supplies from **St Kew Harvest Farm Shop** (see page 45) and walk to Delphi Bridge, a secluded spot near the village of St Breward. Immortalized in Daphne du Maurier's novel, the legendary **Jamaica Inn** (Bolventor, PL15 7TS, T01566-86250, jamaicainn.co.uk) is open most days for breakfast, lunch and dinner and has the added attractions of a pirate museum and playground.

Don't miss

Bodmin & Wenford Railway
Bodmin General Station, Bodmin, PL31 1AQ, T0845-125 9678, bodminandwenfordrailway.co.uk. Mar-Dec. All-day rover tickets £11.50 adult, £6 child (3-16), £30 family.
This six-mile train ride on Cornwall's only full-size railway operated by steam locos links directly with the Camel Trail (see page 38) at Boscarne Junction, Cardinham Woods (see page 52) via a footpath from Colesloggett Halt or Lanhydrock (see below) via a path from Bodmin Parkway. Restored to 1950s nostalgia, the main station is in Bodmin (Bodmin General), where you'll find a souvenir shop and workshop viewing area.

Carnglaze Caverns
St Neot, PL14 6HQ, T01579-320251, carnglaze.com. Year round Mon-Sat 1000-1700 (Aug till 2000). £6 adult, £4 child, £17.50 family.
Join a 45-minute guided tour to a subterranean lake deep within old slate-mining caves.

Colliford Lake Adventure Park
Bolventor, PL14 6PZ, T01208-821469, collifordlakepark.com. Daily from 1030. £6 adult, £5 child (3-12), £19.80 family.
This is Bodmin on the wild side, whichever way you look at it. At one extreme you've got the 50-acre Moorland Kingdom with walking trails and wildlife hides and, at the other, there's Kids' Kingdom, an indoor adventure zone with ball pit, net mazes and drop slide. Woodland Kingdom has more energy-sapping stuff and there's also a Beast of Bodmin display.

Lanhydrock
Nr Bodmin, PL30 5AD, T01208-265950, nationaltrust. org.uk. Garden year round daily from 1000; house Mar-Nov Tue-Sun from 1100. £10.40 adult, £5.20 child (5-17), £26 family.
A magnificent estate with vast grounds and an imposing gatehouse, the interior of Lanhydrock itself is surprisingly unpretentious and reflects the day-to-day – albeit very wealthy – lifestyle of a Victorian family. Children can follow a quiz trail to explore the 50-odd rooms which include a nursery and the servants quarters 'below stairs'. Craft activities are held in the old stables across the courtyard from the café, while paths weave through park and woodland to the banks of the River Fowey (keep your eyes peeled for otters). Back near the car park there's a woodland play area.

Launceston

Five minutes off the A30 and you could be dawdling through countryside like this – rolling hills, emerald fields and wooded slopes just to the north of Launceston. The town itself is also worth a detour – if only to trade car for train and take a ride on the Launceston Steam Railway.

Get your bearings
Launceston is just across the Devon-Cornwall border within earshot of the A30. You can also reach it by striking north through the Tamar Valley on the A388 from Callington. Just to the west of

Launceston, the A395 branches off the A30 to link with the A39 Atlantic Highway. Launceston is Cornwall's only walled town. Climbing to the top of the Norman castle (english-heritage.org.uk, Apr-Oct daily from 1000, £3.50 adult, £1.50 child) is a good way to stretch your legs if you've been couped up in a car for hours.

The main attractions
The Launceston Steam Railway (Launceston, PL15 8DA, T01566-775665, launcestonsr.co.uk,

Spot an otter

Tucked away in beautiful rolling countryside, the Tamar Otter & Wildlife Centre is just a few miles north of Launceston and makes a welcome diversion off the relentless A30. You'll see two types of otter here – European and Asian short-clawed. Both are shy and secretive, so try to visit during feeding times (1200 and 1500), when keepers do their rounds of the enclosures, handing out offcuts of cod from local fish and chip shops and offering titbits of information on each otter's life history. The otters emerge from their hiding places, chattering excitedly, squirming like eels in their pools and pestering the keepers for food. Peacocks, guineafowl and geese amble around the park and there are also various owls in aviaries. You can attempt to hand-feed fallow deer and wallabies on a woodland walk and there's a nature trail too. Peaceful, uncrowded and refreshingly simple, the centre has a café, gift shop and picnic area.

Tamar Otter & Wildlife Centre
North Petherwin, Launceston PL15 8GW, T01566-785646, tamarotters.co.uk. Apr-Oct daily 1030-1800. £7 adult, £3.50 child (3-15), £18 family.

European otter.

Easter and Oct half term, plus May-Sep Sun-Fri, from 1100, call for fares) operates narrow gauge steam locos through the Kensey Valley back and forth to **New Mills Farm Park** (Launceston, PL15 8SN, T01566-777106, newmillsfarmpark.com, Easter-Sep 1030-1700, £3). You can also reach the farm park by car (not nearly as much fun). Once there, kids can get stuck into good-value food at the Hungry Farmer Café before running riot in the indoor/outdoor play areas.

Three miles west of Launceston, there's more fun and games at **Trethorne Leisure Park** (Kennards House, PL15 8QE, T01566-86324,

trethorneleisure.com, Feb-Nov daily from 1000, around £8) – one of Cornwall's biggest play zones with a huge amount to do whatever the weather.

Nearby, at **Hidden Valley Discovery Park** (Tredidon, PL15 8SJ, T01566-86463, hiddenvalleydiscoverypark.co.uk, Apr-Oct 1000-1700, £6.50 adult, £5.50 child (4-15), £22 family) allow at least two hours to solve clues leading to crystals hidden in an attractive woodland park. Each crystal is worth a certain amount of time in the Vault where you tackle challenges to win a prize. Treasure hunts are available in three difficulty levels.

Main photo: The white stuff –
shark biscuit at Gwithian Sands.
Opposite: The last stand at Treyarnon
Beach; sailing at Stithians Lake.

Northwest Cornwall

It doesn't matter if you're shark biscuit (surf speak for bodyboarder), a grommet (young surfer) or a macker-carving dude (someone pretty good cutting smooth turns on big waves), the northwest coast is Cornwall's surf central, with fantastic beaches almost non-stop from Trevose Head to the Hayle Estuary.

Newquay hogs the limelight. It's one of Europe's premier surf spots with legendary Fistral Beach hosting international competitions. The sprawling resort is awash with teenage surf heads lured by a frothy cocktail of Atlantic breakers, alcopops and nightclubs. But don't let Newquay's brash reputation put you off. There are plenty of quiet family beaches here, while attractions like the Blue Reef Aquarium and Newquay Zoo top the must-do lists of most children. New developments are driving the resort up-market, while Newquay's airport ensures that the resort remains well and truly on the map.

It's not without stiff competition though. A few miles to the north, **Watergate Bay** comes up trumps for many families, thanks to its superb beach, adrenaline-charged Extreme Academy and family-friendly hotel – not to mention the culinary delights of Jamie Oliver's Fifteen restaurant.

Further north still, **Mawgan Porth** has the Bedruthan Steps Hotel (about as family-orientated as they come) and is close to both the Crealy Great Adventure Park and the spectacular beach at Bedruthan Steps (where adventures are inspired by nature). More sandy beaches fringe the granite headland of **Trevose Head**, near Padstow, where you can learn to surf at sheltered Harlyn Bay or run wild in the dunes at Constantine while the Atlantic beats its steady thunder on the rocky reefs offshore.

Six miles south of Newquay, **Holywell Bay** is another sensational, dune-backed beach with the added family appeal of a fun park. **Perranporth** is a busy resort, while **St Agnes** – or 'Aggie' – spills down to pretty Trevaunance Cove in a tumble of rose-clad cottages, galleries and cafés.

Porthtowan has a thriving surf scene and one of the region's most hip beach cafés, in contrast to the quieter beach at **Portreath**. Continue south past this former mining port and you enter a spectacular stretch of National Trust coastline, dramatic cliffs finally bowing to the stoic little lighthouse at **Godrevy Head**, where several miles of glorious beach curl west along broad St Ives Bay.

Here to there

The Northwest Cornwall chapter of *Cornwall with Kids* covers the Atlantic shoreline from Trevose Head to St Ives Bay, including beaches as far west as Hayle. For Carbis Bay and the beaches of Porthminster and Porthmeor, see the section on St Ives (page 110). Inland, Northwest Cornwall coverage extends roughly to the A39/A30 and south beyond Redruth to Stithians Lake. The Coast-to-Coast cycle trail between Portreath and Devoran is also covered in this chapter (see page 70). For Truro, see page 178.

Trevose Head – St Ives Bay

N

2 km
2 miles

You must

❶ Learn to surf at Harlyn Bay.

❷ Cycle the Portreath Tramroad through Cornwall's World Heritage mining site.

❸ Follow in a giant's footsteps at Bedruthan Steps.

❹ Run wild and get wet at Crealy Great Adventure Park.

❺ Count seals at Godrevy Point.

❻ Talk to the animals at Paradise Park.

❼ Scoff Jamie Oliver's pasta at Fifteen.

❽ Get savvy with surf and beach safety at Lusty Glaze beach, Newquay.

❾ Sail a dinghy at Stithians Lake.

❿ Sprint across the vast sands at Perranporth or Holywell Bay.

From top left: kite flying at Constantine Bay; beach lifeguard on patrol at Gwithian Sands; bucket of crabs; Godrevy Lighthouse; surfing at Harlyn Bay; living jewels in a Portreath rock pool; getting the sand and sea between your toes at Watergate Bay.

Fun & free

Fly a kite

The strongest gust ever recorded at a low-level site in England was at Gwennap Head, the most southerly headland on Cornwall's Penwith peninsula, where wind speeds reached 118 mph on 15 December 1979 (tip: don't pitch your tent here). The coast of Cornwall is officially the windiest place in England, which also makes it prime kite-flying territory. On the northwest coast unwind your strings at beaches like **Gwithian**, **Perranporth** and **Watergate Bay**.

Watch the birdies

During spring and autumn the **Hayle Estuary RSPB Reserve** is a magnet for migrant waders and gulls, while in summer you may be lucky enough to spot an osprey. It's winter, however, that really sees the estuary getting all of a flutter as up to 18,000 birds (from lapwings to teals) descend on the mudflats.

Run wild in the dunes

The sand dunes at **Constantine Bay** on Trevose Head are scribbled with paths – an open invitation to a picnic and a mega-game of hide and seek.

> **Keep your eyes (and ears) open for the Gannel Crake, a mysterious creature whose terrible cry echoes across Newquay's Gannel Estuary.**

Spot a seal

Walk to **Godrevy Head**, find a safe place to sit on the cliffs and train your binoculars on the rocky shore below. Grey seals can often be seen 'spy-hopping' or squirming in the surf.

Delve into Cornish history

A little gem, **St Agnes Museum** (Penwinnick Rd, T01872-553228, stagnesmuseum.org.uk, Easter-Oct daily 1030-1700) covers everything from fishing and folklore to tin mining and turtles.

I've lived in Cornwall for 20 years. I came here on holiday and married a Cornish girl. Portreath is my favourite beach – it's good for swimming and has rock pools full of wildlife. For something fun and free, take a field guidebook to one of the Cornwall Wildlife Trust's nature reserves – they're all over the county and you'll learn loads. My top three places to see wildlife are Godrevy for seals, Portreath's North Cliffs for peregrine falcons and Gwithian Towans for adders. As for the best fish and chips in Cornwall – it has to be Mac's Fish Bar, 9 Higher Fore St, Redruth, T01209-218715.

Gary Zammit
Wildlife ranger, Feadon Farm, Gwel an Mor, nr Portreath, T01209-842354, gwelanmor.com.

Visit Tehidy Country Park

Why? Sometimes you just feel like a change from the beach. Carpeted in bluebells during spring, this woodland oasis is bursting with wildlife. Stroll the pushchair-friendly Pink Trail around North Cliffs and you will discover majestic beech trees over 200 years old. Tehidy was formerly the estate of the Bassett family, which developed Portreath as a port for exporting tin ore. The easy Purple Trail loops around ornamental lakes near the Bassett mansion.

Where? From the A30, take the Pool exit and follow brown tourist signs. The Mineral Tramways cycle trail (see page 70) also passes through the park.

How? Tehidy Country Park Visitor Centre & Café is open year round daily 0930-1700. Cornwall County Council, T01872-222000, cornwall.gov.uk.

Hell & back

The B3301 between Portreath and Hayle condenses everything that is fabulous about Cornwall's coast into a few miles. Dawdle and stop often. There's a small car park at Hell's Mouth Café where, after crossing the road, you are just a few steps from dizzy cliff-top views of smugglers' coves and rocky islets wrapped in filigrees of surf. Fulmars pirouette on updraughts, basking sharks tack back and forth through turquoise waters, while flowers – thrift in spring, heather in summer – blush the cliffs pink. A little further on, the road unravels from the cliff tops; a right-hand turn leads past surfing bays and a string of sandy coves to Godrevy Head and its offshore lighthouse.

Out & about Northwest Cornwall

Best beaches

The beaches described here are found east to west, from Trevose Head to the Hayle Estuary. For St Ives' beaches, see pages 110-113.

Trevone Bay
🔵 🔵 ➕ 🔵 🅿️

Just two miles west of Padstow, Trevone is a small sandy bay that's popular with families and surfers. Walk up on to the cliffs to the north and you can peer (with caution) into Round Hole – the result of a collapsed sea cave roof.

Harlyn Bay
🔵 🔵 ➕ 🔵 🔵 🅿️ 🔵

Tucked into the lee of Trevose Head, Harlyn Bay is often sheltered when west-facing beaches are being pummelled by breakers. A perfect family beach, it has gorgeous golden sand, shallow streams to dam, a surf school and snack bar.

Mother Ivey's Bay
🅿️

Overlooked by two caravan parks (Harlyn Sands and Mother Ivey's – see page 79), this beautiful bay faces northeast and, like Harlyn Bay, is a sheltered option for young families. The Padstow lifeboat station is at the far end of the beach, but there are no facilities (unless you're staying at one of the caravan parks), so you will need to park at Harlyn Bay and walk 20 minutes or so along the coast path.

Booby's & Constantine Bay
🔵 ➕ 🔵 🅿️ 🚗 ❗

South of Trevose Head (where you can walk along the cliffs to the lighthouse), the beaches feel the full brunt of the Atlantic and take on a more rugged appearance. Booby's is the first – and probably the least family-friendly – in a long string of spectacular sandy beaches extending all the way to Newquay and beyond. Rocky reefs and strong currents make swimming dangerous at Booby's, but at low tide the beach merges with Constantine where you're as likely to hear the piping of oystercatchers as the scream of excited children surfing, flying kites or running wild across acres of pristine sand. Parking and facilities are located at the Constantine end of the bay, where the superb little Snak Attak van serves fresh coffee, pasta pots, muffins and cookies right by the beach.

Treyarnon Bay
🔵 ➕ 🔵 🅿️ 🚗 ❗

A popular surf beach south of Constantine Bay, Treyarnon has a mixture of sand and rocky outcrops. Be wary of strong currents. There's a Snak Attak beach bar in the car park and a good choice of accommodation nearby, including the Treyarnon Youth Hostel (see page 78).

Porthcothan

A narrow wedge of sand backed by dunes, Porthcothan has decent surf, but take care at low tide when dangerous currents can whip around the headlands.

Bedruthan Steps

Cornwall's very own Twelve Apostles, Bedruthan Steps might not be quite on the scale of Australia's natural wonder, but it is still an impressive beach, dominated by gnarled sea stacks. Be warned, though, that not only is access via a very steep flight of steps, but swimming is dangerous due to strong currents. A fine beach to explore, but be alert to tides as it's easy to get cut off. There's a National Trust car park with shop and tea room at Carnewas. Paths lead from here across flower-speckled cliff tops to a vantage point overlooking the beach.

Mawgan Porth

A shark-fin-shaped wedge of sand between Bedruthan Steps and Watergate Bay, Mawgan Porth is a favourite spot for swimmers and surfers, but usually remains less crowded than beaches further south. There is easy access to the beach, with toilets and parking nearby. The exceptionally family-friendly Bedruthan Steps Hotel (see page 80) is perched on the cliffs above.

Watergate Bay

This glorious stretch of surf-raked coast sees stylish Cornwall riding the crest of a wave. Not only is it home to Jamie Oliver's Fifteen restaurant (see page 83), but the upmarket Watergate Bay Hotel (see page 80) and adrenaline-charged Extreme Academy (see page 72) also preside over its two-mile stretch of pristine sand. Watergate Bay is not a particularly pretty beach – there are no interesting nooks and crannies and it's backed by crumbling cliffs that march austerely northwards – but it is one of those run-wild-and-free Atlantic beaches that are a signature of north Cornwall. The B3276 loops down to the beach at the Watergate Bay Hotel and a car park that backs onto the main beach complex – a grandstand-style building that houses the excellent Beach Hut and Venus Café (see pages 82-83) as well as Fifteen. You certainly won't go hungry at Watergate Bay. Burning off calories shouldn't be a problem either – the Extreme Academy organizes surf lessons, there are trampolines set up by the lifeguard station and you can also try your luck at kite surfing. Newquay's attractions, meanwhile, are just a few miles away across the bay.

This glorious stretch of surf-raked sand sees stylish Cornwall riding the crest of a wave.

Out & about Northwest Cornwall

Porth Beach
Practically a northern suburb of Newquay, Porth is a busy coastal resort with several good hotels. The beach has a good-size swathe of sand even at high water. When the tide ebbs, it's sometimes possible to walk around the headland into neighbouring Lusty Glaze beach. A wide stream flows along the northern edge of Porth beach, which is bordered by Porth Island – connected to the mainland by a footbridge and the site of an Iron Age settlement. Smugglers' caves near the base of the island are well worth exploring at low tide when Whipsiderry beach (just to the north of Porth) is revealed.

Newquay
From east to west, Newquay's main town beaches are **Lusty Glaze**, **Tolcarne**, **Great Western** and **Towan** – all four merging into a continuous ribbon of sand at low tide. From quiet pilchard fishing village to bustling (some would say rowdy) holiday resort, Newquay has everything from holiday parks and plush apartments to boat trips and attractions like the Blue Reef Aquarium and Newquay Zoo (see pages 74-75). And then, of course, there's the surf. Located on the town's western outskirts, Fistral, see below, is Newquay's prime spot for serious wave-

riding. Try the more sheltered town beaches if Fistral is too fiesty. Not only are they ideal for novice surfers, but they are also good, albeit frequently crowded, family beaches. As well as surfing lessons, Lusty Glaze Adventure Centre (see page 71) runs a Junior Baywatch programme of basic surf rescue techniques and rock-pooling for children aged eight to 14. Tucked next to the harbour, Towan is usually the most sheltered of the town beaches and also has excellent facilities: a sound choice for young families. Tolcarne and Lusty Glaze have a dog ban, May to September.

Fistral Beach
If the surf's up, Fistral will be packed. Europe's most famous surfing beach, this iconic strip of sand is located just to the west of Newquay's Towan Head. Fistral has probably the most reliable surf of any beach in Cornwall with waves typically peaking at around 4 to 8 ft. South Fistral tends to be more protected than the northern end of the beach, where large barrelling waves can develop at low tide. With big swells and a southeast offshore breeze, Fistral's legendary Cribbar (a monster wave reaching up to 30 ft in height) pounds the reefs off Towan Head. Located right on the beach, the International Surf Centre at Fistral is a surfer's

paradise – book a surf lesson, kit yourself out with gear from Fat Face or watch the action from the comfort of the Blu Bar.

Crantock Beach
Located at the mouth of the Gannel Estuary, Crantock has plenty of sand and dunes (ideal for beach games and a picnic), but swimming is dangerous due to strong currents. During summer, a ferry runs to the beach from near the Fern Pit Café on Pentire Head.

Porth Joke
Tiny Porth Joke (or 'Polly Joke') is wedged between West Pentire and Kelsey Head. A lovely little cove with good surf – but no facilities and a 15-minute walk from the car park.

Holywell Bay
Just three miles down the coast from Newquay, this large sandy beach is given a family-friendly boost by the nearby fun park (see page 74), which features a range of pay-as-you-play attractions, such as F1 Carts and Adventure Golf. The main access to the beach follows a shallow stream (great for sailing boats or paddling) or you can hit the sands by following paths through the dunes. There's plenty of space at Holywell Bay, even at high tide. One of

Left to right: Trevone Bay looking towards Trevose Head; golden sands near Godrevy Lighthouse; cliff top view of Bedruthan Steps.

the highlights of the beach, however, is only accessible at low tide when you can walk to a sea cave at the northern end of the bay. Venture inside (with a torch and an eye on the tide) and you'll find a terrace of rock pools filled by water seeping through multicoloured rocks – a 'holy well' renowned for its healing qualities.

Perranporth

At low tide, Perran Bay is fringed by three miles of surf-scoured beach, from dune-backed **Penhale Sands** and **Perran Sands** in the north to the lively resort town of Perranporth where the main street is crammed with beach shops, cafés and amusement arcades. Stranded at low water, a small island known as Chapel Rock (in front of the main beach) has a natural sea pool that will appeal to littl'uns in search of a calmer alternative to Perranporth's surf. There are also rock pools and caves at the base of nearby cliffs.

Trevaunance Cove

A small cove hemmed in by cliffs at St Agnes, Trevaunance is

pebbly at high tide, but reveals sand and rock pools as the water recedes. Surfing is good, and there's a small car park near the Breakers Beach Café.

Chapel Porth

Sharing over a mile of sand with Porthtowan at low tide, Chapel Porth shrinks to a small, secluded cove at high water. The cliff tops are littered with tin mining ruins, including the chimney stack of Wheal Coates.

Porthtowan

A popular surfing beach with easy access and good facilities, Porthtowan has a surf school, board hire, a well-stocked beach shop and the trendy Blue Beach Bar (see page 82). The beach is backed by a small area of dunes, behind which you'll find a pleasant sandy playground. Check out the rock pools either side of the bay.

Portreath

An interesting beach with a harbour at one end (built to serve the mining industry in the 18th century) and wild cliffs

riddled with caves at the other, Portreath is a mixture of sand and shingle with rock pools and a natural swimming pool by the pier. Park by the beach where you'll find cafés and a surf shop.

Hayle Sands

Hayle Sands is the collective name for the beaches stretching three miles from Godrevy Point to Hayle Estuary. Approaching from the east, the B3301 skirts dramatic cliffs at Hell's Mouth (see page 65) before dropping down to St Ives Bay. A right turn leads to a National Trust car park and the excellent Godrevy Café (see page 82). Stretching away to the south are the unblemished, surf-strafed sands of **Gwithian Towans** and **Hayle Towans** (also accessible across dunes and from various holiday parks further south). Continue past Godrevy Café towards the lighthouse and the coastline becomes rockier and more varied, with secluded coves that are wonderful for swimming, snorkelling and kayaking in calm conditions. And, as is so often the case with Cornish beaches, it just gets better and better as the tide goes out.

Out & about Northwest Cornwall

Action stations

Boat trips
Padstow boat trips: see page 50.

Newquay boat trips
South Quay, Newquay, T01637-878886, newquay-harbour.com. May-Sep daily 1000-1800. £5. One- or two-hour cruises aboard the 12-passenger *Kernow Belle*, *Tamarisk* or *Island Maid*, with a chance to spot seals and catch mackerel. Speedboat trips also available (T0781-398 5273).

Cycling
Coast to Coast Trail
Linking historic mining harbours on the north coast (Portreath) and south coast (Devoran), this 11-mile route follows the old Portreath tramroad (worked by horses as early as 1812) and the Redruth and Chasewater Railway line, built in the 1820s to transport copper ore from Gwennap to Devoran. Weaving through ancient woodland and heathland, the scenic trail is largely off-road and surprisingly level. You can also embellish your ride with various loops on the newly extended network of Mineral Tramways. See below for routes and cycle hire companies.

Mineral Tramways
Whether you choose to cycle, walk or ride a horse, this network of trails, centred around Camborne and Redruth, provides mainly level, traffic-free access to one of Cornwall's historic mining regions. There are 30 miles of track in total – several linking with the Coast to Coast Trail (see above). Options include the 7½-mile Great Flat Lode Trail, the 2½-mile Tehidy Trail (through Tehidy Country Park) and the 5½-mile Portreath Branchline Trail (a useful link between Portreath and the Great Flat Lode Trail).

The Bike Barn
Elm Farm Cycle Centre, Cambrose, Portreath, TR16 5UF, T01209-891498, cornwallcycletrails.com. Year round daily from 1000. Bikes from £12, child trailers and tag-a-longs £8. The main cycle hire centre for the Coast to Coast Trail and Mineral Tramways, the Bike Barn offers guided rides and children's activity packs, as well as a picnic area, farm shop and children's play area.

Bike Chain Bissoe Bike Hire
Old Conns Work, Bissoe, TR4 8QZ, T01872-870341, cornwallcyclehire.com. Year round daily from 0930. Adult bike £12-15/day, child's bike £8/day, tag-a-long £10/day. Located towards the southern end of the Coast to Coast Trail, Bissoe Bike Hire has a café and good range of bikes.

Go karting
St Eval Kart Circuit
St Eval, Wadebridge, PL27 7UN, T01637-860160, cornwallkarting.com. Sat 0930-dusk, Mon-Fri call for details. Cub kart £4/5 mins, Bambini kart £7/10 mins, Cadet kart £8/10 mins, Junior kart £10/10 minutes, Pro kart £22/15 mins.
Unleash the Jenson Button in your three-year-old at this supremely child-friendly go-karting circuit where electric Cub karts are suitable for kids aged three to five. Step up a gear and six- to eight-year-olds can take a spin in Bambini karts capable of reaching 12 mph over a 200 m circuit. Cadet Karts (for eight- to 11-year-olds) can top 20 mph, while Junior Karts (12- to 16-year-olds) push the needle to a thrilling 35 mph. Big boys (and girls), meanwhile, can play at being Stig in 70-mph Pro-Karts (16+).

Horse riding
Chiverton Riding Centre
Silverwell, TR4 8JQ, T01872-560471, chivertonriding.co.uk. Daily 0800-2200, call for details.
Pony Club-approved school near St Agnes, with indoor and outdoor facilities, and a lot going on for children, such as introduction to ponies courses and stable and grooming days.

Cornish Riding Holidays
Wheal Buller Riding School, Buller Hill, Redruth, TR16 6SS,

T01209-211852, cornish-riding-holidays.co.uk. Year round, call for details of lessons, hacks and rides. This family-run horse-riding centre has lessons available most days (minimum age five). Rides and hacks, also daily, strike out along the Mineral Tramways and Coast to Coast trails. Pony-mad children can join week-long riding holidays.

Reen Manor Riding Stables

Reen, Perranporth, TR6 0AJ, T01872-573064, reenmanorstables.com. Year round, £15/30-min ride, £25/hr ride, £50/2-hr beach ride.

From beginners' lessons to exhilarating hacks across three miles of sandy beach, Reen Manor caters for all abilities. Thirty-minute rides are for under-10s on lead reins.

Kitesurfing
Mobius Kite School

Perranporth, T08456-430630, mobiusonline.co.uk. £65/2½-hr intro session, £100/1-day BKSA/IKO beginner course (minimum age 12). Learn to kitesurf at Perranporth, Hayle, Marazion or Pentewan. Mountain bike hire also available.

Multi activity
Lusty Glaze Adventure Centre

Lusty Glaze Rd, Newquay, TR7 3AE, T01637-872444, lustyglaze.co.uk. Junior Baywatch (2 hrs) £25 child (8-14), Baywatch Babes (2 hrs) £20 child (3-8); call for rates and minimum ages for coasteering, zip wire, abseiling and rock climbing; for

kitesurfing see Mobius Kite School (above); for surfing, see page 72. Newquay's privately owned Lusty Glaze Beach is an enticing spider's web of zip wires, abseiling ropes and obstacle courses, luring adrenaline junkies from miles around. It also offers surfing, kitesurfing, coasteering and mountain biking, but it's the adventure centre's highly acclaimed Junior Baywatch programme that will appeal most to families. Children are taught how to be surf-savvy, learning not only how to avoid riptides and rocks, but also basic techniques of surf rescue. They'll get to grips with the RNLI Beach Lifeguard flag system and gen up on their rockpool-critter ID skills. It's a fun and worthwhile way to spend a couple of hours on the beach. There's even a version for younger kids called Baywatch Babes.

Quad biking
The ATV centre

Blackwater, TR4 8HJ, T01872-560753, atv-centre.com. Easter-Sep daily 1000-1800, Oct-Easter 1000-1700. Minimum age 6. From £12/10 mins. Three dirt-track circuits with coaches on hand for novices.

Surfing

See pages 72-73.

Tree climbing
Mighty Oak Tree Company

Nanswhyden, nr Newquay, T07890-698651, mighty-oak.co.uk.

Introductory climbs £120/group of 1-4 people (minimum age 4). Rekindle a childhood passion with a rope- and harness-assisted arboreal adventure.

Water sports
Stithians Lake

Menherion, Redruth, TR16 6NW, T01209-860301, swlakestrust.org.uk. Mon-Thu, Sat 0900-1700. Taster sessions (2 hrs) call for rates; RYA Junior Stage 1-4 sailing courses (2 days) and RYA Youth Stage 1-2 windsurfing courses (2 days) £275 or £145 for groups of 3+; BCU 1 Star kayaking courses (1 day) £180 or £80 for groups of 3+. Minimum age 8 for all courses; wetsuits and buoyancy aids included in rates. Wet 'n' Active days £45. Hire rates: Pico dinghy £16/hr, windsurf £24/hr, Canadian canoe or double kayak £16/hr, kayak £10/hr, rowing boat £15/hr. Camping £6 adult, £3 child (5-14), £14 family. Water sports with no added salt, Stithians Lake is the perfect venue for learning how to sail or windsurf. You can enrol on a RYA-accredited course or try a taster session – Wet 'n' Active Days for children aged eight and above run every Tuesday during summer holidays. Alternatively, splash out on a Junior Cadet Week – five action-packed days of sailing, windsurfing, kayaking and raft building for children aged eight to 16.

Wildlife safaris
Feadon Farm Wildlife Centre

Gwel an Mor, see page 11.

Falmouth & Porthtowan Surf School
Lessons and transport to and from
north-coast beaches, see page 177.

Fistral Beach Surf School
Fistral Beach, Newquay, TR7 1HN,
T01792-360370,
fistralsurfschool.co.uk.
£35/2-hr lesson, family courses.

Surf schools

Blue Wings Surf School
Tower Rd, Newquay,
TR7 1LZ, T01637-874445,
bluewingssurfschool.co.uk.
£20/2-hr lesson, £35/day (2 lessons).

Breakers Surf School
Breakers Beach Café, Trevaunance
Cove, St Agnes, T07725-842196,
surf-lessons.co.uk. £24/2-hr lesson,
£40/day, 5-day course £100.

Dolphin Surf School
Eliot Gardens, Newquay, TR7 2QE,
T01637-873707, surfschool.co.uk.
£30/2-hr lesson, £40/day (2 lessons),
2-day course £70, 3-day course £90.

The Escape Surf School
Fore St, Newquay, TR7 1HD, T07967-
497117, escapesurfschool.co.uk.
£30/2-hr lesson.

Extreme Academy
On The Beach, Watergate Bay,
TR8 4AA, T01637-860543,
watergatebay.co.uk.
£30/2-hr lesson; private surf lesson
£150 for groups of 2-4 people;
surf-and-hire (morning lesson, then
keep your kit for rest of day) £40.
Introduction courses to kitesurfing,
surf kayaking, kite buggying and
stand-up paddleboarding £30-100.

Gwithian Academy of Surfing
Godrevy House, Prosper Hill,
Gwithian, TR27 5BW, T01736-
757579, surfacademy.co.uk.
Surf shop at Sandsifter Café.
£28/2-hr lesson, £50/day
(2 lessons), 2-day course £80.

Harlyn Surf School
Grenville Rd, Padstow,
PL28 8EX, T01841-533076,
harlynsurfschool.co.uk.
£35/2-hr lesson; surf 'n' hire
£49/day; stand-up paddleboarding
£90/day; Ultimate Beach
Experience (surf lesson, stand-up
paddleboarding lesson, kayak hire)
£110; Awesome Foursome (surf
lesson, stand-up paddleboarding
lesson, Camel Trail cycle hire and
Padstow speedboat trip) £120.

King Surf
Betty's Surf Shop, Mawgan Porth,
T01637-860091, kingsurf.co.uk.
£30/2½-hr lesson,
£50/day (2 lessons).

Lusty Glaze Adventure Centre
Lusty Glaze Beach, Newquay
TR7 3AE, T01637-872444,
adventure-centre.org.
£30/2½-hr lesson; Junior surfing
for children (7-16); private lessons
£50/hr (8-12), £55/1½ hrs (13-16).

National Surfing Centre
Fistral Beach, Newquay,
TR7 1HY, T01637-850737,
nationalsurfingcentre.com.
£30/2½-hr lesson,
Junior Surfer Scheme (8-17).

Newquay Surfing School
Newquay, T07592-
736820 or 07970-684167,
newquaysurfingschool.com.
Children's lessons from £15, plus
regular 2½-hr lessons from £25.

Overhead Surf
Tolcarne Beach, Newquay,
T01637-850808,
overheadsurf.co.uk.
Runs Animal Surf Academy lessons
on Fistral beach (animal.co.uk).
£25/2½-hr lesson.

Over the top – learning to surf with the Extreme Academy at Watergate Bay.

Reef Surf School
10 Berry Rd, Newquay, TR7 1AR,
T01637-879058, reefsurfschool.com.
Operates from Newquay's
Great Western Beach.
£25/2-hr lesson,
£35/day (2 lessons).

Shore Surf School
46 Mount Pleasant, Hayle, TR27 4LE,
T01736-755556, shoresurf.com.
£25/2½-hr lesson.
Offers 'surfaris' to any of
Cornwall's surfing locations.

The Winter Brothers Surf School
Headland Hotel, Fistral Beach,
Newquay, T01637-879696,
winterbrothers.com.
£25/2hr lesson,
£40/day (2 lessons).

Out & about Northwest Cornwall

Big days out

Blue Reef Aquarium

Towan Beach, Newquay, TR7 1DU, T01637-878134, bluereefaquarium.co.uk. Daily from 1000. £9.20 adult, £7.20 child (3-14), £30.80 family.
Sharks lurk just metres away from the bucket-and-spade brigade at Newquay's Towan Beach, but don't worry – they're all behind glass at this stunning aquarium which features a Tropical Shark Lagoon and huge reef display with walk-through tunnel. Other highlights include seahorses, cuttlefish and giant Pacific octopus – try to see them during one of the interesting feeding-time talks.

Crealy Great Adventure Park

Tredinnick, Wadebridge, PL27 7RA, T01841-540276, crealy.co.uk. Apr-Oct daily 1000-1800. From £12.95, £12.45 for groups of 4 or more, children under 92 cm tall free, reduced prices available online and during winter. Return free for a week.
Located in lovely countryside south of Padstow, this mildly wild adventure park is largely a glorified playground with slides, zip wires, sand pits and climbing nets. There's a handful of thrill rides, including a swinging pirate ship, a log flume and twin racing waterslide. The Beast (minimum height 105 cm) is hyped as Crealy's 'big one' – a stomach-churning 15-m-tall tower-drop that actually elicits fewer squeals than the waterslide. It's Crealy's tameness, however, that makes it so appealing – kids run free from one play area to the next and queues rarely reach Disney proportions. The Water Walkerz (giant floating orbs that you zip your child inside) are £3.50 a go – a bit cheeky when you've already forked out over £50 for a family ticket. Crealy is still good value though – particularly when you factor in the farm animals, shire horse rides, indoor play areas and Swampmonster's Eco-Adventure (a streamside nature trail). Seasonal highlights include a summer sunflower maze, Pumpkinfest and Easter egg hunt.

Dairyland Farm World

Nr Newquay, TR8 5AA, T01872-510349, dairylandfarmworld.com. Daily 1000-1700. £7.95, under-3s free, £33 family (up to 5 people).
Milk Clarabelle with her realistic udders, pat a pet and ride in a Lamborghini (that's a type of tractor by the way). Dairyland is a gold-top, full-fat farm park with vast indoor and outdoor adventure play areas offering everything from drop slides and soft play to pony rides and nature trails.

Slide rules – the all-action Crealy Adventure Park.

Holywell Bay Fun Park

Holywell Bay, TR8 5PW, T01637-830095, holywellbay.co.uk. Apr-Nov dates and times vary. Rides and attractions from 50p to £4.
Holywell Bay Fun Park is free to enter, but don't expect a cheap day out once the kids get wind of the array of pay-as-you-play attactions – go karts, crazy golf, bumper boats, trampolines and gold panning to name a few.

Lappa Valley Railway

St Newlyn East, TR8 5LX, T01872-510317, lappavalley.co.uk. Apr-Nov from 1030. £9.50 adult, £7.50 child (3-15), £30 family.
This narrow gauge steam train chuffs along to the old tin-mining site at East Wheel Rose, where you will find the mine's renovated engine house, a café,

Hit or miss?

Treasure Park
Tolgus Mill, Redruth, TR16 4HN,
T01209-218198, treasureparks.
com. Year round Mon-Sat 0930-
1730; Sun 1000-1630. Free entry.

Some might argue that the
biggest gems in North Cornwall
are its beaches, but there's no
denying the rainy-day appeal of
Treasure Park. Located on the
road to Portreath, it's awash with
gold and jewellery. Kids can pan
for gold, scoop for gems, paint a
'Pot of Gold', explore the history
of Cornish mining at Tolgus Tin
and follow Nugget's Adventure
Treasure Trail. There are also
jewellery workshops, a picnic
area and café.

Far left: Yellow tang at Blue Reef Aquarium.
Left, from top: Shire horse, Crealy; snowy
owl, Paradise Park; meerkat, Newquay Zoo.

☘ **Free** play

Does the weather forecast look
bleak? Some attractions, like
Crealy, offer a week of free return
visits when you purchase a single
admission ticket so you can make
good use of their indoor play areas
when the weather turns against you.

crazy golf, canoeing lake, brick-
path maze, play castle and two
additional miniature railways.

Newquay Zoo

Trenance Gardens, Newquay, TR7
2LZ, T01637-873342, newquayzoo.
org.uk. Apr-Sep 0930-1800, Oct-Mar
1000-1700. £10.95 adult, £8.20 child
(3-15), £32.90 family.
A three-acre African Savannah,
which sees wildebeest and
warthog rubbing shoulders with
ostrich and zebra, is the latest
addition to Newquay Zoo. A
collection of intriguing critters
from the Philippines, including
the Visayan warty pig, have also
joined the zoo's exotic cast of
over 130 species. Junior Keeper
days are available for eight- to
14-year-olds, while daily feeds
and talks take place at the
otters (1100), macaques (1200),
meerkats (1230), tropical house
(1345), big cats (1430) and
penguins (1545).

Paradise Park

16 Trelissick Rd, Hayle, TR27 4HB,
T01736-751020, paradisepark.org.
uk. Daily from 1000. £10.99 adult,
£8.99 child
(3-14), £38.50 family.
Home to the World Parrot Trust,
Paradise Park boasts huge
freeflight aviaries where you
can handfeed lorikeets with
nectar. Parrots hog the limelight
at this excellent park, but you
will also see penguins, owls,
eagles and local rarities
like the chough.
Non-feathered
friends include
alpacas, otters
and red pandas.
On rainy days
let your own
wild things
loose in the
all-weather
Jungle Barn.

Out & about Northwest Cornwall

More family favourites

Blue Hills
Wheal Kitty, St Agnes, TR5 0YW,
T01872-553341, bluehillstin.com.
Apr-Oct Mon-Sat 1000-1600.
£5.50 adult, £3 child.
At Cornwall's only tin producer
you can follow the entire process,
from extraction, crushing and
smelting to pouring ingots and
casting finished products.

Cornish Birds of Prey Centre
Meadowside Farm, Winnards Perch,
St Columb Major, TR9 6DH, T01637-
880544, cornishbirdsofprey.co.uk.
Easter-Oct daily 1000-1700. £6.50
adult, £5 child (3-13), £23 family.
Eyeball hawks, owls, falcons,
vultures and eagles and watch
them fly at 1200 and 1430.
Falconry experiences (minimum
age 14) are also available.

Cornish Mines & Engines
Pool, nr Redruth, TR15 3NP,
T01209-315027, nationaltrust.org.uk.
Easter-Nov, Mon, Wed-Fri, Sun 1100-
1700; Jul-Aug also Sat. £6.40 adult,
£3.20 child (5-17), £16 family.
Climb three flights of stairs to
reach the top of Taylor's Engine
– a mighty beam engine once
used to pump water from the
mines. You can also walk under
a 35-m-tall chimney stack and
visit the discovery centre, where
a short film provides a gritty and,
for children, quite complicated
introduction to Cornish mining.
Other sites (like Geevor, see page
100) are more child-friendly.

Screech Owl Sanctuary
Goss Moor, nr Indian Queens,
TR9 6HP, T01726-860182,
screechowlsanctuary.co.uk. Feb-Nov
daily 1000-1700 (1800 spring and
summer), flying displays 1100, 1300
and 1600. £7.50 adult, £6.25 child
(3-15), £24.50 family.
A right hoot, this superb little
sanctuary is home to over 140
owls and hawks from 50 species.
As well as guided tours and
falconry displays, a hand-tame
area allows you to touch and
stroke the birds. Find out about
the owl hospital and Siberian
eagle owl breeding project.

Spirit of the West
Retallack, St Columb Major, TR9 6DE,
T01637-881160, wildwestthemepark.
co.uk. May-Sep, Sun-Fri from 1030.
£7 adult, £5 child, £22 family.
Gold panning, pony rides and all-
action shoot-outs in the streets.

Springfields Fun Park
St Columb, TR9 6HU, T01637-881224,
springfieldsponycentre.co.uk. Easter-
Oct. £7.95 adult, £6.95 child (3-16),
£26.95 family.
Springfields promises a fun day
out with pony and train rides,
duck racing, bottle-feeding
lambs and bunny cuddling.

Trenhayle Maze
Trenhayle Farm, Hayle TR27 6HQ,
T01736-755631, maize-maze.com.
Jul-Aug daily 1000-1800.
£4.75 adult, £3.75 child, £18 family.
Maize maze, crazy golf, go karts,
trampolines, assault course etc.

Rain check

Cinemas
Plaza
Lemon St, Truro, T01872 272894.
Regal
Fore St, Redruth, T01209-216278.

Indoor play & amusements
Bombadinga's
Wilson Way, Pool, Redruth, TR15 3RX
T01209-219555. Daily 1000-1800.
Café and pirate-themed soft play for
children under nine.

The Bull Pen
Dairyland Farm World, see page 74
for contact details. Daily from 1000.
Soft play and ball pool for littl'uns;
adventure zone for older children.

Country Skittles
Townshend, Hayle, TR27 6ER, T01736-
850209, countryskittles.com. School
holidays Mon-Sat 1400-2300, Sun
1200-2230. Nine-pin skittle alleys,
crazy golf and shooting gallery.

Jungle Barn
Paradise Park, see page 75 for contact
details. Daily from 1000. Soft play,
drop slides, ball pool, toddlers' area
and café, all with a jungle theme.

Newquay Tenpin Bowling
Porth Lodge Hotel, Porthbean Rd,
Newquay, TR7 3LT, T01637-874483.
porthlodgehotel.co.uk.

Indoor swimming pools
Carnbrea Leisure Centre
Station Rd, Redruth, TR15
3QS, T01209-714766,
carnbrealeisurecentre.co.uk.

Oasis
Hendra Holiday Park, Newquay, TR8
4NY, T01637-875778, oasis-hendra.
co.uk. Daily 1000-1800. Heated indoor
and outdoor pools with water flumes,
river rapid ride, fountains, geysers,
water cannon and toddlers' area;
pizza bar and restaurant.

Waterworld
Trenance Leisure Park, Newquay,
TR7 2LZ, T01637-853829,
newquaywaterworld.co.uk. Tropical
fun pool, two water flumes, water
play hut and erupting volcano. Next
to Newquay Zoo. Soft play sessions
for toddlers Tue, Thu, Fri 1015-1145.

Pick of the pitches

Bedruthan Steps Camping

Bedruthan Steps, T01637-860943, bedruthanstepscamping.co.uk. Jul-Aug. Call for rates.

The coast path borders this picture-perfect clifftop site overlooking the famous 'stepping stones' of the giant Bedruthan. Just turn up and pick a spot on the five-acre field. Facilities are limited to toilets, showers and a small kiosk selling local food and snacks.

Berryfields Farm Campsite

Berryfields, Porthcothan Bay, PL28 8PW, T01841-520178. Call for rates.

Originally a strawberry farm, this peaceful site (with 65 pitches for tents and caravans) has an excellent café with some of the best Cornish cream teas you'll taste anywhere. Located close to Porthcothan beach, the campsite also has a gift shop, games room and crazy golf.

Gwithian Farm Campsite

Gwithian, TR27 5BX, T01736-753127, gwithianfarm.co.uk. Apr-Sep. £12-24/pitch (2 people), plus £5 extra adult, £2 extra child, £1 dog.

You can almost smell the surf at this friendly campsite 10 minutes' walk from Gwithian's golden sands. After a day on the beach, the family shower room is a welcome change from the limb-crunching cubicles you find at many sites. Kids will enjoy befriending the resident goats and guinea pigs – not to mention the ice cream vendor (daily) and fish and chippie van (Sun) that visit the site. A fresh fish van also turns up (Tue) and there's a good pub opposite.

Tollgate Farm

Perranporth, TR6 0AD, T01872-572130, tollgatefarm.co.uk. £4-6 adult, £2-3 child (6-14), £5-7 tent.

A well thought out family site, Tollgate Farm has a large play area, as well as a paddock where kids can pet and feed miniature pigs, pygmy goats and guinea pigs. The nearest beach is a 20-minute walk through dunes to Perran Bay.

Treago Farm Holidays

Crantock, TR8 5QS, T01637-830277, treagofarm.co.uk. Year round (shop May-Sep). £6-8 adult, £3-4 child.

Tucked into a sheltered valley just inland from Porth Joke

and Crantock, this idyllic site has the best of both worlds – peaceful, unspoilt countryside and easy access (along footpaths) to stunning beaches. Old farm buildings house a cosy bar, games room and shop.

Also recommended

Beacon Cottage Farm

St Agnes, TR5 0NU, T01872-552347, beaconcottagefarmholidays.co.uk. Apr-Sep. £15-21/pitch (2 adults), plus £4.50 extra adult, £3 extra child. Small secluded site on working farm, close to the sea.

Cottage Farm Park

Treworgans, Cubert, TR8 5HH, T01637-831083, cottagefarmpark. co.uk. Apr-Sep. £11-15/pitch (2 adults), plus £6.50-7.50 extra adult, £3.50-4.50 extra child.

Peaceful site, a 20-minute walk to the beach at Holywell Bay.

Silverbow Park

Perranwell, TR4 9NX, T01872-572347, chycor.co.uk/parks/silverbow. Apr-Sep. £12-24/pitch (2 adults), plus £3-6 extra adult, £2.50-4.50extra child (2-12).

Quiet, immaculate site close to Perranporth; landscaped gardens and heated pool.

Bedruthan Steps Camping.

Sleeping Northwest Cornwall

Best of the rest

Bassets Acre
Portreath, TR16 4JU, T01209-842367, bassetsacre.co.uk. Four-bed apartment £375-925/wk.
Six apartments (sleeping up to seven) in a Georgian house with heated indoor pool, play area and sub-tropical gardens.

Blue Chip Newquay
T0844-561 2001, bluechipnewquay.co.uk. Check online for special offers.
Stylish crash pads for discerning surfers. Over 150 luxury self-catering apartments and houses, from Crantock to Watergate Bay.

The Harlyn Inn
Harlyn Bay, PL28 8SB, T01841-520207,

Cottage agents
See also page 186.

Around Kernow Holidays
T01872-571575, ak-hols.co.uk.
Cottages, apartments and chalets in and around Perranporth.

Cornwall Coast Holidays
T0208-4407518,
cornwallcoastholidays.com.
Luxury cottages and apartments overlooking Fistral Bay, Newquay.

Cornwall Holiday Homes
T01209-715358,
cornwall-holidayhomes.co.uk.
Self-catering in Portreath.

Duchy Holidays
T01872-572971,
duchyholidays.co.uk.
Wide range of properties from Newquay to Porthtowan.

harlyn-inn.co.uk. Standard cottage (sleeping 6) £250-1100/wk.
Idyllic location on Harlyn Bay. Quality B&B and smart new three-bedroom self-catering cottages. The pub's restaurant welcomes families and there's even a beach shop next door.

Tolcarne Beach Village
Tolcarne Beach, Newquay, TR7 2QN, T01209-712651, tolcarnebeach.co.uk. Two-bedroom apartment £520-1250/wk.
Stylish, bright apartments with private balconies overlooking a great family beach.

Trengove Farm Cottages
Cot Road, Illogan, TR16 4PU, T01209-843682, trengovefarm.co.uk. Two-bedroom cottage from £275-675/wk.
Seven character cottages on a working farm near Portreath.

Trevone Beach House
Trevone, PL28 8QX, T01841-520469, trevonebeach.co.uk. B&B £35-40 adult, £25-30 child (2-12).
Comfortable, nine-room guest house just a short stroll from Trevone Bay. Great breakfasts and a warm welcome.

YHA Treyarnon Bay
Treyarnon, PL28 8JR, T0845-371 9664, yha.org.uk. From £13.95 adult, £10.50 child (under 18).
Superb location perched above Treyarnon Bay. Seventy-bed hostel with family rooms, an excellent café and a handy drying room for soggy wetsuits.

Park life

If you yearn for a good value, home-from-home break on Cornwall's northwest coast you can't go wrong with a holiday park. But which one to choose? Leave it to the kids and they'll probably go for the one with the best swimming pool complex. The Oasis at **Hendra Holiday Park**, for example, has the full works – flumes, river rapids ride, water cannon and geyser. Proximity to a beach is another key factor. A short stroll from glorious beaches, **Atlantic Coast Caravan Park**, **Mother Ivey's Bay Caravan Park** and **St Ives Bay Holiday Park** both score highly on the barefoot-and-carefree front. Other parks have a more rural setting – **Tehidy** is perfect for woodland walks and getting back to nature, while **White Acres** overlooks a lake.

Not all holiday parks are large and rowdy. **Sun Haven Valley** keeps things simple with a playground and small games room in place of the usual clubs, bars and organized entertainment. If it's five-star facilities you're after, though, opt for a fully fledged park like **Monkey Tree**, **Newperran** or **Trevornick**, where 'extras' can include anything from free kids' clubs and on-site shops and restaurants to fishing lakes and golf courses.

As far as accommodation is concerned, the des-res of most holiday parks is the static caravan, typically with two or three bedrooms, lounge, kitchen, shower/bathroom and a good spattering of mod cons such as flatscreen TV, microwave, double glazing and central heating. You might be able to upgrade to one with a deck, ideal for those summer evening barbecues. Many parks also offer more spacious chalets and timber lodges or allocate space for you to hook up your own caravan or pitch a tent.

Finally, look for parks with green credentials. **Trevella**, for example, has its own nature reserve and has received the Gold David Bellamy Conservation Award for 10 years in a row.

Atlantic Coast Caravan Park scores highly on the barefoot-and-carefree front.

Holiday parks

Atlantic Coast Caravan Park
Upton Towans, TR27 5BL, T01736-752071, atlanticcoastpark.co.uk.

Carnevas Holiday Park
Porthcothan, PL28 8PN, T01841-520230, carnevasholidaypark.com.

Crantock Beach Holiday Park
Crantock, TR8 5RH, T0871-641 0197, parkdeanengland.co.uk.

Harlyn Sands Holiday Park
Trevose Head, PL28 8SQ, T01841-520720, harlynsands.co.uk.

Hendra Holiday Park
Newquay, TR8 4NY, T01637-875778, hendra-holidays.com.

Holywell Bay Holiday Park
Holywell Bay, TR8 5PR, T0871-641 0197, parkdeanengland.co.uk.

Mawgan Porth Holiday Park
Mawgan Porth, TR8 4BD, T01637-860322, mawganporth.co.uk.

Monkey Tree Holiday Park
Rejerrah, TR8 5QR, T01872-572032, monkeytreeholidaypark.co.uk.

Mother Ivey's Bay Caravan Park
Trevose Head, PL28 8SL, T01841-520990, motheriveysbay.com.

Newperran Holiday Park
Rejerrah, TR8 5QJ, T0845-166 8407, newperran.co.uk.

Newquay Holiday Park
Newquay, TR8 4HS, T0871-641 0197, parkdeanengland.co.uk.

Perran Sands Holiday Park
Perranporth, TR6 0AQ, T0871-231 0871, havenholidays.com.

Perran Springs Holiday Park
Goonhavern, Truro, TR4 9QG, T01872-540568, perransprings.co.uk.

Porth Beach Tourist Park
Porth, TR7 3NH, T01637-876531, porthbeach.co.uk.

Riverside Holiday Park
Lane, Newquay, TR8 4PE, T01637-873617, riversideholidaypark.co.uk.

St Ives Bay Holiday Park
Upton Towans, TR27 5BH, T01736-754523, stivesbay.co.uk.

Sun Haven Valley Holiday Park
Mawgan Porth, TR8 4BQ, T01637-860373, sunhavenvalley.com.

Tehidy Holiday Park
Illogan, Redruth, TR16 4JQ, T01209-216489, tehidy.co.uk.

Treloy Touring Park
Newquay, TR8 4JN, T01637-872063, treloy.co.uk.

Trenance Holiday Park
Newquay, TR7 2JY, T0500-131243, trenanceholidaypark.co.uk.

Trencreek Holiday Park
Newquay, TR8 4NS, T01637-874210, trencreekholidaypark.co.uk.

Trevella Park
Crantock, TR8 5EU, T01637-830308, trevella.co.uk.

Trevornick Holiday Park
Holywell Bay, TR8 5PW, T01637-830531, trevornick.co.uk.

Treworgans Holiday Park
Cubert, Newquay, TR8 5HH, T01637-830200, treworgansholidaypark.co.uk.

Treyarnon Bay Caravan Park
Treyarnon Bay, PL28 8JR, T01841-52068, treyarnonbay.co.uk.

Watergate Bay Touring Park
Watergate Bay, TR8 4AD, T01637-860387, watergatebaytouringpark.co.uk.

White Acres Holiday Park
Newquay, TR8 4LW, T0871-641 0197, parkdeanengland.co.uk.

Sleeping Northwest Cornwall

Bedruthan Steps Hotel

Mawgan Porth, TR8 4BU, T01637-860555, bedruthan.com. DB&B £79-145 adult, £20-36 infant (1-2), £40-73 child (3-6), £53-97 child (7-12).

Don't feel intimidated by the smart, contemporary style of this cliff-top hotel – it's as child-friendly as they come. In fact, with its indoor and outdoor play areas, daily entertainment, heated pools, OFSTED-registered clubs and special mealtimes, children could be forgiven for thinking that it was made exclusively for them. In a way it was. But grown-ups get a fair share of goodies too. There's the sumptuous Ocean Spa and the award-winning Indigo Bay Restaurant (for adults only), as well as exemplary childcare for those moments when you crave some 'me time'. The simple but tastefully decorated bedrooms often have spectacular sea views and they come in all shapes and sizes – from spacious family rooms to villas and apartments.

Rosehill Lodges

Porthtowan, TR4 8AR, T01209-891920, rosehilllodges.com. Two-bed lodge (sleeping 4) £482-1580/wk.

A five-minute walk from Porthtowan and nuzzled in wildlife-rich woodland, these classy timber lodges have private hot tubs, glass-covered decks, log burners and outdoor heated drench showers – just the job for rinsing off children and wetsuits after a day on the beach. Each lodge is also equipped with handy extras like buckets and spades, softball tennis and badminton sets. And they're green too, thanks to solar panels and grass roofs.

Sands Resort Hotel

Watergate Rd, Porth, TR7 3LX, T01637-872864, sandsresort.co.uk. B&B £50-79 adult, £12 baby, £16-24 infant (1-2), £25-39 child (3-6), £36-55 child (7-14).

A genuinely family-friendly hotel, Sands does more than most to make parents and children feel welcome and well catered for. Most of the rooms are suites, with separate children's sleeping areas. There are sports facilities, play areas and children's clubs for all ages; the Surf Shack has wetsuits and boards, while two beach adventure centres are just minutes away. Little ones get pre-dinner entertainment; grown-ups get a health spa.

Watergate Bay Hotel

Watergate Bay, Newquay, T01637-860543, watergatebay.co.uk. Family suites £215-385/night B&B. Check online for other room rates.

Behind the quite traditional Victorian-looking façade of this hotel lies Cornwall's ultimate base for surf and chic. Watergate Bay Hotel is right on the beach, with its own watersports centre and no less than four places to eat, including the Hotel Brasserie and Jamie Oliver's Fifteen (see page 83). The hotel has playrooms, an indoor/outdoor swimming pool, supervised Kids' Zone, children's activities and evening entertainment, plus a baby-listening service. Bright, contemporary family suites feature a king-size bedroom and bunk room for children. Plasma televisions and DVD players come as standard – for those rare moments when you can tear yourself away from the ocean views. Interconnecting rooms, some with balconies overlooking the bay, are also available. Outside there's a lovely terrace with steps leading down to the beach.

Also recommended
Crantock Bay Hotel

West Pentire, TR8 5SE, T01637-830229, crantockbayhotel.co.uk. Hotel gardens lead to coast path and sandy beach.

The Esplanade Hotel

Fistral Bay, Newquay TR7 1PS, T01637-873333, newquay-hotels.co.uk. Just 50 m from beach; indoor and outdoor pools, games room, great food and surf centre.

Gwel an Mor

Portreath. See page 11.

The Headland

Fistral Bay, Newquay TR7 1EW, T01637-872211, headlandhotel.co.uk. Breathtaking views; village of self-catering cottages.

Local goodies

Callestick Farm

Callestick, Truro, TR4 9LL, T01872-573126, callestickfarm.co.uk. Summer Mon-Sat 0930-1730, Sun 1100-1700; winter Wed-Sat. You've probably slurped it at countless places across Cornwall – now visit the farm to find out how Callestick ice cream is made. There's a viewing gallery above the farm's ice cream factory where you can watch – with the help of an explanatory DVD – the entire process from Friesian milk to frozen tub. As well as sampling the sweet sensation at the dairy parlour, you can indulge in other local foods at the farm's café and deli. A typical summer menu will have savoury specials like tomato, basil and cream cheese tart or Cornish brie, bacon and cranberry sauce baguettes. Farm animals are another big attraction at Callestick, with chickens, pigs, calves, sheep dogs and the resident shire horse all vying for attention. Utimately, though, there's only one thing on the minds of most visitors to this small, friendly farm – which of the 26 flavours of Callestick ice cream to sample. Purists will probably plump for clotted cream vanilla, while those with more daring palates can choose from butterscotch and pecan, lemon curd, crunchy toffee or white chocolate and raspberries.

◉ **Ice** spy

Download a treasure hunt from Callestick's website (callestickfarm. co.uk), solve eight clues at the farm (there are questions for both older and younger children) and you can claim a free ice cream cone.

Healey's Cornish Cyder Farm

Penhallow, TR4 9LW, T01872-573356, healeyscyderfarm.co.uk. Year round, daily from 0900. Free admission. No-one's suggesting you initiate the kids to Cornish Scrumpy or Rattler (that's your holiday treat). Instead, they'll get a kick out of the tractor rides, meeting farm animals and completing the quiz on a tour through the Cyder Farm's press house, bottlery, jam kitchen and museum. There's also a suitably fruity farm shop and restaurant.

Trevaskis Farm

Conner Downs, Hayle, TR27 5JQ, T01209-714009, trevaskisfarm.co.uk. Summer daily 0900-1800; winter, daily 0900-1700; organic kitchen garden May-Oct; restaurant Mon-Sat breakfast 0830-1030, lunch from 1200, afternoon teas 1500-1700, evening meals from 1800, Sun roasts 1200-1800.
There are no less than 70 crops on this 28-acre pick-your-own farm – from strawberries, raspberries and plums to peas, beans and pumpkins. Armed with baskets, kids can plan a soft-fruit safari, bolting for poly-tunnels, if it rains, and gleaning juicy snippets of information from interpretation boards on how each variety has been grown. There are even recipe suggestions and cooking tips but, if you can't wait to taste the fruits of your labours, head for the restaurant, which serves delicious homemade apple pie and clotted cream, plus a full range of snacks and meals. The children's menu (dishes £5.95-6.25) includes home-made sausages and lasagne, while Sunday roasts (with pork and gammon from the farm's rare-breed Cornish lop pigs) range from £6.95 for a child's serving to £10.95 for an adult's portion. There's also a fabulous farm shop with baker, butcher, fishmonger and deli.

Market days

Perranporth Country Market
Memorial Hall, Friday 0900-1100.

Redruth Country Market
Town Centre, Friday 0800-1400.

Stithians Produce Market
New Road, Saturday 0900-1100.

Truro Farmers' Market
Lemon Quay, Saturday 0900-1600.

Quick & simple

The Beach Hut

Watergate Bay, TR8 4AA, T01637-860877, watergatebay.co.uk. Sun-Thu 1000-1700, Fri-Sat 1000-late, snacks available throughout the day.
This busy, friendly café has picture-window views of the beach and serves breakfast, lunch and dinner. For a pre-surf energy boost, kids will demolish the sweet waffles with crispy bacon and maple syrup (£2.70-5.40) on the breakfast menu. For lunch, try the Cornish cheese fondue, the stir-fried squid or a gooey bowl of nachos (all £5.50). Mains on the children's menu cost £3.95 and include an excellent homemade burger, sole goujons and penne pasta. For grown-ups there's crab linguini (£13.95), Fowey mussels (£7.50/half-kilo) and a seriously filling fish pie (£12), plus various steak, curry, fish and chicken dishes. If you have room for pudding, squeeze in Will's Crème Brûlée (£4.65) or a Kids' Extreme Ice Cream with cream, marshmallows and chocolate (£2.80). For an afternoon snack,

the Beach Hut's hot chocolate £2.90) and chocolate fudge brownie (£3.50) are legendary.

Blue Beach Bar & Brasserie

Beach Rd, Porthtowan, TR4 8AD, T01209-890777, blue-bar.co.uk. Food served daily 1200-2100, brunch Sat-Sun 1000-1200.
Blue has a fantastic beach location that's perfect for sunset gazing. The chips 'n' dips (£5.50) makes a great snack but, for something more substantial, try one of the burgers (from £8.75), stonebaked pizzas (from £5.50) or a special like pan-fried seabass on wilted spinach (£13.50). The kids' menu has posh fish and chips (battered pollock with hand-cut chips and minted pea puree) for £5, as well as pasta and bangers and mash.

Carnewas Tearoom

Nr Bedruthan, St Eval, PL27 7UW, T01637-860563, nationaltrust.org.uk. Feb-May and Oct-Dec daily 1100-1600; May-Sep daily 1030-1700.
You can't go wrong with a National Trust tea room after a bracing cliff-top walk and this one is smack in the middle of some of North Cornwall's most stunning coastal scenery.

Godrevy Café

Godrevy Towans, Gwithian, TR27 5ED, T01736-757999. Daily 1000-1700, plus evenings in summer.
A bright and breezy cabin, simple, tasty food and a great location in the dunes at

Godrevy's National Trust car park (with views across St Ives Bay) – it's small wonder that this café is so popular. Expect to pay around £3.95-7.50 for light bites, ranging from local fish to Mediterranean mezzé.

Palms Oasis

New Portreath Rd, Bridge, nr Redruth, TR16 4QL, T01209-842255, palmsoasis.co.uk. Sun-Mon 0830-1700, Wed-Sat 0830-2200.
Home-cooked food, an exotic terrace, kids' pottery painting and a bunny-petting ranch: it doesn't get much better than this...

Schooners Bistro

Trevaunance Cove, St Agnes, TR5 0RY, T01872-553149. Daily 1000-2100.
Perched above the cove at St Agnes, Schooners has a grandstand view of the Atlantic, whether you're lounging on the deck in the sunshine or huddled inside while waves burst on the rocks below. For lunch, there's a good range of toasted ciabattas (from £4.95), while dinner mains (from £8.95) include local steamed mussels, grilled mackerel fillets and lamb shank.

Tin Fin

Beach Rd, Perranporth, TR6 0JL, T01872-572117. Daily 1030-2130.

Fish & chips

Try the **Jolly Fryer** (Beach Rd, Porthtowan) for fish and chips on the beach. **Morrish's** (Bucketts Hill, Redruth) has a secret batter recipe handed down over three generations, while **Pickwick** (St Pirans Road, Perranporth) uses the freshest fish and local potatoes cooked in beef dripping.

Colourful, relaxed and friendly, this seaside bistro serves good quality, locally sourced dishes, often with a Mediterranean twist. The tapas is excellent. Children eat free with an adult meal (1730-1900, except Wed).

Also recommended
The Mermaid Inn
Alexandra Rd, Porth, TR7 3NB, T01637-872954.
Good pub grub at Porth beach.

Sandsifter Café
Godrevy Towans, TR27 5ED, T01736-758384, sandsiftervenue.com.
Contemporary café overlooking the beach at Godrevy.

Venus Café
Watergate Bay, T01637-860297; Tolcarne Beach, Newquay, T01637-876028, venuscompany.co.uk.
Excellent children's box meals and a great range of locally sourced snacks to eat alfresco or take away to the beach.

The Watering Hole
Perranporth Beach, TR6 0JL, T01872-572888, the-wateringhole.co.uk.
Lively beach bar with a big menu and summer barbecues.

The Windswept Café
South Fistral Beach, TR7 1QA, T01637-850793, windsweptcafe.co.uk.
This cool café serves great pasta, seafood (try the fishcakes) and smoothies, and you'll be blown away by its location – perched right above the beach.

Fifteen Cornwall
Watergate Bay, TR8 4AA, T01637-861000, fifteencornwall.co.uk. Daily 0830-1030, 1200-1700, 1815-2400.
Buzzing at lunchtime with surf-tussled children, Jamie Oliver's pukka beach restaurant is very popular with families and you'd be wise to book. Bright, lively and trendy (spot Jamie's spray-can signature in magenta paint on one of the walls), Fifteen has friendly service, front-row views of the beach and, of course, fabulous food. Children are welcome for breakfast and lunch, but seven-to 12-year-olds are only allowed for dinner from 1815 to 1900. A Mini Brekkie fry-up for kids costs £4.50, while lunchtime dishes start at around £6.50 (or you can choose a three-course set menu for £26). In the evening

tuck into the Tasting Menu (£55), which uses lamb, seafood and other local produce in irresistible Italian recipes. It's totally delish.

New Harbour Restaurant
Newquay Harbour, T01637-874062, finns2go.com. Daily from 1200.
Superb seafood – from crab sarnies to dressed lobster – served at lunch and dinner.

The Terrace
Gwel an Mor, Portreath. See page 11.

Menu bites
• Bruschetta of grilled Cornish sardines with roasted peppers, capers, herbs and Amalfi lemon £8.95
• Roasted Cornish salted hake with panzanella (a lovely rustic Tuscan bread and tomato salad) £17.95
• Tom's amazing smashed meringue, vanilla mascarpone and prosecco poached apricots £6.40
Examples from Fifteen's lunch menu.

Posh pasta at Fifteen – taglierini vongole (clams).

Contents

Portheras Cove, near Pendeen.

West Cornwall

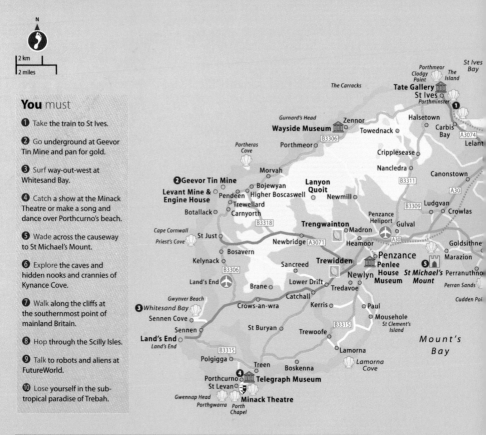

N

2 km
2 miles

You must

1. Take the train to St Ives.

2. Go underground at Geevor Tin Mine and pan for gold.

3. Surf way-out-west at Whitesand Bay.

4. Catch a show at the Minack Theatre or make a song and dance over Porthcurno's beach.

5. Wade across the causeway to St Michael's Mount.

6. Explore the caves and hidden nooks and crannies of Kynance Cove.

7. Walk along the cliffs at the southernmost point of mainland Britain.

8. Hop through the Scilly Isles.

9. Talk to robots and aliens at FutureWorld.

10. Lose yourself in the sub-tropical paradise of Trebah.

St Ives Bay
Porthmeor
Clodgy Point
The Island
The Carracks
Tate Gallery
St Ives
Porthminster
Halsetown
Carbis Bay
Lelant
A3074
Gurnard's Head
Zennor
Towednack
Wayside Museum
Cripplesease
Portheras Cove
Porthmeor
B3306
Nancledra
Canonstown
Morvah
Bojewyan
Lanyon Quoit
B3311
2. Geevor Tin Mine
Levant Mine & Engine House
Pendeen
Higher Boscaswell
Newmill
A30
Ludgvan
Crowlas
Trewellard
Penzance Heliport
B3309
Botallack
Carnyorth
Trengwainton
Madron
Gulval
Cape Cornwall
St Just
B3318
Newbridge
A3071
Heamoor
A30
Goldsithne
Priest's Cove
Bosavern
Trewidden
Penzance
Marazion
Kelynack
Sancreed
Penlee House Museum
St Michael's Mount
Perranuthno
B3306
Newlyn
Land's End
Brane
Lower Drift
Tredavoe
Perran Sands
Gwynver Beach
Catchall
Cudden Poi
3. Whitesand Bay
Crows-an-wra
Kerris
Paul
Sennen Cove
Mousehole
St Clement's Island
Sennen
St Buryan
Trewoofe
B3315
Land's End
Mount's Bay
Land's End
B3315
Trewoofe
Lamorna
Polgigga
Treen
Boskenna
Lamorna Cove
Porthcurno
4. Telegraph Museum
St Levan
Gwennap Head
Porthgwarra
Porth Chapel
Minack Theatre

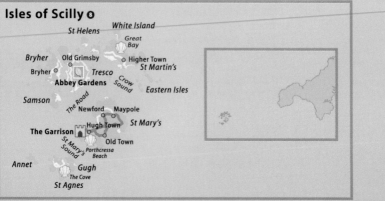

Isles of Scilly

St Helens
White Island
Great Bay
Bryher
Old Grimsby
Higher Town
Bryher
Tresco
St Martin's
Abbey Gardens
Crow Sound
Samson
Eastern Isles
The Road
Newford
Maypole
The Garrison
Hugh Town
St Mary's
St Mary's Sound
Old Town
Porthcressa Beach
Annet
Gugh
The Cove
St Agnes

Three Burrows
Tresillian
A39
Mawla
Blackwater
A390
A390
Truro
Portreath
B3301
A39
St Clement
Illogan
Chacewater
Threemilestone
Scorrier
St Day
A30
Kea
Malpas
St Michael Penkevil
Godrevy Island
Navax Point
B3298
Twelve Heads
Baldhu
Old Kea
Godrevy Point
A3047
Redruth
Bissoe
Playing Place
Gwithian
Kehelland
Tuckingmill
Carnbrea
Carharrack
Carnon Downs
Penpol
Trelissick
Philleigh
B3301
Roseworthy
Cambourne
Carnkie
Gwennap
Perranarwothal
A39
Devoran
Penpol
B3289
Phillack
A30
Connor Downs
Barripper
Lanner
B3393
Feock
Copperhouse
Carnhell Green
Four Lanes
Penhalvaen
Ponsanooth
Burnthouse
Mylor Bridge
St Just in Roseland
Gerrans
Hayle
B3303
Praze-an-Beeble
Penmarth
Stithians
Lake
Stithians
Penryn
Carrick Roads
A3078
Praze
B3280
Burras
Carnkie
Longdowns
Mabe Burnthouse
Flushing
St Mawes
St Erth
Fraddam
B3280
Penmarth
B3297
Porkellis
Mabe Burnthouse
Falmouth
National Maritime Museum
Bohortha
Leedstown
Drym
Crowan
A39
Townshend
Relubbus
B3303
Releath
Nancegollan
A394
Wendron
Sewogan
Treverva
Budock Water
Penjerrick
Pendennis Castle
Zone Point
St Hilary
Godolphin Cross
Crowntown
Gyllyngvase
Swanpool
Trescowe
Maenporth
Falmouth Bay
Germoe
Ashton
Breage
Sithney
B3297
Trewennack
Constantine
Mawnan Smith
Praa Sands
A394
Rinsey
Helston
Gweek
Porth Navas
Trebah Gardens
Glendurgan
Rosemullion Head
Prussia Cove
Helford Passage
Mawnan
Trewavas Head
B3304
Flambard's Experience
National Seal Sanctuary
Helford River
Porthleven
The Loe
Mawgan
Helford
St Anthony-in-Meneage
Gillan Creek
Porthleven Sands
Garras
St Martins
Manaccan
Nare Point
Loe Bar
B3293
Newtown
Tregidden
Porthallow
Berepper
Goonhilly Earth Station
Gunwalloe
Cury
Cross Lanes
Future World @ Goonhilly
Traboe
Roskilly Farm
Porthoustock
Poldhu Cove
Mullion
Goonhilly Downs
St Keverne
B3293
The Manacles
Polurrian Cove
B3296
Penhale
Trelan
Lowland Point
Mullion Island
Mullion Cove
A3083
Gwenter
Coverack
Chynhalls Point
Predannack Wollas
Lizard Nature Reserve
Kuggar
Kennack Sands
Black Head
Vellan Head
St Ruan
Ruan Minor
Grade
Cadgwith
Kynance Cove
Llandewednock
Pentreath Beach
Lizard
Hot Point
Lizard Point
Lizard Lighthouse Heritage Centre

Main photo: Embracing the surf scene at Whitesand Bay.
Opposite: Geevor Tin Mine and Penzance harbour.

The Far West

The journey to the road's end may be long and tiring. It may be fraught with crawling traffic and toilet stops, but there's something undeniably liberating and otherworldly about arriving in Penzance on the A30. Perhaps it has something to do with those exotically planted roundabouts on the town's outskirts.

Yet, in many ways, **Penzance** is only the beginning – the hub from which a web of minor roads fans out across the Penwith Peninsula to a whole 'island' of holiday opportunities in hidden fishing villages, old mining communities, organic farms, cliff-top retreats and surf spots.

If you're lucky, Penzance is also a departure point for daytrips or longer visits to the **Isles of Scilly** aboard a British International helicopter or the plucky little *Scillonian III*. Lying just 28 miles to the southwest, this idyllic archipelago seems to have a toehold in the tropics, with brilliant turquoise seas, powder-white beaches and rampant plantlife.

If you're sticking to the mainland, though, the natural thing is to keep heading west from Penzance on the A30 until it finally fizzles out at **Land's End**. Before you reach the mighty, wave-chewed toe of Britain, however, you can't help but notice all those enticing signs luring you down side lanes to places like **Porthcurno** (with its show-stopping line-up of beach, Minack Theatre and Telegraph Museum) or **Sennen Cove** (surf central and all-round beach beauty).

Closer to Penzance, fishing villages like **Newlyn** and **Mousehole** add weight to postcard stands with their colourful trawlers and cutesy harbourfronts, while **Marazion** is the stepping-off point for **St Michael's Mount** – the crowning glory of the region, if not the entire county.

Further west, towards The Lizard, you'll find rocky nooks and blousy bays like Prussia Cove and Praa Sands. Head inland from Penzance and the B3071 weaves past prehistoric remains to **St Just** – gateway to Cape Cornwall and the starting point for a spectacular coastal drive on the B3306, linking historic mining settlements before reaching **St Ives**. If there's one thing worth driving all the way to the far west of Cornwall for, it's this beautiful harbour town with its dazzling beaches and dynamic arts scene.

Here to there

The Far West chapter of *Cornwall with Kids* covers the Penwith Peninsula (stretching west from St Ives to Cape Cornwall, south to Land's End, then east to Penzance) and Mount's Bay (east from Penzance to Praa Sands). For information on beaches east of Praa Sands, refer to the chapter on The Lizard (see pages 114-133). St Ives is covered in detail on pages 110-113, while the Isles of Scilly section starts on page 134. See also Northwest Cornwall (pages 60-83) for attractions within easy reach of the far west.

St Ives – Mount's Bay

Out & about The Far West

Fun & free

Stroll into a good book

Antonia Barber's much-loved children's classic, *The Mousehole Cat* (Walker Books) describes the epic tale of an old fisherman called Tom and his cat, Mowzer, as they set sail into a terrible storm. The gripping yarn get's an extra splash of reality if, afterwards, you stroll around **Mousehole** (pronounced 'Mowzel'), the fishing village near Penzance on which the book is based. A Cornish folktale by Charles Causley, *The Merrymaid of Zennor* (Orchard Books) has its roots in a small village near St Ives where a church chair bears the carving of a mermaid.

Cue *Jaws* music – but don't worry, basking sharks are harmless.

Spot a basking shark

Basking sharks are becoming an increasingly common sight around Cornwall during summer. Growing to a length of up to 11 m, these gentle, plankton-eating giants can be spotted from clifftops anywhere along the coast. Look for the broad, triangular dorsal fin breaking the surface. With binoculars, you might also be able to spot the white gape of the shark's mouth. If you join a boat trip in search of basking sharks and other wildlife (see page 98), be sure to choose an operator that's signed up to guidelines for minimal disturbance (wisescheme.org).

For a day away from it all I love nothing more than Prussia Cove, diving off the rocks or snorkelling around the gullies. A day surfing at Sennen Cove is the children's choice, followed by fish and chips from Jewell's in Newlyn – eaten sitting on a bench overlooking Mount's Bay. If we're feeling greedy, a Jelbert's home-made vanilla ice cream with a flake and a dollop of clotted cream goes down a treat! As for walks, one of our favourites is to head east along the coast path from Marazion to Perranuthnoe – it's exhilarating with the sea pounding the rocks below. Great fun on a calm summer's day is the walk along the causeway to St Michael's Mount as the tide starts to come in – see how far, and how wet, you get! Another fun and free pastime, rock-pooling is one of our specialities. My grandparents taught us well and there's no better place than Prussia Cove. Prise a limpet off the rocks, tie a length of cotton around it (and perhaps a tiny stone as a weight), dangle in a pool, then sit and wait. Before long you'll have a bucket full of blennies...

Philippa Penney
Property Manager, Classic Cottages, T01326-555555, classic.co.uk.

Get an early start and watch the fish being landed at Newlyn Harbour, cluttered with its fleet of long-liners and crabbers.

Take a walk on the wild side

Discover how wildlife thrives in the old mining landscape around Geevor and Levant. You can pick up a leaflet or booklet at Geevor Tin Mine's reception describing a two-hour walk that weaves through a fascinating array of habitats. Depending on the season (late spring or summer is best), you'll see Cornish hedges ablaze with wildflowers, heathland fussed over by stonechats, an insect bank where mining bees burrow into an old spoil heap, coastal grassland flickering with butterflies, cliff-top views of seabirds and, perhaps, basking sharks and dolphins, a reptile slope where adders and lizards enjoy sunbathing and old mine buildings where bats have taken up residence.

Ancient wonders

It requires a bit of tracking down, but delve into the lanes between Madron and Morvah on the Penwith Peninsula and you should spot the Neolithic tomb of **Lanyon Quoit** poking above the hedgerows. There's a small parking layby from where you can walk to the imposing three-legged structure. The capstone alone weighs over 13 tons and stands 2 m above ground – it used to be higher, but one of the 'legs' collapsed during a storm in 1815 and only three were used in the reconstruction. For more prehistoric detective work, head to **Chysauster Ancient Village** (TR20 8XA, T07831-757934, english-heritage.org.uk, Apr-Oct daily from 1000) located just over two miles northwest of Gulval (near Penzance) on the B3311. You have to pay a modest admission fee (£3 adult, £1.50 child) to explore the remains of this 2000-year-old Iron Age settlement and its unique stone-walled homesteads known as 'courtyard houses'. Other ancient sites include the **Boscawen-un Stone Circle** (near the village of Drift) and the replica Iron Age round house at **Bodrifty** (bodrifty.co.uk) signposted from Newmill beween Penzance and Zennor.

Heavy rock – Lanyon Quoit burial chamber dates from 4000-3000 BC.

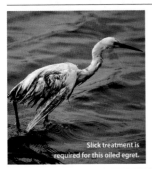

Slick treatment is required for this oiled egret.

Visit Mousehole Wild Bird Hospital

Why? It provides a lifeline to sick or injured birds, like this oiled egret, and relies entirely on donations and the support of visitors. There's no admission fee, but anything you spend in the gift shop will go towards caring for birds until they are ready to be returned to the wild or, if that's not possible, providing a long-term home for them at the sanctuary. Residents range from ducks and gulls to lapwings and turnstones. The hospital rose to fame in 1967 when it treated over 8000 oiled sea birds following the *Torrey Canyon* disaster.

Where? Mousehole Wild Bird Hospital, Raginnis Hill, Mousehole, TR19 6SR, T01736-731386, mouseholebirdhospital.org.uk.

How? The hospital is open year round daily 1030-1430.

Out & about The Far West

Get to the point

Distil everything that is magical about a family holiday in Cornwall – from surf, sand and rock pools to wild headlands and cutesy fishing villages – and you could well end up with this wonderful walk to **Land's End**. Following the South West Coast Path, the route starts at Gwynver, descending to a wave-pummelled beach at the northern end of Whitesand Bay. At low tide you can then stroll the best part of a mile along the entire scimitar curve of mainland Britain's most westerly beach, playing chicken with the waves, flying a kite, or simply enjoying the sensation of bare feet sinking into powder-soft sand. Approaching **Sennen Cove**, you'll reach a lifeguard-patrolled zone where it's safe to swim or surf (wetsuits and boards can be hired from the surf shop), but be sure to leave enough time to explore the rock pools near the lifeboat ramp. Continue through the village, stopping at The Blue Lagoon for fish and chips, or Breakers Café for a pasty. Peruse the local crafts in the Round House Gallery, then rejoin the coast path for the steady climb to an old coastguard lookout. There's a superb view across Whitesand Bay from here, but it's to the west that your eyes are drawn – to heather-capped cliffs rearing from a filigree of waves and marching west towards Land's End. Follow the clifftop path, passing the remains of Maen Castle, an Iron Age fort, then celebrate your arrival at the edge of Britain with ice creams at the First and Last House. There's an RSPB Discovery Centre just below the Land's End signpost where, for free, you can use telescopes to scan for dolphins, seals and basking sharks. The walk from Gwynver to Land's End is around two miles. Buses run from Land's End to Sennen Cove and Penzance.

Opposite: Maen Cliffs near Land's End.
This page: shrimping at Sennen Cove; rusty chain
in the harbour; a fisherman returns to shore; distant Gwenver
Beach merges with Whitesand Bay; heather-clad clifftops;
Sennen Cove fishing boats; body boarding at Whitesand Bay.

Out & about The Far West

Best beaches

The beaches described here are found anticlockwise, from just west of St Ives to Praa Sands. For St Ives' beaches, see pages 110-113; for beaches on The Lizard, see pages 118-119.

Portheras Cove

A strong contender for wildest beach in the west, Portheras is a sandy cove on a spectacular stretch of otherwise cliffy coast between St Just and St Ives. You can park near Pendeen Lighthouse and walk across to Portheras at low tide, but a more exciting approach is from Chypraze Farm, tucked down a narrow lane off the B3306 between Pendeen and Morvah. Park in the small field by the farm, drop £2 in the box at the farmhouse, then follow the short, fairly steep track towards the sea. At first, all you can see are waves breaking on the rocky, offshore Kenidjacks and the white dome of Pendeen Lighthouse poking above a distant headland. Keep walking (looking out for adders which like to bask on these slopes) and a crescent of sand slowly comes into view. The path enters a gully where you boulder-hop across a tea-coloured stream, then you're confronted by a sign warning of strong currents and fragments of metal from an old shipwreck. Portheras is not the kind of place for swimming or bare feet. But what a beach! Surf lacing smooth banks of fine golden sand, seals cruising the breakers; brilliant tuquoise sea and jumbled granite boulders that wouldn't look out of place in the Seychelles – Portheras is a beach to sit and stare, enjoy a secluded picnic and play chicken with the waves. Just be very careful, though, as surf can unexpectedly sweep high up the beach, funnelled by a channel carved by the stream.

Priest's Cove (Cape Cornwall)

Topped by the chimney of an old mining engine house, Cape Cornwall (the only cape in England and Wales) has a small rocky beach snagged with Atlantic flotsam, from old ropes to worn chunks of driftwood covered in goose barnacles. It's a wonderfully wild and remote place – perfect for walks and picnics in the kind of solitude you rarely find at Land's End.

Whitesand Bay

Just shy of Land's End, mainland Britain's most westerly beach has child appeal by the bucket load: a mile-long swathe of sand, turquoise sea white-ribbed by breakers and the cutesy fishing village of Sennen Cove with its surf school, fish and chips and lifeboat station. Scrawl your name in house-size letters across acres of rippled sand, learn to surf, play beach cricket or frisbee, build a dam to hold back the tide and befriend a shaggy 14-stone Newfoundland called Bilbo – the adorable canine contingent of Sennen Cove's beach lifeguard crew (you'll probably see him riding around on the back of a quad bike). You could also try dipping a net in the rock pools near the lifeboat ramp, spotting seals by the harbour, walking across the bay at low tide to Gwynver Beach (where the surf is usually at its wildest) or striking out in the opposite direction, across the cliffs, to Land's End (see page 92). You'll need to arrive early during high season if you want to bag a space at Sennen Cove's main car park overlooking the beach. This is also where you'll find the Sennen Surfing Centre (see page 99) and Beach restaurant (see page 108); an ice cream van is usually parked by the slipway, while just across the road is the Old Success Inn (see page 108). If this car park is full, try the one at the other end of the village, near the Round House Gallery. Otherwise, you'll have to park at the top of the hill and walk down to the beach.

Porthgwarra

A Cornish smugglers' cove if ever there was one, Porthgwarra even has a 'secret' tunnel leading from the slipway (just don't tell

Praa Sands.

Portheras Cove.

Whitesand Bay.

the kids it was excavated by miners to help farmers transport seaweed to their fields for use as fertiliser). A crabbing boat still operates from Porthgwarra, working the inlets along this dramatic and secluded stretch of coast south of Land's End. The cove has sand at low tide and swimming is safe as long as you stay close to shore. A small shop sells snacks and drinks.

Porth Chapel
Ⓟ
This sandy cove has no facilities and requires a steepish walk, starting either at the car park near St Leven's church or by following the coast path from Porthgwarra (15 minutes) or Porthcurno (30 minutes).

Porthcurno
Ⓟ Ⓟ Ⓟ Ⓟ Ⓟ
The best family beaches hold secrets back, revealing them one by one as the tide ebbs and flows – and Porthcurno is a master of suspense. Stunning even by Cornish standards, it nestles beneath the stone ramparts of the cliff-top Minack Theatre, brilliant turquoise waters lapping its sweep of white sand or pounding the cliffs in a magnificent procession

of curling, spray-whipped breakers. Then, as the tide drops, the beach slowly creeps along the rocky coast, stranding an enticing string of rock pools and knee-deep lagoons. Tiny coves appear and, if you're lucky, a spit of sand emerges to form the perfect ephemeral wicket for beach cricket – best played as the tide turns again and fielders are sent splashing into the encroaching waves in pursuit of the ball. Porthcurno's most unusual secret is that it was once the site of the first transatlantic submarine cable telegraph station – a museum in the village (see page 101) reveals all. Keep your eyes peeled for basking sharks near Porthcurno – particularly if you venture west along the coast path towards Land's End.

Lamorna Cove
Ⓟ Ⓟ Ⓟ Ⓟ
A rocky cove approached along a beautiful wooded valley, Lamorna is sheltered and south facing with good rock-pooling.

Mousehole
Ⓟ Ⓟ Ⓟ Ⓟ
A tiny, sandy cove is exposed at low tide in this picture-postcard, yet unspoilt, fishing village.

Marazion
Ⓟ Ⓟ Ⓟ Ⓟ Ⓟ Ⓟ
Better known as the stepping-off point for walking across to St Michael's Mount (see page 102), Marazion is also a fine beach in its own right, with gently sloping sand and fine shingle.

Perran Sands
Ⓟ Ⓟ Ⓟ Ⓟ Ⓟ
A wide sandy beach near the village of Perranuthnoe with just a strip of shingle at high tide.

Prussia Cove
Ⓟ
Remote and tricky to reach, Piskies Cove and Bessy's Cove are linked by the coast path to Kenneggy Sands; a good spot for adventurous rock-poolers.

Praa Sands
Ⓟ Ⓟ Ⓟ Ⓟ Ⓟ Ⓟ Ⓟ
One of Cornwall's most popular family beaches, Praa Sands (pronounced locally as 'Pray Sands') has a mile of golden sand, excellent swimming, great rock pools at the western end and even a dollop of surf when there's a south-coast swell. A spattering of beachfront shops, a café and watersports centre makes Praa a doddle for a relaxed day out.

Stunning even by Cornish standards, Porthcurno nestles beneath the stone ramparts of the cliff-top Minack Theatre, brilliant turquoise waters lapping its sweep of white sand or pounding the cliffs in a magnificent procession of curling, spray-whipped breakers.

Out & about The Far West

Action stations

Boat trips
Elemental Tours

Penzance, TR18 2LL, T01736-811200, elementaltours.co.uk. Atlantic Adventure (2 hrs) £30 adult, £22 child (5-14), £95 family; Ocean Safari (3 hrs) £35 adult, £30 child (10-14); Evening Cruise (2 hrs, summer only) £25 adult, £15 child; land safaris (4 hrs) £35 adult, £25 child (10-14). Hold on tight for a wave-skipping, wind-in-your-face high-speed RIB ride in search of whales, dolphins, seals, basking sharks and seabirds. Enthusiasts can venture far offshore on three-hour Ocean Safaris, but the shorter Atlantic Adventure is a better bet for young families. It cruises the waters of the Penwith Peninsula, taking in famous landmarks like St Michael's Mount, the Minack Theatre and Land's End. Elemental Tours also offer 4WD land-based safaris, bouncing around remote parts of Penwith in search of its wildlife, culture and industrial mining heritage.

Marine Discovery Penzance

Penzance, T01736-874907, marinediscovery.co.uk. Bay Discovery (1-1½ hrs, minimum age 3) £18 adult, £14 child, £55 family; Marine Discovery (2-2½ hrs, minimum age 6) £32 adult, £24 child (6-15), £100 family; Ocean Discovery (2½-3 hrs, minimum age 12) £38. These adrenaline-charged cruises operate out of Penzance Harbour aboard the jet-powered RIB *Shearwater*. The crew know the area intimately and you are almost guaranteed sightings of grey seals and a variety of seabirds. The most popular trip is the Marine Discovery which, depending on weather conditions, surges west to Land's End via Porthcurno, or east towards Rinsey Cove. Both options return by an offshore route to boost your chances of spotting common, bottlenose and Risso's dolphins, porpoises, basking sharks, sunfish and, if you're very lucky, a minke whale. Maximizing your chances of a whale or dolphin encounter, the Ocean Discovery tour ventures further offshore, taking in Wolf Rock Lighthouse and wildlife-rich shoals and reef. The Bay Discovery cruise, meanwhile, is more suited to younger families and flits across the bay from Cudden Point to Mousehole, with a stop at St Michael's Mount. Trips depart Penzance Harbour from either South Pier or Albert Pier, depending on the tide.

Mermaid Pleasure Trips

The White Shed, Ross Bridge, Wharf Rd, Penzance, TR18 4AH, T07901-731201, cornwallboattrips.com. Mackerel fishing (2 hrs) £12 adult, £8 child (5-7), £2 infant (under 5). Seal Cove trips (2 hrs, summer and school holidays, daily 1300 and 1500) £10 adult, £8 child (5-12), £5 infant (2-4). Wildlife Adventure (1-2 hrs) from £16 adult, £12 child (4-12), £50 family. Having worked on local ferries and lifeboats, skipper Adrian Thomas knows the seas around Penzance like the back of his hand. He's also lived on St Michael's Mount, so a cruise aboard his boat, *Mermaid II*, is a great opportunity not only to catch mackerel, observe seals and haul in lobster and crab pots, but also to learn about the history and legends of this beautiful stretch of Cornish

Surf's up – Praa Sands.

See life

Warmed by the Gulf Stream, the seas around West Cornwall are positively squirming with life. Join a boat trip and you could find yourself bobbing alongside bottlenose dolphins or racing towards a rendezvouz with a pod of leaping Risso's or common dolphins. Harbour porpoises tend to make more fleeting appearances, while any sighting – no matter how brief – of an orca, minke whale or fin whale is a bonus. Grey seals, meanwhile, are the staple sighting of wildlife cruises – they breed in local sea caves and can often be seen dozing on rocky outcrops. Summer visitors include basking sharks (see page 90), sun fish and leatherback turtles. Turning your binoculars skyward, you'll be able to tick off seabirds such as gannets, fulmars and puffins.

coast. The 33-ft boat is licensed to carry 35 passengers for summer cruising and up to 18 for fishing trips. For something a little zippier, Mermaid also offers wildlife-watching cruises on its fast RIB, *Misty Blue*. The one-hour trip makes for Cudden Point in search of seals, while the two-hour adventure heads west to the Runnelstone at Land's End, eyes peeled all the way for whales, dolphins and sharks.

Cycling
First & Last Trail
Part of this trail includes a level, mainly traffic-free link between Penzance and Marazion, with views of St Michael's Mount.

Mount's Bay Cycle Hire
Station House, Marazion, T01736-363044.

Pedals Bike Hire
The Wharfside Shopping Centre, Penzance, TR18 2GB, T01736-360600.

Horse riding
Land's End Trekking Centre
Trevescan Farm, Sennen, TR19 7AQ, T01736-871989. Year round. Roam the cliffs around Land's End on horseback or take a more gentle farm ride.

Surfing
Global Boarders Surf School
North St, Marazion, TR17 0EA, T01736-711404, globalboarders. com. Surf Experience Days £75. Operating from Marazion, Global Boarders takes you to the beach with the best surf conditions

that day – transport, two surf sessions and all gear included.

Sennen Surfing Centre
Sennen Cove, TR19 7AD, T01736-871561, sennensurfingcentre.com. £25/2-hr lesson, £20/family course (minimum 4 people), £50/2-day course, £75/3-day course, £90/4-day course, £100/5-day course. Located beneath the Beach restaurant (see page 108), this well-established surf school is a short sprint from the waves at Whitesand Bay.

Smart Surf School
Sennen Cove, T01736-871817, bluelagoonsurf.com. £20/2-hr lesson. Small, friendly surf school located on the seafront.

Stones Watersports
Praa Sands, T01736-762991, praasands.info. Year round, daily 1000-1800. Call for rates. More than just a surf shop, Stones can arrange scuba diving, windsurfing and water skiing. Sit-on sea kayaks can also be hired on the beach.

Geevor Tin Mine

Pendeen, TR19 7EW, T01736-788662, geevor.com. Jan-Jun and Sep-Dec Sun-Fri 0900-1700 (1600 Nov-Mar); Jul-Aug daily 0900-1700; mine tours hourly 1000-1600. £9.50 adult, £4.50 child (5-16), £27 family. Geevor Tin Mine really evokes the atmosphere of Cornwall's rich industrial heritage – pick up hard hats at the ticket office and you know you're in for something authentic.

A working mine until 1990, Geevor's tunnels are now open to visitors but first you need to navigate the mine building – a vast metal skeleton of rusted beams, pipes, plankways and colossal stone-grinding cauldrons. Don't worry – the route is clearly marked and quite safe. Every now and then you come across a friendly member of staff who will demonstrate an aspect of the tin-mining process. You'll get to weigh up a nugget of tin ore against a similarly-sized lump of granite; you'll learn about giant stone crushers and watch tin ore being separated from sandy waste on large, juddering sorting tables. It all makes perfect sense to children – a ginormous, smashing, sieving, sorting machine that could almost have been hatched from the mind of Willy Wonka.

Eventually you reach a door where more smiling ex-miners hand out overcoats and direct you to the underground section of the tour – a 300-year-old mine that was only discovered in 1995. Bent double (even a nine-year-old will have to duck in places) you shuffle along dank tunnels, passing narrow shafts and cramped chambers where costumed mannequins reenact the grim realities of mining three centuries ago. One of the figures rather alarmingly comes to life – at least, that's how it seems in the dim light until you realise it's another of Geevor's engaging miners waiting to chat to you about what it was like to work in the modern mine.

Plans are afoot to build a new, bigger underground experience, but for now this is an utterly mesmerising insight into the very heart of Cornwall's World Heritage mining site.

All mine – panning for gold at Geevor.

Back above ground you can pan for fool's gold, explore sheds full of machinery and even have a go at hand drilling.

Land's End Landmark

Land's End, Sennen, TR19 7AA, T0871-720 0044, landsend-landmark.co.uk. Easter-Oct, from 1000, Nov-Easter from 1030. £10.95 adult, £6.95 child, £24.75 family all-inclusive, or pay for individual attractions, from £3 adult, £2 child. Dr Who gets everywhere (as you'd expect with a Time Lord), but do you really need to see him, along with the Daleks and Cybermen at Land's End? It's just one of the exhibits at Land's End Landmark which also includes an interactive display on Britain's coasts, a rattling 'motion cinema' show reinacting an air-sea rescue, a restored 200-year-old farm (with craft workshops), the Land's End Trading Co (get your ceramic VW campervans here) and a free exhibition on people who have made the intrepid journey from Land's End to John O'Groats. New attractions are added all the time, so check the website for the latest news. It all adds up to a fun day out – don't forget to pop outside, check out the view and have your photo taken beneath the famous signpost (John of Groats 874 miles, New York 3147 miles). There's also a 'wreckreation' playground and an observation post manned by RSPB volunteers.

Minack Theatre

Porthcurno, TR19 6JU, T01736-810181, minack.com. Open to visitors Nov-Mar daily 1000-1530; Apr-Oct Mon, Tue, Thu, Sat, Sun 0930-1700, Wed, Fri 0930-1130. £3 adult, £1.20 child (under 16), free for under-12s. Call or check website for forthcoming productions. Cornwall's iconic open-air theatre, clinging to the cliffs above Porthcurno, is well worth a visit even if you're not planning on taking in a show (several family-friendly productions are scheduled each season). As well as the triumphant setting, there's an interesting exhibition about the theatre's creator, Rowena Cade, as well as a coffee shop and dazzling sub-tropical rockeries.

More family favourites

Levant Mine & Beam Engine

Trewellard, Pendeen, TR19 7SX, T01736-786156, nationaltrust.org.uk. Mar-Oct days vary (engine is steaming Jul-Sep Tue-Fri and Sun, 1100-1700). £5.80 adult, £2.90 child, £14.50 family.
Still standing proud on the cliff edge, Levant is Cornwall's only working steam-powered beam engine. Underground tours and a short film help to tell its story.

Trewidden Garden

Penzance, TR20 8TT, T01736-351979, trewiddengarden.co.uk. Feb-Sep Wed-Sun; Jul-Aug daily 1030-1730. £5 adult, children free.

Rain check

Cinemas
Savoy
Causewayhead, Penzance, TR18 2SN, T01736-363330.

Indoor swimming pools
Penzance Leisure Centre
St Clare, TR18 3QW, T01736-874744.

Museums
Penlee House Gallery & Museum
Morrab Rd, Penzance, TR18 4HE, T01736-363625, penleehouse.org.uk. £3 adult, children free.
Victorian home with impressive collection of paintings and museum artefacts relating to the history and culture of West Cornwall. Children's workshops take place during school holidays and there's also a café, gift shop and play area.

Porthcurno Telegraph Museum
Eastern House, Porthcurno, TR19 6JX, T01736-810966, porthcurno.org.uk. Apr-Oct daily 1000-1700; Nov-Mar Sun-Mon. £5.50 adult, £3.10 child, £13.20 family.
Fascinating museum all about communications and Porthurno's famous undersea cable. Second World War tunnels to explore, quiz trails, play tables and plenty of hands-on, touch-screen displays.

Wayside Museum
Old Zennor St, Zennor, TR26 3DA, T01736-796945. Apr-Oct daily from 1030. £3.25 adult, £2 child, £10 family. Reopened after flood damage in 2009, this wonderful time-capsule has themed areas including a watermill, cobbler's shop and blacksmith.

Ten-pin bowling
Grand Casino
Promenade, Penzance, TR18 4HH, T01736-363824.

Riddled with enticing pathways this peaceful, 15-acre garden is particularly impressive during spring when the magnolias are in bloom. Nearby Trengwainton is a peaceful woodland garden.

Don't miss St Michael's Mount

It's a cliché, but getting here really is part of the adventure. Few landmarks in Cornwall are more evocative, or enticing, than St Michael's Mount, especially at low tide when a cobbled causeway emerges from the sea, extending an irresistible invitation to walk across to the rocky islet crowned with its medieval castle and church. Better still, wait for an ebbing tide, roll up your trousers and wade across.

Once on the island, you may be surprised to find a thriving little community (home to 30 islanders), complete with harbour, sub-tropical gardens, shops, café and restaurant.

Collect children's quiz sheets before walking up the steep, but short, path to the castle. If you look carefully, you'll find a cobblestone in the shape of a heart which, according to legend, once beat in the chest of the giant Cormoran – a big bully prone to snacking on the island's cattle until he was lured into a pit and slain by a local lad called Jack (the original giant killer). A more uplifting legend refers to a vision of the Archangel St Michael that appeared to fishermen in the year 495.

The views from the summit of St Michael's Mount are spectacular, while the castle itself is a small but fascinating window on the past, with cannons and suits of armour dating from the War of the Roses and the Civil War, when the fortress was under seige.

The Mount's religious roots go back to the Norman invasion, when the island was granted to the Benedictine Abbey of Mont St Michel in Brittany. There's an exquisite chapel deep inside the castle which has been the family home of the St Aubyn family since the 17th century. Don't miss the elegant rococo-style Blue Drawing Room or the Chevy Chase Room with its 17th-century frieze depicting hunting scenes described in the *Ballad of Chevy Chase*.

Wade to go – barefoot to St Michael's Mount.

At low tide a cobbled causeway emerges from the sea, extending an irresistible invitation to walk across to the rocky islet.

Mount a plan

St Michael's Mount

Marazion, nr Penzance, TR17 0HS
T01736-710507 or 710265 (tide and ferry
information), stmichaelsmount.co.uk,
nationaltrust.org.uk. Late Mar-Jun Sun-Fri
1030-1700; Jul-Aug Sun-Fri 1030-1730;
Sep-early Nov Sun-Fri 1030-1700, last
admission 45 mins before castle closing time.
£6.60 adult, £3.30 child (5-17), £16.50 family.

Getting there

On foot At low tide, follow in the footsteps
of pilgrims and giants as you walk across the
causeway to St Michael's Mount. It only takes a few
minutes, but you should wear sensible shoes as
the cobbles are slippery and uneven. Bear in mind
that the climb to the castle is steep and cobbled
and, therefore, unsuitable for pushchairs.
By boat At high tide small motor boats ply back
and forth between the Mount and three landing
points along the shore at Marazion. One-way fares
£1.50 adult, £1 child.

Sleeping The Far West

Higher Pentreath Farm
Praa Sands, TR20 9TL, T01736-763222. Easter-Oct. Rates around £8-12/pitch.

Unzip your tent each morning to an invigorating view over mile-wide Praa Sands. The facilities at this campsite might be quite basic (a converted barn for a toilet and shower block, plus a tiny shop), but its location more than compensates. It takes just five minutes to stroll down the (steep) hill to the beach where there are cafés, pubs and shops.

Kelynack Caravan & Camping Park
Kelynack, St Just, TR19 7RE, T01736-787633, kelynackholidays.co.uk. Mar-Oct. £6-7 adult, £3-3.50 child (3-12); bunk barn from £12 adult, £6 child; static caravans £175-475/wk.

This small, secluded site offers a range of accommodation, including 45 touring pitches, a cluster of holiday homes and a self-contained four-bedroom bunk barn. A food van serves cooked breakfasts and evening meals, while everyday groceries, home-made cakes, sandwiches and picnic hampers are available at the shop. Children will find plenty to do at Kelynack. As well as a playground and wood to explore, they'll be forever fussing over the small herd of friendly donkeys and a lone Shetland pony called Pedro. Kelynack is also well located – hop on a bus at the end of the road and you can be in Land's End or St Ives within the hour.

Kenneggy Cove Holiday Park
Higher Kenneggy, Rosudgeon, TR20 9AU, T01736-763453, kenneggycove.co.uk. May-Oct. £17.50-23/pitch (2 adults), plus £4 extra person.

A quiet, well-tended site with 60 touring pitches and nine holiday homes, Kenneggy Cove Holiday Park is just a 12-minute walk from the coast path and Kenneggy Sands, a secluded beach (with sand and rock pools) between Perranuthnoe and Cudden Point.

Noongallas
Gulval, Penzance, TR20 8YR, T01736-366698, noongallas.com. Jul-Aug. £5 adult, £2.50 child (under 16).

Snug in the depths of the Penwith countryside with views of Mount's Bay, this back-to-nature campsite is one of the very few in Cornwall that permits campfires (don't forget your marshmallows). There's a relaxed, almost festival-like, atmosphere here – families get together for communal barbecues, while children make a bee-line for the nearby woods, building camps and damming the stream. As you might expect, facilities are few and far between (just a small shower and toilet block). However, if you don't mind basic camping, this is the ideal site for a relaxed holiday.

Tower Park Caravans & Camping
St Buryan, TR19 6BZ, T01736-810286, towerparkcamping.co.uk. Mar-Oct. £12.50-17/pitch (2 adults), plus £3.50 extra adult, £2 extra child (5-15); yurts £180-280/wk; static caravans £230-440/wk (up to 4 people).

Handy for both Sennen Cove and Porthcurno, Tower Park is a couple of minutes' walk from the village of St Buryan with its general store and pub. The site is divided into seven level fields of mown grass, sheltered by trees and Cornish hedges. As well as camping pitches and five static caravans, Tower Park has two Mongolian yurts for hire.

Trevedra Farm
Nr Sennen Cove, T01736-871818, cornwallfarwest.co.uk/trevedra. Apr-Oct. £4.50/adult, £2/child (5-15).

Occasionally windy, but with a superb location above Whitesand Bay, Trevedra has direct access to the steep coastal path leading to Gwynver Beach (see pages 92 and 94). Book early to secure a pitch in the field with sea views. Trevedra gets busy during summer, so don't expect total peace and quiet – especially if a group of surfers pitch up next to you. The site is kept immaculately clean

Porthcurno and the Minack Theatre.

by the friendly owners and there is a well-stocked shop and a handy snack van.

Treverven Touring Caravan & Camping Park
Treverven Farm, St Buryan, TR19 6DL, T01736-810200, chycor.co.uk/camping/treverven. Easter-Oct. Call for rates.

You can see the sea from this lovely, elevated site two miles west of Lamorna Cove. A farm track delves into a wooded valley, thick with ferns and wildflowers and ringing with birdsong in spring and summer, while a traffic-free country lane leads directly to the coast path, 10 minutes' walk away. On-site facilities include a children's play area and snack van.

Also recommended
Bone Valley Holiday Park
Heamoor, Penzance, TR20 8UJ, T01736-360313, bonevalleyholidaypark.co.uk. Easter-Oct. Call for rates.

Sheltered site close to Penzance.

Secret Garden Carvan & Camping Park
Bosavern House, St Just, TR19 7RD,

T01736-788301, secretbosavern.com. Mar-Oct. £14/pitch (2 adults), plus £2 extra person.

Tiny, intimate site with just 12 pitches within the old walled garden of a 17th century house.

Sennen Cove Camping & Caravanning Club Site
Higher Tregiffian Farm, St Buryan, TR19 6JB, T01736-871588, campingandcaravanningclub.co.uk. Mar-Nov. £5.80-8.90 adult, £2.60-2.80 child, £17.50-22.10 family, plus £7 non-member fee.

Immaculate site with midern facilities and children's playfield.

Trevair Touring Park
South Treveneague, St Hilary, TR20 9BY, T01736-740647, trevairtouringpark.co.uk. Easter-Oct. £2-6/tent, £5 adult, £2-3 child (3-16), static caravans £160-290/wk.

Peaceful, three-acre site with sub-tropical palms and lush lawns, surrounded by woodland.

Farm favourite
For camping in style, try Boswarthen Farm, near Madron – it's the only Feather Down Farm site in Cornwall. See pages 12-13 for details.

Holiday parks

Mount's Bay Holiday Park
Marazion, TR17 0HQ, T01736-710307, mountsbay-caravanpark.co.uk.
Small family-run park with 18 caravans and a heated outdoor swimming pool just 50 m from the beach at Marazion.

Praa Sands Holiday Park
Praa Sands, TR20 9SH, T01736-762201, haulfryn.co.uk or hoseasons.co.uk.
Five minutes' walk from the beach, Praa Sands Holiday Park is being redeveloped into a smart new retreat for families and couples. In addition to top-of-the-range caravans, facilities include an indoor heated swimming pool, nine-hole golf course, restaurant and terrace bar with sea views.

River Valley Country Park
Relubbus, TR20 9ER, T01736-763398, surfbayholidays.co.uk.
As well as pitches for touring caravans and tents, River Valley Country Park has holiday homes and luxury lodges (some with hot tubs). The park is located in a quiet valley close to Marazion and Praa Sands and offers breakfast packs on arrival.

Praa Sands Holiday Park.

Sleeping The Far West

Best of the rest

Atlantic House
Sennen Cove, T01326-555555, classic.co.uk. £546-1449/wk.
This gorgeous, open-plan New England-style property sleeps seven and is crisp, fresh and uncluttered – exactly how you wished your own home could be. The path to surf-sensation, Whitesand Bay, is steep, but the views more than compensate.

Queens Hotel
The Promenade, Penzance, TR18 4HG, T01736-362371, queens-hotel.com. B&B from £60 adult, £15 child.
Handy if you need to spend a night in Penzance prior to sailing to the Isles of Scilly, this Victorian seafront hotel has family rooms and a children's menu.

Rosudgeon Farm
Prussia Cove, T01702-475075, rosudgeonfarm.com. £400-850/wk.
A 15-minute walk from Prussia Cove, this fine farmhouse with its three crisply converted barns (sleeping up to six) is set around a courtyard, with wonderful coastal views and opportunities for cliff-top walks.

YHA Castle Horneck
Alverton, Penzance, TR20 8TF, T0845-371 9653, yha.org.uk. From £15.95 adult, £11.95 child (under 18).
Recently refurbished, this smart hostel occupies a Georgian manor house on the outskirts on Penzance and has family rooms, a café, self-catering kitchen and landscaped woodland gardens.

Splashing out

Tregenna Castle Estate
St Ives, TR26 2DE, T01736-795254, tregenna-castle.co.uk. Check online for special offers.
Standing proud above St Ives, this 72-acre estate has a luxury hotel, 70 self-catering cottages and apartments and a collection of wooden lodges (each with jacuzzi and sauna). Leisure facilites include an 18-hole golf course, two heated swimming pools, tennis courts, croquet and a spa. Tregenna also boasts one of Cornwall's best kids' programmes, with a packed schedule of treasure hunts, discos, craft modelling, cooking, wildlife activities and soft play.

See also **The Cove**, page 109.

Cottage agents
See also page 186.

Cornish Riviera Holidays
Westcotts Quay, St Ives, TR26 2DY, T01736-797891, cornishrivieraholidays.co.uk.
Portfolio of over 70 fishermen's cottages and harbourside flats in the heart of St Ives.

Furthest West Cornish Holidays
Treen, TR19 6LQ, T01736-810452, furthestwest.com.
Three properties in Sennen Cove and two in Treen, between Porthcurno and Penberth.

Higher Chellew Holiday Cottages
Nancledra, TR20 8BD, T01736-364532, higherchellew.co.uk.
Four cottages with sunny patios in a rural location, about halfway between St Ives and Penzance.

St Aubyn Estates
The Manor Office, Marazion, TR17 0EF T01736-710507, staubynestates.co.uk.
Eight lovingly restored seaside boltholes (sleeping up to 10) in Nanjizal, Porthgwarra and the Marazion area.

Trevarthian Holiday Homes
Marazion, TR17 0EG, T01736-710100, trevarthian.co.uk.
Beachside self-catering apartments close to the sandy beach and children's playground at Marazion.

Sennen Cove has several holiday properties, including Atlantic House on Marias Lane.

Eating The Far West

Local goodies

Bill & Flo's
Trevarrack, nr Lelant, TR26 3EZ,
T01736-798885.
Home-grown veg and salad,
plus local meats, cheese, honey,
cider and apple juice.

Chegwidden Farm Shop
St Levan, TR19 6LP, T01736-810516,
chegwiddenfarm.com.
Delicious rare-breed sausages,
bacon and burgers, along
with a good selection of
fresh vegetables, cheeses
and other local produce. The
farm also offers top quality
accommodation at The Granary.

Higher Trenowin Farm Shop
Nancledra, TR20 8BE, T01736-
362439. Sun 0900-1300.
A family-run farm between
St Ives and Penzance, Higher
Trenowin Farm runs a single
suckler beef herd and stocks
its farm shop with free-range
hen and quail eggs, seasonal
vegetables, herbs and salads,
cakes, jams and preserves, as
well as local ice cream from
Zennor (see opposite).

Trevathan Farm Shop
St Endellion, PL29 3TT, T01208-
880164, trevathanfarm.com.
Daily from 1000.
Pick your own fruit and veg or
find it in the farm shop, together
with farm-fresh beef, lamb and
eggs, plus lots of other Cornish
goodies – jams, chutneys,

Fishy business

The **Pilchard Works** at Newlyn
(pilchardworks.co.uk) uses only
line-caught fish – look out for their
distinctive tins of pilchards and
mackerel, decorated with Newlyn
School paintings.

honey, cheeses, fudge and
clotted cream. Children can
pamper the fluffies in the pets'
corner, while grown-ups peruse
the country wines, Cornish beer
and scrumpy. Afterwards, treat
them to Treleavens ice cream or
go the whole hog and sit down
to a traditional Sunday roast or
cream tea in the restaurant.

Trevelyan Farm Shop
Perranuthnoe, TR20 9PP,
T01736-710410.
Organic farm shop selling a
good range of meat, dairy,
vegetables and fruit products,
plus preserves, bread and cakes.

Dating from the 13th century, the pasty
became established as the staple diet of
miners across Cornwall. A portable
and durable convenience food, its
crimped crust was used as a handle
which was later discarded due to
the high levels of arsenic in many
Cornish tin mines.

Perfect pasties

The **Genuine Cornish Pasty Association** is a group of more than 40 pasty
makers in Cornwall, baking around 86 million pasties each year – check online
for a list of members (cornishpastyassociation.co.uk). They know exactly what
makes a proper Cornish pasty. For starters, it has to be a 'D' shape, crimped on
one side – never the top. The filling should be chunky with no less than 12.5%
roughly cut chunks of beef, plus swede or turnip, potato and onion, with a
light pepper seasoning. Glazed with milk or egg, the pastry casing should be
golden with no splits. And, finally, it should always be made in Cornwall.

Market days

Lamorna Produce Market
Village Hall, Friday 0900-1300.

Penzance Country Market
St Johns Hall, Alverton Street,
Thursday 0830-1145.

Penzance Farmers' Market
St John's Hall, Alverton Street,
Friday 0900-1400.

Sennen Farmers' Market
Sennen School, Tuesday
0800-1200.

St Erth Farmers' Market
Methodist Church, Saturday
1000-1200.

St Ives Farmers Market
Lower Stennack, Thursday
0900-1400.

Ice cream

Milking the legend of the Zennor
Merrymaid (see page 90) **Moomaid
of Zennor** (moomaidofzennor.co.uk)
creates sumptuous ice cream and
sorbet using milk and cream from
the dairy herd at Tremedda Farm.
There's a Moomaid parlour on the
harbourfront at St Ives.

Eating The Far West

Quick & simple

Beach

Sennen Cove, TR19 7BT, T01736-871191, thebeachrestaurant.com. Mon-Sat 1000-1630, 1845-2045; Sun 1000-1730.
Located right above Whitesand Bay, the Beach restaurant practically dabbles its toes in the Atlantic. There's a surf shop underneath it, so no excuses for not working up an appetite for lunchtime bites such as crab soup (£7.25), steak sandwich (£10.95) or cauliflower cheese (£7.45) – best enjoyed on the large terrace with views of the beach and distant Cape Cornwall. The children's menu features fish goujons and chips (£5.95) and meatballs with pasta (£6.45). An all-day snack menu includes tapas, pizza, cream teas and cakes. You can also order takeaway pizzas from £7.25. Dinner is an altogether more refined affair with main courses costing around £13-22. Try the delicious smoked haddock risotto for starters (£7.25), followed by hake with herb crust and ratatouille (£16.45). Much of the seafood is fresh off the restaurant's boat, *Rosebud*.

Old Success Inn

Sennen Cove, TR19 7DG, T01736-871232. Food served 1200-1400, 1800-2100.
A pub alternative to the nearby Beach restaurant (above), this 17th-century fisherman's inn is a local watering hole with a good range of Cornish bitters and ciders, a cosy bar and old pictures of the Sennen lifeboat. There's also a pool table and photos of big waves – no doubt to appease the surf crowd – but this busy pub is also a good bet for families. The menu features light bites such as fish goujons (£6.75), sandwiches (from £4.50) and jacket potatoes (from £4.95). Mains include local bangers and mash (£7.95), fish pie (£9.75) and wholetail scampi (£8.95), while the kids' menu is equally 'safe' with fish and chips, casserole or pasta from £4.75. Only serious surfers deserve the Big Fudge Sharer (£6.95) – a mountain of warm chocolate fudge cake, vanilla ice cream, whipped cream, marshmallows and chocolate flake.

Poolside Indulgence

Jubilee Pool, Wharf Rd, Penzance, TR18 4HH, T0777-999 8590, poolside-indulgence.co.uk. Daily from 1000.
Just imagine a long summer's evening, fresh tasty food, a poolside table and lights twinkling across the bay... This irresistible little café is as close to the Mediterranean as Penzance gets – and the menu reflects just that. Overlooking Jubilee Pool, one of the best preserved lidos in the country, and beyond to St Michael's Mount, Poolside Indulgence serves freshly made salads, hot ciabatta and pastas

Poolside Indulgence overlooks the lido.

for lunch, while the evening menu turns to tapas, with individual dishes (calamari, whitebait, olives, garlic prawns, Spanish tortilla etc) from £3.25.

Renaissance Café

Wharfside Shopping Centre, Market Jew St, Penzance, TR18 2GB, T01736-366277. Daily 0900-late.
Just across from the main car park in Penzance, the Renaissance commands views across the harbour to St Michael's Mount and serves some of the town's best pizza and pasta.

Fish & chips

Captain's (Daniel Pl, Penzance) has been established for over 50 years. Also try **Jewell's** (The Strand, Newlyn), **Jeremy's** (Market Sq, St Just), **Beck's** (Longstone Hill Carbis Bay), **The Kingfisher** (Wharf Rd, St Ives) and **The Blue Lagoon** on the seafront at Sennen Cove.

Sandbar

Praa Sands, TR20 9TQ, T01736-763516, sandbarpraasands.co.uk. Mon-Fri from 1100, Sat-Sun from 1000.
Smack bang on the golden, surf-raked beach of Praa Sands, the Sandbar has an oceanfront view to rival any of the beach cafés on the North Cornwall coast. Lively and popular, it serves snacks and beach bites from £2.75, decent home-made burgers, locally caught fish and other mains (from £7.50) and a Sunday lunchtime carvery (£8.95 for adults, £5.95 for children).

Also recommended
The Cook Book

St Just, TR19 7JZ, T01736-787266, thecookbookstjust.co.uk.
Home-made cakes, cream teas, soups, baguettes, salads and breakfast – with a second-hand book store upstairs.

Count House Café

Geevor Tin Mine, Pendeen, TR19 7EW, T01736-788662. Free entry.
Simple, tasty food and picture-window views of the Atlantic. Few places serve a better pasty in a more spectacular location.

The Cove Café

Praa Sands, TR20 9TQ, T01736-763751, cafecove.co.uk.
Opened in 2009, this bright and cheerful café/takeaway is just above the car park at the eastern end of Praa Sands and has an outdoor seating area overlooking the beach.

The Gurnard's Head

Nr Zennor, St Ives, TR26 3DE, T01736-796928, gurnardshead.co.uk.
A perfect pitstop if you've been out stomping the cliff paths between St Ives and St Just, the 'Gurn' has a relaxed atmosphere, fine views and good simple food, using fresh local ingredients.

Posh nosh

The Cove

Lamorna, TR19 6XH, T01736-731411, thecovecornwall.com. Brunch 1030-1200, light bites and afternoon tea 1430-1800 , children's tea 1800-1930, dinner 1900-2200.
With just 15 stylish self-catering apartments, this exclusive hotel peeps through the trees at Lamorna Cove. It combines all the comforts of a luxury hotel (heated outdoor pool, sauna, in-room beauty treatments, baby listening etc) with the convenience of your own apartment, but if a week's stay (£600-2742) is out of the question, then at least treat yourself to a meal here. Open to non-residents, The Cove's terrace bar is a gorgeous spot to enjoy a cream tea (£6.50) or a light snack, such as a plate of mezze or charcuterie (from £6.95). Lunch and dinner dishes (taken on either the terrace or in the restaurant) typically fuse local ingredients with a touch of the Mediterranean. For starters (from £5.95), try the Newlyn crab and cockle linguine with garlic and chilli, sardines pan-fried with sherry and almonds or hand-dived scallops with pancetta, leeks and cream. Dinner mains (around £13-23) include wild mushroom risotto, Cornish beef fillets with béarnaise sauce and red mullet fillets with a fricassee of squid and samphire. Children's meals (all £5.95) are home-made and organic – choose from grilled chicken, poached salmon, burger or fish and chips, pasta and pizza.

Longships Restaurant

The Land's End Hotel, Lands End, TR19 7AA , T01736 871844, landsendhotel.co.uk. Daily 1200-1400, 1900-2030.
Open to non-residents of the Land's End Hotel, the Longships Restaurant & Bar are located in the conservatory, where window seats bag stunning views of the sea. Sandwiches and paninis are available at the bar, while the very reasonable lunchtime Evergreen Menu (two courses £6.95, three courses £8.95) features soup, salad, pâté or melon for starters and steak pie, poached salmon, roast dinner or a vegetarian dish for main courses. The evening à la carte menu, meanwhile, has a classic selection of starters (mussels, baked mushrooms etc), followed by an equally traditional range of mains, featuring fish, steak and chicken. Expect to pay from around £15 to £20 for two courses.

St Ives

How do you sell a day out at a modern art gallery to children? You could mention that the Tate St Ives is renowned for its child-friendliness and has family activities that sometimes spill onto Porthmeor Beach.

You could add that St Ives is the epicentre of Cornwall's thriving art scene and that a visit to the Tate embodies the region's creativity. Or you could simply slip in the gallery as part of a fun-filled day trip that starts with a train ride on the St Ives Bay Line, an hour or two on Porthminster Beach, followed by a spot of browsing and crabbing along the harbourfront as you amble towards the Tate.

Get your bearings

St Ives has everything you could possibly want in a Cornish seaside town -- from bustling harbour and beautiful beaches to great food and fine art. Small wonder it's heaving with tourists during the high season. The trick for a stress-free visit is to leave your car behind and explore on foot.

The 12-minute train ride from St Erth on the **St Ives Bay Line** (T08457-484950, firstgreatwestern. co.uk, return tickets £4 adult, £2 child) provides dreamy views across the bay towards Godrevy Point and some great birdwatching as you trundle past the Hayle Estuary. The train stops at Porthminster Beach, just south of the harbour, but you could also get off at Carbis Bay and stroll into town along the coast path (about 20 minutes).

St Ives Tourist Information Centre (Street an Pol, TR26 2DS, T01736-796297, visit-stives. co.uk) is located close to the main shopping area behind the harbour. Follow The Wharf around the harbour to Smeatons Pier or cross over the narrow peninsula separating the harbour from Porthmeor Beach. At the tip of this short stub of land, the so-called Island conceals tiny Porthggwidden Beach.

Get all arty

Seek inspiration in Cornwall's myriad galleries, then equip your kids with a sketch pad, pencils and paints for an art session at a colourful fishing harbour like St Ives. On the beach, make collages from strandline finds, fashion silly faces from shells and seaweed and build sandcastles modelled on St Michael's Mount. Don't forget that it costs nothing to visit the Falmouth Art Gallery (see page 176), or that the Tate St Ives (see page 112) is free for under 18s. If you're stuck for ideas, there's an excellent giftshop in the Tate St Ives, brimming with books, postcards and art kits guaranteed to get the creative juices flowing.

Let's go to... St Ives

Hit the beach

A slightly quieter alternative to the busy town beaches in St Ives, **Carbis Bay** is a dune-backed, Blue-Flag beauty, covering acres of sand with just the right consistency for sandcastles. The swimming here is generally sheltered and safe.

Another regular contender in the Blue Flag awards, **Porthminster** is a stunning beach with fine golden sand gently shelving into a sheltered corner of St Ives Bay. Deservedly popular with families, it boasts safe swimming, fabulous cafés (see opposite), mini golf, beach huts and an almost Mediterranean vibe, thanks to its sparkling waters and exotic palms.

Tucked up along the seafront right in the thick of things, **Harbour Beach** is a great place to paddle, dig and muck about in shallow, calm waters – although you do have to watch out for boats coming and going. Young families also love **Porthgwidden**, the smallest of the town beaches at St Ives, east-facing and sheltered between the harbour and The Island.

On the west side of the town, just below the Tate Gallery, **Porthmeor Beach** reaps some hefty Atlantic swells and is one of the region's most popular surf spots. Lessons are available from the St Ives Surf School (T01736-794633). There are also rock pools either end of the half-mile-wide, lifeguard-patrolled bay.

Take to the water

Self-drive motor boats can be hired along the harbourfront during summer. For organized boat trips, **St Ives Pleasure Boat Association** (T07821-774178, stivesboats.co.uk) operates two-hour fishing trips in St Ives Bay (£14 adult, £10 child), as well as cruises out to Seal Island (£9 adult, £6 child) – a 90-minute jaunt westward to see a colony of Atlantic grey seals. For sailing times, check out the noticeboards near the lifeboat station. Boats include the *James Steven* (an old lifeboat originally powered by oar and sail) and the *Dolly Pentreath*, a traditional Cornish fishing lugger.

Carbis Bay.

Visit the gallery

You may catch your children casting wistful glances at Porthmeor Beach, but you can't leave town without at least a stab at some contemporary art appreciation in the **Tate St Ives** (Porthmeor Beach, TR26 1TG, T01736-796226, tate. org.uk/stives, Mar-Oct daily 1000-1720, Nov-Feb Tue-Sun 1000-1620, £5.75 adult or £8.75 if combined with a visit to the Barbara Hepworth Museum & Sculpture Garden, free for under 18s).

The fact is, this curvaceous vision of clean-cut modernism presiding over Porthmeor's Bohemian surf scene is actually quite family friendly. Activity packs, talks, events and a team of helpful staff aim to make everything fun and accessible to children. And, even if your visit doesn't coincide with a family activity, kids can pick up free I-Spy sheets and set off on a search for abstract shapes and patterns. A family trail guide, meanwhile, will help parents make sense of the exhibits and frame pertinent questions to bemused children. In the studio, kids can get creative on the Tate's website, with activites linked to the current exhibition.

A family trail at the nearby **Barbara Hepworth Museum & Sculpture Garden** on Barnoon Hill (see Tate St Ives for contact details) provides an intriguing journey through a verdant garden 'sprouting' abstract works of art.

All sounds too high-brow? The **St Ives Museum** (Wheal Dream, TR26 1PR, T01736-796005, Easter-Oct Mon-Sat from 1000, £1.50 adult, 50p child) has a more down-to-earth collection of fishing nicknacks and the like. And,

Porthmeor Beach.

if you just want somewhere indoors for the kids to burn off energy, make tracks for the **Play Zone** (Carbis Bay Holiday Park, TR26 3HW, T01736-799499, daily from 1000).

Canvas & cottages

The beaches and galleries of St Ives are just a short stroll from **Ayr Holiday Park** (T01736-795855, ayrholidaypark.co.uk, Apr-Sep, £5.50-19.25/pitch, plus £4-6.25 adult, £2-3 child) – a popular cliff-top campsite and touring park with excellent facilities and chest-swelling views across the bay.

St Ives Cottages (T0800-328 8051, stivescottages.co.uk) has a small collection of character properties, many with that all-important parking space and some right on the harbourfront.

Located off the B3306 between Zennor and St Ives, **Trevalgan Holiday Farm** (St Ives, TR26 3BJ, T01736-796529, trevalgan.co.uk, £230-650/wk) has four cottages sleeping up to six, plus a wealth of facilities to keep families happy – from a play barn and pets corner to garden toys and baby gear.

Lavish living near Porthmeor Beach, **Sail Lofts** (T01736-799175, thesaillofts.co.uk, £310-2599/wk) has two-, three- and four-bedroom open-plan boutique apartments with subtropical courtyard garden, outdoor shower, surf board storage, plasma televisions and iPod docks. See also Tregenna Castle Estate, page 106.

Grab a bite

A sunny, beachside café with a zesty menu, fusing local seafood with imaginative Asian and Italian recipes, **Porthminster Beach Café** (St Ives, TR26 2EB, T01736-795352, porthminstercafe.co.uk, daily during spring and summer from 0900, closed Mon during winter) is the hottest reservation in town. It's not cheap – haddock and chips will set you back £10.95, while the monkfish curry is a whopping £18.95.

Nestled beneath the grassy slopes of the Island on the other side of St Ives, the sister property, **Porthgwidden Café** (T01736-796791, porthgwiddencafe.co.uk, daily from 0900) serves breakfasts and light lunches from around £4.

Among the plethora of restaurants and cafés along the harbourfront, **Slipways** (Fish St, T01736-799950) and **The Wave** (St Andrews St, T01736-796661) are both highly recommended. Try the **Pizza Patio Restaurant** (Fore St, T01736-798235) for excellent pizza and pasta from £7.25 (takeaway pizzas from £5.95).

Main photo: Kynance Cove – the gem in the Lizard's glittering crown. Opposite: On the trail at Trebah Gardens, stream jumping at Kennack Sands.

The Lizard

You won't find much in the way of big, blousy beaches on the Lizard. Instead, its crinkle-cut coast is riddled with the kind of coves, creeks and fishing hamlets that have smugglers' den written all over them. The Lizard is a land of adventure, helped in no small part by several of Cornwall's top attractions.

Adrenaline addicts can binge on the rides at Flambards, time travellers can explore new frontiers at Future World, while close encounters with marine mammals await visitors to the National Seal Sanctuary.

All three big days out are within easy reach of **Helston**, a small market town at the gateway to the Lizard. Apart from a rather splendid playground next to the boating lake, there's little to waylay holidaying families in this modest town. Most visitors slingshot through its roundabouts and continue south on the A3083, a seriously exciting road that hugs the perimeter fence of **RNAS Culdrose** (look out for helicopters) before dropping like a stone towards the village of **Lizard** and its iconic headland.

Rising like an exclamation mark at mainland Britain's most southerly point, Lizard Lighthouse has a fascinating new heritage centre and is the starting point for some of Cornwall's finest cliff walks – the sea chewing over the coastline, stiff-winged fulmars riding the ocean breeze and, if you're lucky, a Royal Navy ship sidling out into the Atlantic.

Backtrack slightly and you can delve off the A3083 to **Kynance Cove** (everyone's favourite Lizard pin-up), **Cadgwith** (a fairytale fishing village) and **Mullion** – gateway to a string of sandy inlets and the stoic little harbour at **Mullion Cove**.

Back at RNAS Culdrose, the B3293 branches eastwards and, soon after, a sideshoot wriggles up to **Gweek** where the contented honks of the sanctuary's seals echo across the mudflats of the **Helford Estuary**. Lose yourself in the knot of lanes around this idyllic waterway and, hopefully, you'll find yourself unravelling at hidden gems like **Helford Passage** or **Mawnan** – a stone's throw from magical **Trebah Gardens**.

Stick to the B3293 and you'll scale **Goonhilly Downs**, where Arthur and his fellow satellite dishes sprout from the Lizard like white mushrooms. Roskilly's ice cream calls nearby as the road continues east to **Coverack** and south to **Kennack Sands** – that rarity on the Lizard: a big golden beach.

Here to there

The Lizard chapter of *Cornwall with Kids* covers the peninsula south from Porthleven and Helston to Lizard Point and east to the Helford River – including attractions on the north bank like the gardens of Trebah and Glendurgan. See pages 174-177 for Falmouth and its beaches (including Maenporth). For Praa Sands, Penzance and other highlights west of Porthleven, see The Far West chapter (pages 88-109). Truro, linked to Falmouth and Helston via the A394, is covered on pages 178-179.

Porthleven – Helford River

Out & about The Lizard

Fun & free

Take a walk on the wild side

Stretching almost four miles from Porthleven to Gunwalloe, Loe Bar is a shingle and flint ridge separating the sea from a freshwater lake called The Loe. It was formed during storms in the 12th century, blocking the Cober Valley and preventing merchant ships from sailing up the estuary to Helston. You can access the Bar from a small car park about halfway along, or by walking two miles along the coast path from Porthleven. The beach shelves steeply and fierce currents strafe the coast (many ships have been wrecked here). Take a picnic and a kite and enjoy this lonely, wild stretch of coast, but don't be tempted to swim. Birdwatchers will enjoy strolling the woodland paths around Loe Pool.

Watch the choppers

King of spin, RNAS Culdrose is one of Europe's largest helicopter bases with squadrons specializing in anti-submarine warfare and surveillance. Most people are more familiar with its red and grey search-and-rescue Sea Kings, which can often be seen whirring overhead on training missions or dealing with emergencies. You can get a closer look by visiting the air station's free-to-enter Public Viewing Area. The Merlin Café & Gift Shop (Apr-Oct Mon-Fri from 0930) is also located here, along with the departure point for coach tours (T01326-565085).

Unravel a crab line from the harbour walls of fishing villages like Porthleven and Coverack.

> I've lived in Cornwall for 18 years and both of my children were born here. Dollar Cove, near Gunwalloe, is our favourite beach as it has spectacular rock formations and holds many happy memories. At low tide, Castle Beach in Falmouth is fantastic for rock-pooling. Falmouth also has the best fish and chips at Harbour Lights, as well as plenty of things to do on a rainy day, like the maritime museum and Ships & Castles' swimming pool with its river run and slide. For walks, the coast path from Kynance Cove to Lizard Point is stunning.

Nicola Wharton
Garden Team, Trebah Gardens, Mawnan Smith, T01326-252200, trebah-garden.co.uk.

Visit Cadgwith Cove

Why? It's not exactly the kind of beach you're going to stake out with a windbreak for the day, but Cadgwith Cove is still not to be missed. It's a proper little Cornish fishing village, with trawlers and fishing paraphernalia scattered over a shingle beach, thatched cottages and a tiny tin-roofed church clinging to a hillside, and gardens crammed with flowers and flotsam sculptures. The Cornish accents here are as thick as the milkshakes served at Minnie Moon down by the pilot gig boathouse. Above the café, the Crow's Nest gallery has vibrant paintings of the village. Boat trips can be arranged (T01326-290716) and there's a cosy pub with folk music on Tuesday and Friday nights. Don't forget to check out the fishing contest results chalked up by the beach.

Where? Cadgwith (cadgwith.com) is located on the southeast tip of the Lizard.

Walk the Lizard

Located at latitude 49°57'N and longitude 5°12'W, Lizard Point is the most southerly point of the British mainland – a wave-gnawed headland with fierce tidal races and ship-snagging reefs. Walk from the National Trust car park down to the point and you'll see maps in the Lizard Point Gift Shop scrawled with shipwrecks (about 400 vessels have floundered here, including the *Royal Ann* which ran onto Stag Rock in 1720 with the loss of 207 lives).

Built by Trinity House in 1752, the Lizard Lighthouse originally had two towers lit by coal fires. It went electric in 1878 and is now fully automated, with flashes every three seconds that are visible for 25 miles out to sea. A new heritage centre at the lighthouse (see page 124) shines a light on the area's history.

Some of Britain's oldest rocks can be found at the Lizard, including serpentine – pop into PL Casley & Son's stonemason hut at the Point to see some beautiful examples. You might meet the grandson of artist William Casley, renowned for his evocative seascapes of the area.

You'll feel like you are walking into a masterpiece when you set out, east or west, along the coast path from Lizard Point. Eastwards, the trail leads past the sandy cove at Housel Bay and the Coastwatch Lookout at Bass Point before reaching Kilcobben Cove, where the RNLI are planning to replace the existing lifeboat station with a new £6 million facility.

The Lizard's original lifeboat house can still be seen at Polpeor Cove, just to the west of Lizard Point. Continue westwards from here for a spectacular, two-mile walk to Kynance Cove, passing wild Pentreath Beach. With luck, you'll spot a pair of the rare crow-like choughs that nest along this stunning stretch of coast.

From top left: The Lizard National Nature Reserve is home to a wealth of flora and fauna – from thrift to choughs; the old lifeboat house at Polpeor Cove; Lizard Lighthouse; a handful of snails, and the cliff-top approach to Kynance Cove.

Out & about The Lizard

Best beaches

The beaches described here are found west to east, from Porthleven to the Helford River.

Gunwalloe Church Cove

South of Loe Bar (see page 116), the Lizard's coastline rucks up into cliffs, nicked in places by small coves and fishing harbours. Gunwalloe Church is the first of these little havens – a sandy, dune-backed cove with a car park and seasonal café. Good surf rumbles into Gunwalloe on a strong southwesterly and, although lifeguards are on duty during summer months, you should always beware of strong undercurrents and steeply shelving sand. The cove gets its name from the 15th-century church of St Winwaloe, constantly battling against storm-shifted sands at the northern end of the beach. Some of the woodwork inside the church is said to be from the wreck of a Portuguese carrack (sunk here in 1527). Coins from this and other shipwrecks are still found on the beach, so keep your eyes peeled (see Treasure Hunting, page 121).

Poldhu Cove

One of the Lizard's most popular sandy coves, Poldhu lies a short distance to the north of Mullion. A road loops around the back of the cove with a car park providing easy, level access to both the beach and a funky little café perched in the dunes (see page 132). Like Gunwalloe, left, Poldhu gets decent surf when conditions are right – just stay well clear of the rocks either side of the cove. Children enjoy playing in the shallow stream that flows over the beach – it's littered with small flat pebbles that are perfect for stacking into weirs. If it's not really beach weather, Poldhu is still worth a visit. Walk onto the grassy cliff-top and you will find the remains of the Marconi Wireless Station, where Italian, Guglielmo Marconi, sent a wireless message (three dots for 'S' in morse code) across the Atlantic Ocean on 12 December 1901. A few building foundations and the anchor points for aerial masts are all that remain to mark this defining moment – the birth of modern telecommunications. It's a far cry from today's world of Wi-Fi – you might need to help your children make the connection.

Mullion Cove

Although the tiny harbour beach here only appears at low tide, this is a wonderful base for cliff walks and exploring. When it comes to Cornish fishing hamlets, Mullion Cove is as close to picture-book perfection as you'll find. Granite piers embrace a harbour tucked into serpentine cliffs, where whitewashed cottages huddle out of the wind. The cobbled slipway is still strewn with fishing boats and lobster pots, but it was in the 18th century that Mullion Cove thrived as a pilchard fishery (supplemented, no doubt, by smuggling). The harbour master's house used to be a pilchard cellar, while opposite the café are the remains of a Second World War anti-tank wall. Stake out the harbour walls for crabbing (you might be lucky enough to catch a glimpse of a seal or basking shark) and wait for low tide to scramble through the cave that leads from the harbour beach to a neighbouring cove. Offshore you can see uninhabited Mullion Island, a nature reserve with the Lizard's only breeding colonies of kittiwakes, razorbills and guillemots – ask at the harbour about boat trips.

Kynance Cove

The rough diamond in the Lizard's crown, Kynance is the stuff of childhood fantasy. The moment you first glimpse this wild beach on the half-mile walk down from the National Trust car park, countless beach adventures surge to mind – from delving in caves and rock pools to exploring the serpentine stacks and pinnacles that rear above this extraordinarily beautiful cove.

Facilities are limited to a single beach café (see page 132), but it's the remoteness and solitude of Kynance that makes it so compelling. Aim to get there at least three hours before low tide, when sugary sand envelops the bases of the rock formations. Take care when swimming, as strong currents strafe the cove.

Kennack Sands
🏄 🚻 ♿ 🍴 🚰 🅿️

A sheltered bay of sand and fine shingle on the eastern side of the Lizard Peninsula, Kennack Sands has a lovely café with a small sun terrace overlooking the beach (the hot waffles with ice cream are the perfect energy boost after a bodyboarding session). The beach is gently shelving and has good, level access, but can get quite crowded in summer due to the close proximity of holiday parks. There's a challenging stream to dam and some interesting rocky outcrops to explore, while organized activities include horse riding and scuba diving.

Coverack
🏄 🚻 🍴 ♿ 🅿️ 🚤

Low tide reveals plenty of sand at Coverack, an unspoilt fishing village that faces west and enjoys the best of any late afternoon sunshine. The harbour wall is a good spot for crabbing. There's a fleet of about 40 boats here, some of which offer mackerel fishing trips.

Top: View from the café at Poldhu Cove. Above left: Helford Passage. Above right: Kynance Cove

Gillan Creek
🅿️ 🚤

Snaking between wooded banks, this pretty creek has stony beaches – many requiring a 15- to 20-minute walk to reach. A lovely, peaceful area for picnics and skimming stones.

Helford Passage
🏄 🚻 ♿ 🚤 🅿️

Little more than a narrow strip of gritty sand and shingle, Helford Passage enjoys an idyllic location on the northern shore of the Helford River. Crowded with sailing dinghies and motor boats, it feels like the setting for a *Swallows and Amazon*-style adventure on the Helford Estuary – and that's precisely what you'll get if you hire a self-drive boat from Helford River Boats (see page 120) which also operates a ferry to Helford on the south shore. Walk up the hill to the left of the beach at Helford Passage for a prime picnic spot overlooking the estuary, or treat yourself to a meal at the Ferryboat Inn (see page 132), right in the heart of the cluster of whitewashed cottages.

Action stations

Boat trips
Danda & Starfish

Porthleven Angling Centre, Harbour Head, Porthleven, TR13 9JY, T01326-561885, porthlevenangling.co.uk. Fishing trips (2 hrs) £14, coastal cruises (2 hrs) £12 adult, £10 child. Operating from the picturesque harbour at Porthleven, the 27-ft *Danda* and 31-ft *Starfish* ply the coast in search of mackerel, garfish and pollack. Boat trips are also available from local operators in fishing villages further south on the Lizard, such as Cadgwith and Coverack.

Helford River Boats

Helford Passage, T01326-250770, helford-river-boats.co.uk. Apr-Oct. Six-person motor boats £35/hr, £50/2 hrs, £80/half day, £100/day,

Ferry to Helford

Linking north and south shores of the Helford River, the Helford Passage to Helford Ferry operates from early April to late October, daily 0930-1730 and until 2130 during July and August, return fares £5 adult, £2 child (under 14).

£400/wk; kayaks £10/hr, £20/2 hrs, £30/half day, £50/day, £150/wk. You can peek at it from the thickly wooded shoreline, but in order to really soak up the special atmosphere of the Helford River, you need to get afloat and explore the myriad creeks. Kayaks and self-drive motor boats are available for hire from the kiosk by the jetty. No experience is needed and all boats come with life jackets, maps and fuel.

Camel riding
Cornish Camels

Rosuick Farm, St Martin, TR12 6DZ, T01326-231119, cornishcamels.com. May-Aug. Free entry to farm; photo opportunity £5 (no age limit), Camel Experience £18, Camel Trek £50 (both minimum age 14).
Meet big Frank (the dominant male), elegant Jemima, gentle Myrtle, cheeky Jasmine, pretty Camomile and scraggy Maggie – six of a growing herd of Bactrian camels that reside at this organic farm. There are three ways you can 'interact' with them: the Photo Opportunity involves polite introductions, some obligatory grooming

and a quick snap while you sit between a suitable pair of humps; the Camel Experience includes a 15-minute ride around the farm, and the Camel Trek sets out on an hour-long lollop over Goonhilly Downs. All of the riding camels are well trained and, judging by the rate at which they're breeding, very content with life on the Lizard. Rosuick Farm also has a farm shop and café (see page 131), a play area and giant sand pit (presumably to make the camels feel at home). During peak season there are tractor rides around the farm where you can meet other unusual residents, like rheas and wallabies.

Canoeing
Helford River Expeditions

Carwinion House, Mawnan Smith, TR11 5JA, T01326-250258 or 07968-024457, helfordriverexpeditions. co.uk. Apr-Oct. 4-hr expedition £30 (group discounts available).
Canoeing with a conscience, Helford River Expeditions organize paddling trips with a strong environmental ethos. You start by walking through the celebrated Carwinion bamboo

Sea horses at Kennack Sands.

gardens down to a beach where your tandem open-cockpit or sit-on kayaks are waiting. They're easy to manouvre, so you'll soon have them gliding along the peaceful waters of the Helford River, under the watchful eye of your naturalist guide. This Area of Outstanding Natural Beauty is a haven for kingfishers, herons and other waterbirds, and a canoe is the best way to see them. Frenchman's Creek, Gweek, Helford Passage, Durgan and Helford are all within reach (not to mention countless hidden coves). After a barbecue lunch on the riverbank, you return to Carwinion Gardens for a cream tea on the terrace, followed by a tree-planting session – the perfect way to ensure the Helford River stays green and beautiful.

Horse riding
Bosvathick Riding Stables
Bosvathick Farm, Constantine, TR11 5RD, T01326-340367, bosvathickridingstables.co.uk. Tue-Sun. Adult rides £17/hr, children's lesson £13/30 mins (minimum age 6), lead rein rides £10/30 mins (minimum age 4).

Set on a 92-acre farm just to the north of the Helford River, this friendly, family-run yard has an indoor arena for rainy days.

Newton Riding Stables
Newton Farm, Mullion, TR12 7JF, T01326-240388, newton-equestrian.co.uk. Lessons £14/hr, hacks from £13/hr, beginner's sessions (half-hr lesson plus half-hr hack) £15.
This approved Pony Club Centre offers exhilarating beach rides, as well as more sedate countryside hacks for the less experienced.

Poltesco Valley Stables
Treal Farm, Ruan Minor, T01326-240591, poltescovalleystables.com. Lessons £8/30 mins, hacks from £8/30 mins.
Located just a mile from Kennack Sands, Poltesco Valley Stables organizes beach rides at 0900 and 1800 during the summer (you need to be able to canter). For the ultimate rush, combine this with a moorland hack or, if you're new to riding, opt for the more gentle farm ride.

Treasure hunting
Dig a sandcastle or comb the strandline at Gunwalloe Church Cove (see page 118) and you might just strike it rich. According to folklore, the pirate John Avery (aka Long Ben) stashed his booty here. And that's not all. In 1527, the 300-ton Portuguese carrack *San Antonio* floundered on rocks near the cove and spilled her cargo of copper and silver ingots. A Spanish galleon met the same fate in 1785, adding two tons of gold and silver coins to Davy Jones's Locker. Despite search efforts, neither cargo has been recovered. Coins, however, are sometimes found on the beach.

Scuba diving
Kennack Diving
Sea Acres Holiday Park, Kennack Sands, TR12 7LT, T07816-903260, kennackdiving.co.uk. Pool session (minimum age 8) £15, pool session and sea dive (minimum age 12) £50. This PADI dive centre offers a full training programme, including introductory courses for children.

Big thrills and small wonders – the Balloon Race ride and Victorian Village at Flambards.

Big days out

The Flambards Experience

Helston, TR13 0QA, T01326-573404, flambards.co.uk. Apr-Oct daily from 1030 (1015 during high season). £16.50 adult, £11.50 child (3-15), £40 family. Limited opening and rides operating Nov-Mar; from £7.95 adult, £4.50 child (3-15).

With its Hornet rollercoaster and cheek-pummelling Extreme Force and Thunderbolt rides, Flambards is an adrenaline blast for older kids, while littl'uns can get a buzz from gentle alternatives like the Cornish Mine Train. The closest Cornwall gets to a full-blown theme park, Flambards is not as rural or pretty as Crealy, the county's other big fun park (see page 74). Where Flambards really scores, however, is sheer variety.

Kids will stampede towards the big rides, but rein them in for the outstanding Victorian Village. This indoor attraction recreates Victorian life with walk-through streets, shops and houses crafted in exquisite and original detail, without the merest whiff of MDF.

Kids will stare in wonder

(or total disbelief) at the toy shop, which has nothing more high-tech than wooden jigsaw puzzles and rocking horses. There's also a baker, butcher, tobacconist, dairy, pub, school, milliner, boot shop, barber, grocer – each one populated by lifelike characters.

Flambards' Britain in the Blitz Experience is equally spellbinding. Vera Lyn's dulcet tones give way to the whine of air-raid sirens followed by the ominous drone of German bombers overhead; then the shells start exploding and you're transported back to Second World War London – a war-torn world of burning houses, rations and evacuees.

Other undercover exhibits at Flambards cover everything from wedding dresses to Concorde. You won't have time to see everything in a single day. Not when there's also a F1 kart track, crazy golf, radio-controlled boats, the Really Wild Experience (animal show), the Hands On Science Experience, live shows and a chance to meet characters like Peppa Pig and Bart Simpson.

Future World @ Goonhilly

Goonhilly Downs, TR12 6LQ, T0800-679593, goonhilly.bt.com. Mar-Oct daily from 1000. £7.95 adult, £5.95 child (5-16), £26 family. Call for winter opening times and rates.

If your child was plugged into a Nintendo DS or PSP for the entire journey to Cornwall, probably the last thing you want to do is take them somewhere that has a room full of Xbox 360 playstations as one of the attractions. But don't zap FutureWorld from your plans too hastily because it's one of Britain's most imaginative and stimulating science centres.

Goonhilly played a pivotal role in the development of global communications, but it's easy for children (and parents) to get turned off by techno-babble when faced with FutureWorld's ground-floor exhibits on morse code, fax machines, undersea cables, fibre optics, micro-waves and satellites. Fortunately, Professor Dibble, a fictitious inventor based at Goonhilly during the 1960s, comes to the rescue during a 15-minute film where he puts his time-travel machine to the test. Steer your children

Check point

The minimum height requirements for Flambard's big rides are:

70 cm	Canyon River Log Flume
90 cm	Balloon Race
105 cm	Rocking Tugboat
120 cm	Hornet and Thunderbolt
140 cm	Extreme Force

to the film show first, then show them the display of early telephones – completely alien to the mobile generation.

Upstairs you can email an alien (you never know – you might get a reply) and watch a short film on the search for extra-terrestrial life. There are also live web-cam feeds from around the world, but by now you'll be lucky if the kids haven't noticed the video games area. It's like a scene from a zombie movie, dozens of children mesmerized by wall-to-wall screens and jostling for position to get their hands on an Xbox or Wii controller. There's actually a fascinating display here, describing how it all began with the pixel-tastic Atari and games like Pac-Man (the brainchild of Toru Iwatani who was eating a pizza one day to find Pac-Man staring back at him).

FutureWorld also has a planetarium, a gift shop (heaven for technophiles) and a free internet café. The highlight, however, is undoubtedly the FutureWorld Tour where a bus takes you into the restricted zone dominated by the huge satellite dishes of Arthur, Merlin and Guinevere. It's a hop-on, hop-off tour. At the first stop you enter a building buzzing with inventions, from Sinclair's C5 to Apple's iphone. Professor Dibble makes another appearance, this time with a message for how we

Robo Thespian – programme him to blush, snore, wave, recite *Hamlet*, wolf-whistle and sing Rod Stewart's *Do you think I'm sexy?*

shape the future for a better world, then it's back on the bus for the final stop: Project Future. Here, touch-screen monitors allow you to doodle your big idea for the future, but it's Robo Thespian that ultimately steals the show. This animated android is simply wonderful. Programme him to blush, snore, wave, recite *Hamlet*, wolf-whistle, blow a kiss, sing Rod Stewart's *Do you think I'm sexy?* and – best of all – enact key moments from classic movies like *Jaws*, *Psycho*, *Star Wars* and *The Sound of Music*. If there's one thing certain about the future, it's that every kid will want one of these.

Extra terrestrial

Arthur Tours, exploring the heart of Goonhilly's iconic dish, are available at extra cost, along with Segway Tours (minimum height 135 cm).

Out & about The Lizard

Lizard Lighthouse Heritage Centre

Lizard Point, T01326-290202, lizardlighthouse.co.uk or trinityhouse.co.uk. Feb-Mar, Nov-Dec Sun-Wed 1200-1600; Apr Sat-Wed 1200-1600; May-Jun Sat-Wed 1100-1600; Jul daily 1100-1800; Aug daily 1100-1900; Sep-Oct Sat-Wed 1100-1700. Heritage Centre £4 adult, £2 child, £10 family; Heritage Centre and lighthouse tour (minimum height 1 m) £5 adult, £2.50 child, £12.50 family.

Opened in 2009, this excellent new visitor centre has converted the engine room at Lizard Lighthouse into a beacon of interactive, audio-visual wizardry. As well as learning about the history of mainland Britain's southernmost lighthouse (see page 117), you can get hands-on by sounding a foghorn, tracking ships in one of the world's busiest sea lanes, sending messages using morse code, semaphore and signal flags, writing an entry in the weather log book and even building your own model lighthouse. There are fascinating displays on shipwrecks and the history of sea rescue with riveting yarns from lighthouse keepers and their families. To top it all, you can also take a tour of the lighthouse tower, from where there are spectacular views along the Lizard's gnarled coastline.

National Seal Sanctuary

Gweek, TR12 6UG, T01326-221361, sealsanctuary.co.uk. Daily from 1000. £13 adult, £10 child (3-14), £36 family (book online for savings). Home to sea lions, fur seals and otters, this is primarily a rehabilitation centre for common and grey seals rescued around Cornwall's coast. The Seal Rescue Hospital provides a fascinating glimpse into the whole process, from rescue to release, and enables children to see pups at various stages of recuperation. The hospital is usually at its busiest during autumn and winter (the pupping period when young are at their most vulnerable). By the time the summer holidays arrive, most, if not all, of the patients have been treated and released back to the wild (or the sanctuary's convalescence pool). It can be disappointing for children to see the empty hospital pens, but they can still take part in mock medical examinations using a lifelike seal model, complete with head marker tag, blanket and feeding tube. There are also plenty of other exhibits to keep them entranced at this gentle, slow-paced attraction on the banks of the Helford estuary.

Several pools (many with underwater viewing chambers)

Life's a beach

Rescued as a seal pup in the early 1970s after being thrown against rocks during a winter storm, Fatima's head injuries were so severe that it was feared she might not survive. Unable to return to the wild, she has spent a long, happy life at the Seal Sanctuary and, although her eyesight is deteriorating with age, she still enjoys her sprats and conger eel chunks.

Seal survival

If you discover a seal pup that seems to be in distress, or is alone:
DO keep your distance;
DON'T attempt to handle the pup;
DON'T try to put the pup in the sea;
DO call the National Seal Sanctuary.

See the light – a new heritage centre at Lizard Lighthouse reveals all.

Rain check

Cinemas
Flora
Wendron St, Helston, TR13 8PT,
T01326-569977.

Phoenix
Berkeley Vale, Falmouth, TR11 3PL,
T01326-313072.

Craft centres
Mullion Meadows
Mullion, TR12 7HB, T01326-241311,
mullionmeadows.co.uk

Indoor swimming pools
Helston Sports Centre
Church Hill, TR13 8YQ, T01326-563320.

Ships & Castles Leisure Centre
Castle Drive, Falmouth, TR11 4NG,
T01326-212129, shipsandcastles.co.uk.
Rapid river ride, 70-m flume and
ridewave machine.

Museums
Flambards and Future World (see
page 122) both have excellent indoor
attractions. See also Falmouth (page
174-177) for museums.

Save our seals –
but practise on a dummy first.

are home to resident common, grey, hooded and fur seals, while sea lions joined the gang in 2009. Every individual has a heartwarming story of survival which you can read about on the child-friendly information boards. Feeding times and talks are displayed at the entrance.

There's also a quiz trail and a woodland nature walk that leads to an enclosure inhabited by Starsky and Hutch – two frisky and inquisitive Asian short-clawed otters. The Cornish Coast Experience, meanwhile, has dream rock pools teeming with crabs and blennies. A children's play area is nearby, while the grassy bank above the seal pools makes a lovely spot for a picnic overlooking the estuary. Don't forget your pocket money – the sanctuary's gift shops sell cuddly seals in all shapes and sizes, and every penny you spend here helps to fund the vital work of the seal rescue team.

Trebah Gardens
Mawnan Smith, TR11 5JZ, T01326-252200, trebah-garden.co.uk. Daily from 1000. £7.50 adult, £2.50 child (5-15). Arrive by bus (from Falmouth or Helston) for half-price admission. Free entry during winter for National Trust and RHS members.

This beautiful ravine garden leads to a small, secluded beach on the Helford River and, in addition to being a leafy sub-tropical paradise, is quite possibly the most child-friendly of Cornwall's gardens.

Nature trails and quiz sheets are available for various age groups, while Tarzan's Camp provides arboreal adventure thrills for the over-fives, with climbing nets, rope swings and a zip wire tucked away in a shady grove of fir trees. Another play area, Fort Stuart, provides a gentler play option for toddlers.

Even without these extras, however, Trebah is virgin jungle for mini-Tarzans and Janes. Side paths lure you from the main beach track to ponds, streams, and shady tunnels beneath tree ferns. Kids can tiptoe through a Brazilian swamp beneath a canopy of giant gunnera leaves, which block out the sky with their 2-m-wide leaves, or probe a mysterious bamboo maze known as the Bamboozle. At the height of summer, Hydrangea Valley is like something out of Willy Wonka's chocolate factory with blue and pink flower balls scattered everywhere, like an explosion of strawberry and blueberry bonbons – all reflected in Mallard Pond where huge rainbow trout cruise the shallows. Another diversion leads to Koi Pool, a hidden retreat with more whopping great fish and a waterfall.

There are maps to guide you around the garden, but it's more fun following your instincts and seeing where they lead you. A dead-end? A hidden pool? A mossy monster lurking in Dinky's Puddle? Eventually, though, you will reach Polgwidden Cove, an estuary beach of skimming-stone-shingle with a small café selling drinks and ice creams. It's a fine spot for a picnic, gazing out to sea where cargo ships are often moored, waiting to enter Falmouth harbour. It was all a very different place on 1 June 1944, when 7500 American troops embarked here for the D-Day landings at Omaha Beach in Normandy. Trebah now exudes peace and tranquillity. Take your time exploring its hidden secrets, but don't leave it too late to visit the superb Planters Café (see page 131) and gift shop.

More family favourites

Glendurgan
Mawnan Smith, TR11 5JZ, T01326-252020, nationaltrust.org.uk. Feb-Oct Tue-Sat (plus Mon in Aug) 1030-1730. £6.40 adult, £3.20 child (5-17), £16 family.
Like Trebah (above), a slice of sub-tropical paradise, with a sandy beach, fiendish laurel maze and Giants Stride maypole.

Poldark Mine
Wendron, TR13 0ES, T01326-573173, poldark-mine.co.uk. Jul-Aug daily 1000-1730, Sep-Nov and Apr-Jul Sun-Fri 1000-1730. £8 adult, £5 child, £20 family, including guided mine tour (last mine tour 1600). Fascinating tours of an 18th-century tin mine, plus beam engine, museum, panning area, craft activities and play area.

Trevarno
Crowtown, TR13 0RU, T01326-574274, trevarno.co.uk. Daily 1030-1700. £6.50 adult, £2.25 child (under 14), £16 family.
Large estate with magnificent gardens, a fabulous adventure play area and even a reindeer herd and steam railway project.

Garden of delights – Trebah's treasures include (from top left) hydrangeas reflected in Mallard Pond, daisies from South Africa, tree ferns from New Zealand, abundant wildlife (such as this tortoiseshell butterfly), the Tarzan's Camp play area, giant gunnera leaves and the Bamboozle.

Sleeping The Lizard

Pick of the pitches

Boscrege Caravan & Camping Park
Ashton, nr Helston, TR13 9TG, T01736-762231, caravan parkcornwall.com. Mar-Nov. £9.50-18.95/pitch (4 people), static caravans £150-450.

A short drive from Praa Sands (see page 95), this quiet, spacious and well-run site is within easy reach of the Lizard's attractions and has a nature trail and games room.

Chycarne Holiday Park
Kuggar, Ruan Minor, TR12 7LX, T01326-290200, chy-carne.co.uk. Apr-Oct. Camping pitches £6-7.50 adult, £3.50-4.50 teenager (12-16), £1.50-3 infant (up to 12), static caravans and chalets £175-425/wk.

Kennack Sands is just a few minutes' walk from this low-key holiday park with its sheltered, tree-lined camping field, modern shower block, playground and shop. Four- and six-berth holiday caravans and chalets are also available.

Franchis Holidays
Mullion, TR12 7AZ, T01326-240301, franchis.co.uk. Apr-Oct. £10-16/pitch (2 adults), plus £1-1.50 extra person (free for children under 3), static caravans and chalets £225-460/wk.

A couple of miles' drive from Mullion, this peaceful site is a mixture of mown lawns and mature trees, with tent pitches and a few caravans and chalets backing onto woodland. A great location for wildlife and walking.

Gwendreath Holiday Park
Ruan Minor, TR12 7LZ, T01326-290666, tomandlinda.co.uk. May-Sep. £218-486/wk.

Although there's no camping here, this tiny park (with just 17 four-berth holiday caravans) is a great choice for young families. In addition to a play area for under-fives and a field for older children to kick a ball around, a short woodland walk leads to Kennack Sands (see page 119), with its safe swimming and handy beach café.

Little Trevothan Caravan & Camping Park
Trevothan, nr Coverack, TR12 6SD, T01326-280260, littletrevothan.co.uk. Mar-Oct. £10-13/pitch (2 adults), plus £2.50 extra adult, £2 extra child (up to 16), static caravans £180-490/wk.

A secluded 10-acre site with plenty of open space and a playground for children to run around in, Little Trevothan is close to Coverack with its beach, harbour and watersports. The latest addition to the park's accommodation (which includes 70 touring pitches and 40 static caravans) is a Mongolian yurt, sleeping up to four (call for rates).

Several campsites and holiday parks are close to Kennack Sands on the Lizard's southeast coast.

Lower Polladras Touring Park
Carleen, Breage, TR13 9NX, T01736-762220, lower-polladras.co.uk. Apr-Dec. £10-19/pitch (2 adults), plus £2-3 extra adult, £1.50-2 extra child (3-16), static caravans £250-570/wk.

Located north of Helston, Lower Polladras is ideally placed for exploring West Cornwall. A small site with just 39 touring pitches and a group of three very smart, contemporary-styled caravans (sleeping four), it's also the proud recipient of a Gold David Bellamy Conservation Award – recognition of its environmental policy and nature walk.

Skyburriowe Farm
Garras, nr Helston, TR12 6LR, T01326-221646, skyburriowefarm.co.uk. Easter-Oct. £8.50-15.50/pitch, B&B from £28 person.

A delightful, family-run dairy

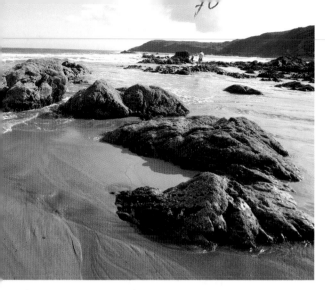

farm, Skyburriowe has shifted the cows off two fields to create a spacious campsite bordered by trees and hedges that are bursting with wildlife. A brand new toilet block features a family shower room. If camping doesn't appeal but you still fancy a rural bolthole, the 120-year-old farmhouse offers B&B as well as self-catering in a separate two-bedroom cottage.

Budget break

Premier Inn
Clodgey Lane, Helston, TR13 8WE, T0870-111 2810, premierinn.com. Rooms from £75, check online for special offers and meal deals.

OK, so you won't find a Premier Inn in a prime beachfront position with lots of leisure facilities – their town-outskirts locations are handy rather than handsome. However, for a budget hotel, Helston's Premier Inn is excellent value for money and even comes with a 'Good Night Guarantee'. Squeeze in extra children's beds and the rooms are still quite spacious with bright, immaculate bathrooms, air conditioning, Freeview TV and tea- and coffee-making facilities. Kids receive an inflight-style goodie bag and there are some great deals at Table Table – the hotel's bar and restaurant – where children can tuck into Sunday roasts for just £1 (with a full-paying adult) or wolf down a Kids' Meal Deal (main and dessert) for only £4.99. The menu is pretty good too, with organic dishes, gourmet burgers, make-your-own pizzas, chicken wraps, pasta and fish and chips. There are other Premier Inns at Bodmin, Hayle, Liskeard, Newquay, St Austell and Truro.

Holiday parks

Mullion Holiday Park
Nr Mullion, TR12 7LJ, T0844-335 3450, parkdeanholidays.co.uk.
Located on the main A3083 between Helston and Lizard Point, this fun-packed park is close to top attractions and stunning beaches like Kynance Cove. Facilities include indoor and outdoor swimming pools, play areas, go-karts, children's clubs (for tots to teens), evening entertainment, a bar and grill, nature trail and crazy golf.

Retanna Holiday Park
Edgcumbe, TR13 0EJ, T01326 340643, retanna.co.uk.
Peaceful caravan park between Helston and Falmouth.

Sea Acres
Kennack Sands, TR12 7LT, T0844-335 3450, parkdeanholidays.co.uk.
More relaxed than its sister park near Mullion (see above), Sea Acres is just up the lane from Kennack Sands and has an indoor pool, nature trail, play area and pitch 'n' putt. It's also the base for Kennack Diving (see page 121).

Seaview Holiday Park
Gwendreath, Kennack Sands, TR12 7LZ, T01326-290635, seaviewcaravanpark.com.
Small park with 15 caravans, nine chalets and an indoor pool. Great views and a short walk to the beach.

Silver Sands Holiday Park
Gwendreath, Kennack Sands, TR12 7LZ, T01326-290631, silversandsholidaypark.co.uk.
Well-run tent and caravan park with conservation award. Short stroll to Kennack Sands.

Sleeping The Lizard

Cool & quirky

Lizard Lighthouse Cottages

Cornish Cottages, T01326-240333, cornishcottagesonline.com. Cottages (sleeping 4-8) £298-1126/wk.
Never mind the foghorn (which has a range of three miles) – the Nanny State Alert at these six newly refurbished ex-lighthouse keepers' cottages rings loud and clear! Granted, this is not somewhere to let children roam at will, but no one can deny the thrill of living in the shadow of Cornwall's most famous lighthouse, walking straight from your front door onto the cliff tops. Surrounding a large courtyard, the cottages are well equipped with all mod cons.

Best of the rest

Heath Farm Cottages

Ponsongath, nr Coverack, TR12 6SQ, T01326-280521, heath-farm-holidays.co.uk. £240-820/wk.
These six beautifully restored cottages are arranged around a courtyard and have the added child appeal of copious farm animals, fresh eggs to collect and a woodland to explore.

Mudgeon Vean

St Martin, TR12 6DB, T01326-231341, mudgeonvean.co.uk. Call for rates.
Snug in a rolling patchwork of fields and ancient woodland, this gorgeous 18th-century farm has three cottages for hire. Home to chickens, ducks, pigs, and pygmy goats, the farm also has a wild side, best explored on the Woodland Walk.

Also recommended
Polurrian Hotel

Mullion, TR12 7EN, T01326-240421, polurrianhotel.com.
Cliff-top luxury, with swimming pool, spa and a footpath to a sandy beach. Choice of 39 hotel bedrooms and eight self-catering bungalows.

Trelowarren Estate

Mawgan, TR12 6AF, T01326- 221224, trelowarren.com. See also page 133.
Choose from 18 properties on this 1000-acre estate with pool, craft centre, restaurant and walks down to the Helford River.

Cottage agents

See also page 186.

Cadgwith Cove Cottages

T01326-290764, cadgwithcovecottages.co.uk.
Thatched-cottage heaven in the idyllic fishing village that inspired a million jigsaw puzzles.

Mullion Cottages

T01326-240333, mullioncottages.com.
Excellent choice of properties on the Lizard Peninsula, from flats to cottages and farmhouses.

Porthleven Holiday Cottages

T01326-574270, porthlevenholidaycottages.co.uk.
Collection of 12 cottages (sleeping up to eight) around the unspoilt harbour in Porthleven.

Eating The Lizard

Minnie Moon

Cadgwith, TR12 7JX, T01326-290539,
minniemoon.co.uk. Easter-Nov.
Landed, cooked and prepared
daily, Minnie Moon's succulent
crab finds its way into delicious
baguettes (a snip at £6) or you
can buy whole dressed crab and
lobster. Thick creamy milkshakes
(£1.75) are also a treat.

Pull the udder one – of course
we make Cornwall's best ice cream.

Sweet sensations from the Lizard
Peninsula include **Heatherbell
Honey** (cornwallhoney.com) and
Helford Creek Apple Juice
(helfordcreek.co.uk), freshly
pressed at Mudgeon Vean Farm
(see opposite).

Planters Café

Trebah Gardens (see page 125).
Daily 1000-1600. Free entry.
A champion of local producers,
this fabulous café is famous for
its freshly made flans and soups.
If you're visiting the gardens,
pick up a Boathouse Box –
a portable picnic for £6.

Rosuick Farm

Cornish Camels (see page 120).
May-Aug. Free entry.
Organic farm shop and café
selling meat, vegetables and

other local produce, and serving
light lunches, teas and home-
made cakes.

Roskilly's

Tregellast Barton Farm, St Keverne,
TR12 6NX, T01326-280479, roskillys.
co.uk. Farm open daily; restaurant
1000-1800 (summer), 1100-1600
(winter), closed Jan. Free entry.
The Creamery is the one part
of Roskilly's farm that isn't open
to visitors, but you can still
watch the legendary ice cream
being made in the Demo Lab
(1330, 1400 and 1430) and even
have a go at making your own
flavour (£45 for up to six people
making one ice cream flavour
and taking eight litres home
with them). If you just want a
taster, Roskilly's ice cream comes
in flavours ranging from clotted
cream vanilla to hoky poky and
costs £1.60 for a single cone or
£2 for two scoops or a tub.

The cows are milked each
afternoon at around 1630 to
1700: 100-odd Jerseys and
Guernseys filing into the barn,

which has a viewing gallery with
faded displays on countryside
wildlife and why milk is good
for you. The milking process is
clinical and efficient, with cows
barely visible beneath a tangle
of hoses, cooling sprays and
machinery. Downstairs you
can stroke the newborn calves
which will lick your hands like
big soppy puppies.

Roskilly's original milking
parlour has been converted into
the Croust House Restaurant,
which serves pizzas, pasties,
salads, pies, cakes, teas and the
farm's very own apple juice.
Evening barbecues are held
weekly during summer, with a
child's size Roskilly's beef burger,
two sausages, chips and beans
for £4.75 and a grown-up's
steak barbecue for £13.50. Don't
forget to leave time for a mosey
around the Bull Pen craft studio
and glass works or a stroll down
to the ponds or withy woods.
Roskilly's also offers self-catering
accommodation in various
converted farm buildings.

Market days

Falmouth Farmers' Market
Prince of Wales Pier, Tuesday
0900-1400.
Helston Farmers' Market
Boating Lake, Saturday 0830-1300.

Eating The Lizard

Ferryboat Inn

Helford Passage, TR11 5LB, T01326-250625. Daily from 1100.
Always busy, this beachfront pub overlooking the Helford Estuary combines traditional pub fare (scampi, steak etc) with more imaginative offerings like grilled sardines and tomato bruschetta (£8.50), baked scallop and crab gratin (£8.95), lemon sole and brown shrimps (£14.95) and courgette, green pea and mint carbonara (£8.95).

Kynance Cove Beach Café

Kynance Cove, TR12 7PF, T01326-290436, kynancecovecafe.co.uk. Dating from the 1920s, this whitewashed café presides over the quintessential Cornish cove (see page 118). Sandwiches, baguettes, jacket potatoes, ploughmans, pasties and a tasty range of salads are all on the menu – just make sure you leave room for the home-made caramel and apple cake; it's one of a mouthwatering selection of sweets that all come with a dollop of Rodda's Clotted Cream

Fish & chips

Try **Thurley's** (Meneage St, Helston), **Roland's Happy Plaice** (Shute Lane, Porthleven) and **The Galleon** (Nancemellyon Rd, Mullion). Or, if you're north of the Helford River, make for the **Harbour Lights** in Falmouth (see page 177).

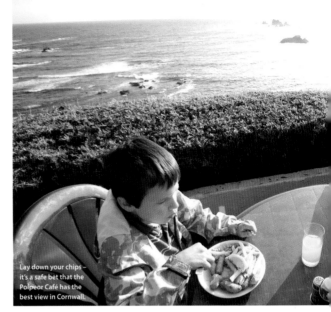
Lay down your chips – it's a safe bet that the Polpeor Café has the best view in Cornwall.

or Kelly's Ice Cream. The café has a small shop selling beach gear and, if you book far enough in advance, there's a cosy cottage for hire next door (from £350 per week), with just enough room for a lucky family of four.

Poldhu Beach Café

Poldhu Cove, TR12 7JB, T01326-240530, poldhucafe. Easter-Sep plus school holidays. Daily 1000-1700.
Tucked into the dunes at Poldhu Cove, this is a proper little 'barefoot and bacon baps' type of beach café. Don't expect much in the way of fresh salads or sandwiches – it's calories that count here. The speciality Poldhu Pixie (£3) has two scoops of Cornish vanilla ice cream, two flakes, a dollop of Cornish clotted cream and a cherry, all in a large waffle cone.

Polpeor Café

Lizard Point, TR12 7NU, T01326-290939. Daily from 1000.
All too often a superb location goes hand in hand with mediocre food and indifferent service – but not here at Britain's most southerly café, right on the cliffs at Lizard Point. Owners Peter and Jackie Hendy are friendly, the food is delicious and it's good value too (healthy-sized children's dishes are just £3.80). If the weather allows, eat outside on the west-facing terrace so you can bask in the glory of a Lizard sunset, sheltered behind a hedge that's not too high to obscure the views. You can't go wrong with the luxury fish pie (£8.95) with local crab and prawns, followed by Granny's Apple Cake and clotted cream (£3.95). Cooked

breakfasts (served until 1230), sandwiches, omelettes, salads, jacket potatoes and cream teas are also on offer. Remember to use the toilet in the National Trust car park before walking down to Lizard Point – there isn't one at the café.

Also recommended
Kennack Sands Beach Café
Kennack Sands, TR12 7LX
T01326-291246.
Handy café opposite the beach car park, serving cream teas, jacket spuds, all-day breakfasts etc. Turbo's Café, next door, serves good pasties and waffles, and has a small terrace overlooking Kennack Sands.

Munchies
Mullion, TR12 7BZ, T01326-241177.
Everything you need for a picnic,

from freshly made sandwiches and pasties to salads, quiche, pasta bowls and cakes.

Porthmellin Café
Mullion Cove, TR12 7ES
T01326-240941.
Harbourside café serving crab sarnies, pasties, cream teas and all day breakfasts.

The Wave
The Cove, Coverack, TR12 6SX,
T01326-281526.
Cosy café with views across Coverack Bay.

Posh nosh

Halzephron Inn
Gunwalloe, TR12 7QB, T01326-240406, halzephron-inn.co.uk. Daily 1200-1400, 1830-2100.
Cornwall Dining Pub of the Year in 2001 and 2005, the Halzephron Inn is just up the lane from Gunwalloe Fishing Cove and the coast path that skirts the wide expanse of Porthleven Sands, south to Halzephron Cove and the rocky Pedngwinian headland. No excuses, then, for not building up an appetite for a meal at this 500-year-old pub. Bag an outdoor picnic table for lunch with panoramic views across Mount's Bay. Ploughmans and salads cost £6.90-14.95, while main courses, like sirloin steak, are £16.25. Daily specials might include starters like smoked haddock and corn chowder

(£6.95) and, for mains, lamb tagine with couscous (£11.95) or pan-fried mackerel fillets on a warm potato, caramelised red onion and asparagus salad (£11.25). The junior menu (from £3.95) has a typical quintet of scampi, chicken goujons, penne pasta, sausages and burger.

The Housel Bay Hotel
Housel Bay, TR12 7PG, T01326-290417, houselbay.com. Call for times.
Perched above a sandy cove just to the east of Lizard Point, this small, romantic hotel has a fine restaurant with menus oozing local flavour and freshness. The bar menu (from £5.95) includes crab salad, fish cakes, haddock and chips, steak, a range of sandwiches and a sumptuous tagliatelle with butternut squash, pine nuts, artichoke hearts, rocket and crème fraiche. For dinner, expect to pay around £20-30 for two courses, choosing from mouthwatering mains like seafood stew, rack of lamb and line-caught sea bass.

New Yard Restaurant
Trelowarren, Mawgan, TR12 6AF, T01326-221595, newyardrestaurant.co.uk. Call for times.
Occupying a converted 18th-century carriage house, this excellent restaurant sources all ingredients from within a 10-mile radius of Trelowarren Estate. Two-course set lunches cost £15.95, while dinner mains start at around £13.

Off the beaten track

Isles of Scilly

Cornwall plays its trump card with these wonderful islands. Just saying the three words 'Isles of Scilly' is enough to make the most jaded traveller go all tingly. The archipelago is only 28 miles southwest of Land's End, but that's far enough to give them an exotic, mysterious feel. And when you arrive – whether it's just for the day or at the start of a two-week island sojourn – you'll wonder whether the Scillies do in fact dabble their toes in the tropics. Abbey Gardens on Tresco is like the Eden Project with the roof off, while the surrounding shallow seas are dazzling turquoise and teeming with sponges and sea fans. All this is nurtured by the Gulf Stream and one of the UK's mildest and sunniest climates. The flip-side, of course, is that anything the Atlantic decides to hurl at Britain reaches the Isles of Scilly first. Witnessing the sea flex its muscles – surf blooming on the headlands above Hell Bay on Bryher – is all part of the adventure. Scilly in the extreme, but unforgettable nonetheless.

Get your bearings

First you need to get there. There are three options for reaching the Isles of Scilly: helicopter, plane or boat (see page 181 for details). Flying is certainly quicker (20 or 30 minutes as opposed to a 2½-hour voyage), but somehow it just feels right to sail to the Scillies. Besides, if you're camping – and the islands have some superb sites – you'll need the *Scillonian III* to transport all your gear. Setting off from Penzance, the 600-passenger ship also affords great views of the southern Penwith coastline and Land's End (try to get an outside seat on the starboard side), as well as potential sightings of dolphins.

Arriving at St Mary's, the largest of five inhabited islands, the *Scillonian III* glides into the harbour at Hugh Town – the hub of island life – and disgorges passengers, luggage and cargo onto the quayside. You'll see smaller boats fussing around her, like worker bees attending their queen. These are the islands' water taxis, a fleet of 10 vessels belonging to the **St Mary's Boatmen's Association** (T01720-423999, scillyboating.co.uk).

A noticeboard on the jetty is chalked up with the day's departures. You can buy tickets from the quay kiosk (daily 0930-1015, 1330-1400, later during high season, returns £7.60 adult, £3.80 child) or the **Tourist Information Centre** (Hugh St, TR21 0LL, T01720-424031, simplyscilly.co.uk). The friendly staff here will also clue you up on anything from tide times to open-top bus tours on the **Island Rover** (T01720-422131, islandrover. co.uk, Mon-Sat, 1015 and 1330, £7).

As well as the tourist office, Hugh Town has a post office, supermarket, chemist and baker, plus various gift shops, galleries, pubs, restaurants and cafés. On the far side of the green, a sports shop sells masks, snorkels and other outdoor gear, while the hardware store stocks basic camping supplies.

Cornwall plays its trump card with these wonderful islands. Just saying the three words 'Isles of Scilly' is enough to make the most jaded traveller go all tingly.

The **Isles of Scilly Museum** (Church St, Easter-Sep, Mon-Fri 1000-1630, Sat 1000-1200) has exhibits charting the islands' fascinating history, from prehistoric times to the present, as well as shipwreck artefacts and a shell collection.

The **Isles of Scilly Wildlife Trust** (T01720-422153, ios-wildlifetrust.org.uk, Mar-Oct, Mon-Wed and Fri-Sat 0930-1630, Thu 0930-1200) has a tiny visitor centre on the quay with aquariums, a touch table, colouring sheets and details of activities, such as rock-pool rambles and nature trails. Next door, **The Pilchard Pit** is a handy spot to pick up sandwiches, pasties and paninis.

Camping on the edge – Troytown Farm on St Agnes is wild, windy and wonderful.

Off the beaten track Isles of Scilly

Pitch your tent

The *Scillonian III* may charge an extra £20 or so for carrying large amounts of camping gear, but that's a small price to pay for pitching your tent and playing the castaway on the Isles of Scilly.

On St Mary's you can set up camp at the Garrison, a ring of fortifications on the headland near Hugh Town. **Garrison Holidays Campsite** (The Garrison, St Mary's, TR21 0LS, T01720-422670, garrisonholidays.com, May-Oct, £7.25-9.75 per person, plus £5 electric hook-up) is sheltered by pine trees and blackberry-laden hedges. Each pitch comes with its own wooden picnic table, and there are clean washrooms and a well-stocked shop. It only takes 10 minutes or so to walk down into Hugh Town, passing the local football field and a ship-themed adventure playground.

Snug in a valley with views of the harbour and neighbouring island of Tresco, **Bryher Campsite** (Bryher, TR23 0PR, T01720-422559, bryhercampsite. co.uk, Apr-Sep, £9.50 per person, plus £20 luggage transfer) is a fabulous spot for those who relish remote camping. The site is not without its home comforts, however. As well as an excellent toilet block and free showers, the cosy Fraggle Rock Bar (see page 140) is just a few minutes' walk away.

St Martin's Campsite (Oaklands Farm, Middletown, St Martin's, TR25 0QN, T01720-422888, stmartinscampsite.co.uk, Mar-Oct, £8-10 per person, plus £8 luggage transfer) is tucked behind hedges in fields once used in the Scillies' famous flower industry. You can virtually roll out of your sleeping bag onto a sandy beach from where there are panoramic views of the archipelago. Facilities include toilets, coin-operated showers and a barn stocked with eggs and seasonal

Islands at a glance

St Mary's Hugh Town (see page 134) is pinched between the Town Beach and the sandy bay of Porthcressa. The Garrison stands proud on a nearby headland, while the south and east coasts are crinkle-cut with idyllic bays, such as Pelistry and Porth Minick. Towards the north, you'll find the Iron Age village of Halangy, while inland there are nature trails at Lower Moors and Higher Moors.

Tresco At low tide you'll land at Carn Near Quay on the southern tip of Tresco, from where it's a short walk to Abbey Gardens (see page 140) and the heliport. Bear right for beachcombing at Pentle Bay or continue past the gardens and Great Pool (a magnet for birds) to New Grimsby with its bike hire, grocery store, post office, art gallery, pub and smart rental accommodation.

St Martin's From Lower Town (with its pub and luxury hotel), the island's single track straddles the island, threading between flower fields and drystone walls – stunning sandy beaches left and right – to Higher Town where you will find craft galleries, cafés, gift shops and even a vineyard. Down at the jetty, St Martin's Dive School (see page 143) organizes guided snorkelling trips.

Bryher Smallest of the five inhabited islands, the coastline of Bryher ranges from the white sands of Rushy Bay and the calm waters of Green Bay (ideal for kayaking) to rugged Shipman Head where Hell Bay is lashed by storm-driven waves. The island has a post office and grocery store, café, campsite, B&Bs, self-catering cottages, a hotel and England's most westerly pub.

St Agnes The 'wild west' of the Scilly Isles, St Agnes has a spectacular campsite overlooking the Western Rocks. Boats slip into the sheltered anchorage at Porth Conger where a short stroll takes you past the Turk's Head pub to The Bar – a causeway between St Agnes and Gugh that reveals an idyllic sandy cove at low tide (see page 142). Walk across St Agnes to find a lighthouse, cafés and farms selling local produce.

Uninhabited islands
Abandoned in 1855, **Samson**, with its twin hills, is the largest of the uninhabited islands and has wonderful sand flats to explore at low tide. The **Western Rocks** and **Eastern Isles** are a spray-whipped haven for grey seals, while seabirds rule the roost on **Annet** (closed to visitors during the summer nesting season).

All in a day's holiday on St Mary's (from top left) – rounding Peninnis Head, detail of a ferryboat's wheel, Hugh Town harbour, setting sail for Tresco, a handful of periwinkles and top shells from the beach at Porthloo, walking to Hugh Town through the gateway to the Garrison, the *Scillonian III* offloading at the quayside.

vegetables. Nearby Highertown has a general store and bakery (see page 140).

If you fancy huddling down on the edge of the Atlantic, ducking the spray, watching glorious sunsets and generally getting away from it all, look no further than **Troytown Farm Campsite** (Troytown Farm, St Agnes, TR22 0PL, T01720-422360, troytown.co.uk, Mar-Oct, £7-9 per person, plus £3-7 charge for tents between 18 July and 29 August, £3 luggage transfer). With views of the Bishop Rock Lighthouse and wave-gnawed Western Rocks, this spectacular site clings to narrow grassy fields above a beach of large cobbles and sand. The farm makes its own ice cream and also keeps campers happy with fresh milk, yoghurt, clotted cream and jacket potatoes (cooked in the farmhouse Aga). Facilities are excellent too, with modern toilets and washrooms.

Cottages & hotels

There's a wide range of cottages and guesthouses on the Isles of Scilly – the tourist board's website (simplyscilly.co.uk) has a search facility. Hotels on St Mary's include the **Star Castle Hotel** (The Garrison, TR21 0TA, T01720-422317, star-castle.co.uk) which has family-friendly garden suites and an indoor swimming pool.

If you want to splash out, the **Flying Boat Club** (Tresco, TR24 0QQ, T01720-422849, tresco.co.uk, from £1375-5000/wk) consists of 12 luxury beachfront houses (sleeping up to 10) with satellite television and membership of an exclusive holiday club with its own restaurant, bar, indoor pool, spa and tennis courts. Tresco's traditional holiday cottages (same contact details as above) are no less desirable, but cost £550-1000 per week for a four-bed bolthole.

Also run by the Tresco Estate, **Hell Bay Hotel** (Bryher, TR23 0PR, T01720-422947, hellbay.co.uk) has rooms from £130 per person, including dinner and bed and breakfast (children between two and 12 pay £50 for high tea and bed and breakfast).

A granite hotel with lovely gardens overlooking

Off the beaten track Isles of Scilly

the quay, **St Martin's on the Isle** (St Martin's, TR25 0QW, T01720-422090, stmartinshotel.co.uk) offers bed and breakfast from £125 per person (£25 for children sharing with two adults). The hotel has a fine restaurant, as well as an indoor pool.

Visit the gardens

Built around the ruins of a 12th-century priory, **Abbey Garden** (Tresco, T01720-424105, tresco. co.uk, daily 1000-1600, £10 adult, free for children under 16) seems to sprout from another world. Exploring the sub-tropical oasis, with its terraces and interconnecting pathways and steps, children can embark a global plant safari. The garden is arranged in geographical zones, so challenge them to find New Zealand tree ferns, orange Namaqua daisies from South Africa, weird succulents from the Canary Islands, bamboo from Asia and banksias from the Australian Outback. There are manmade treasures to find as well. See if you can track down the Shell House with its amazing mosaic, or the statues of Gaia, Neptune and *The Tresco Children*. Just to the right of the garden entrance, the Valhalla Museum, with its extraordinary collection of shipwreck figureheads, is also worth a look. The gardens have a shop, an exhibition about the history of the site and a café with a pleasant outdoor eating area. The food is fine, but you might want to save yourself for Tresco Stores in nearby New Grimsby where the deli counter is groaning with goodies.

Grab a bite

On St Mary's, try **Dibble & Grub** (The Old Fire Station, Porthcressa, T01720-423719) for café snacks right by the beach. **Blues Restaurant** (The Corner House, Hugh Town, T01720-422221, bluesrestaurantscilly.co.uk) is more up-market with signature seafood dishes like roasted Scillonian monkfish with parma ham and baked tomatoes (£16.50). A half-hour stroll from Hugh Town,

Juliet's Garden Restaurant (Porthloo, T01720-422228, julietsgardenrestaurant.co.uk) has views across the harbour and serves a tempting array of light lunches, home-made cakes and evening meals. The local crab salads (£14) are delicious, while generously filled sandwiches (from £3.15) come with a healthy pile of salad. For a sweet treat, try the old-fashioned ginger bread. Bang slap in the middle of St Mary's, **Longstone Heritage Centre** (T01720-423732) has a small café where you can enjoy home-made cakes after perusing displays on the Scilly Isles' history and wildlife. The centre also has a large grassy area that's ideal for picnics – hire bikes in Hugh Town (see page 143) – and it makes a great day out.

On Tresco, the **New Inn** (New Grimsby, T01720-422844, tresco.co.uk) has a tasty lunch menu with sandwiches (from £6.50) and burgers, fishcakes, fish and chips etc starting at around £10. You can also just pop in for Roskilly's ice cream or a wicked hot chocolate.

A must if you're on St Martin's, the **Bakery** (Highertown, T01720-423444, stmartinsbakery.co.uk) rustles up sublime bread, cakes, pasties and pizza – often embellished with its own locally caught and smoked Atlantic salmon. Also on St Martin's, **Little Arthur's Café** (Highertown, T01720-422457) serves home-made food, using local seafood and organic vegetables. A quirky little place with a cosy conservatory half consumed by a grapevine, it has stunning views over the Eastern Isles.

On St Agnes, you must try the ice cream at **Troytown Farm** (see page 138). Just up the lane, **Coastguards Café** (T01720-422197) serves yummy cream teas, while **The Turk's Head** (T01720-422434) is renowned for its pasties.

Bryher's **Fraggle Rock Bar Café** (T01720-422222) is a wonderful spot to relax with a coffee or fruit drink, with views across Kitchen Porth towards Tresco. If you're feeling peckish, it also serves impressive crab doubledecker sandwiches.

Island oasis – Tresco's Abbey Gardens are a paradise for plants, including agapanthus (top left), South African daisies (middle) and succulents (bottom left). Sculptures, including the Tresco Children (opposite), water features and a Shell House dot the gardens and there's a maze of pathways to explore, some leading to the remains of the 12th-century priory (bottom middle).

Beach beauties

The beauty of the Scilly Isles is that you can land on an island and then simply wander off to find your own secluded beach where you may well be making the first and only sets of footprints in the sand. However, two particularly gorgeous beaches worth spending a day on can be found on St Martin's and St Agnes.

Great Bay on St Martin's is like a slice of the Bahamas slipped beneath heather-flushed hills on the island's north coast. The sand is like fine granulated sugar; granite boulders form dramatic bookends to the beach and the water is so clear that snorkellers get goggled-eyed with excitement. Comb the strandline for tiny periwinkle shells and don't forget to bring a picnic – there are no facilities whatsoever.

If anything, **The Cove** on St Agnes is even better. Located on the south side of The Bar that links St Agnes to the smaller islet of Gugh (pronounced Goo), it has squeaky-clean sand, glittering with fine grains of mica. At low tide, long whip-like strands of seaweed are drizzled like honey over the rocks – shallow pools trapped between them crying out for a shrimping expedition. Sheltered from westerly winds that can batter the Atlantic shore of St Agnes, The Cove also has sheltered swimming, and there's always the added excitement of the tide coming in and submerging the sand bar (just make sure you're on the right side of it come high water).

Great Bay, St Martin's.

Action stations

Beachcombing Glass beads from a Venetian wreck are sometimes washed into the cove at Beady Pool, St Agnes.

Birdwatching An RSPB volunteer is often on board the *Scillonian III* to help point out seabirds like Manx shearwater and storm petrel. Take a boat trip to the Annet Bird Sanctuary near St Agnes to see breeding puffins and common terns; Samson and Gugh have nesting gulls and kittiwakes, while the Western Rocks are home to shags, storm petrels and great black-backed gulls. The islands are an important stopover for migrant birds during spring and autumn – join a wildlife tour in autumn to see sanderling, ringed plover and little egret.

Boat trips The **Boatmen's Association** (see page 134) runs two or three 90-minute circular trips each day (usually departing at 1015 or 1400, £11 adult, £5.50 child). The Eastern Isles cruise visits a colony of grey seals and lands at St Martin's; the Norrad Rocks trip noses around rugged islets near Samson (also good for seals) before landing at Tresco or Bryher, while the Annet cruise takes in the bird sanctuary (only available until late July). Two-hour trips (£13 adult, £6.50 child) venture to the Bishop Rock Lighthouse and Western Rocks, visiting shipwreck sites and colonies of seals and seabirds before landing at St Agnes. There's also a two-hour Seabird Special, accompanied by wildlife expert Will Wagstaff (see below), usually running on Sundays and landing at Tresco or Bryher. Other island boat operators include **Bryher Boats** (T01720-422886), **St Agnes Boating** (T01720-422704) and **St Martin's Boating** (T01720-423999).

For day trips visiting two or three islands, contact **Blue Hunter** (T01720-423377), **Calypso** (T01720-422187) or **Crusader** (T07748-243122) – all running 12-passenger launches. For glass-bottom boat trips, hop aboard the **Sea Quest** (T01720-422511). For boat trips with added 'oomph', **Island Sea Safaris** (T01720-422732, islandseasafaris.co.uk) operates a feisty 8-m RIB called *Firebrand* which has an onboard underwater camera for spying on marine life. Four trips are offered: the two-hour Shipwrecks, Seals & Seabirds (£30 adult, £20 child) does what it says on the tin; the one-hour Island Taster (£20) includes a visit to a seal colony, the Evening Gig Race (£12) trails the Wednesday- and Friday-evening island gig race, and the Snorkelling Safari (£35, minimum height 1.5 m) combines a high-speed RIB ride with snorkelling in a sheltered bay.

Craft making The magical light and scenery of the Scilly Isles has inspired numerous artists and there are galleries and craft shops dotted all over the islands. To have a go yourself, wander over to the **Phoenix Craft Workshops** (Porthmellon, St Mary's, T01720-422407, weekday afternoons) where adults and children can get arty making enamel jewellery, kites and seaside mobiles.

Cycling Bikes are an ideal way to explore St Mary's – an easy five-mile circuit of quiet roads taking in fabulous coastal views and secluded beaches. You can hire them from **St Mary's Bike Hire** (The Strand, Hugh Town, T01720-422289, Mon-Sat 0900-1700, £4.50 half day, £7 full day, tag-a-longs from £7). Bikes can also be hired on Tresco (T01720-422849).

Horse riding Saddle up at **St Mary's Riding Centre** (Maypole, St Mary's, TR21 0NU, T01720-423855, horsesonscilly.co.uk) where 30-minute lead-rein rides (£15) are ideal for children or first-timers. Group lessons cost £25, while hacks cost £25-45 and, depending on your level of experience, take to the bridleways, beaches and farm tracks around the east coast.

Rock-pool rambles Two of the best spots are Cove Vean on St Agnes and Porthloo on St Mary's. Check at the **Isles of Scilly Wildlife Trust Visitor Centre** (see page 135) for details of organized rock-pool rambles.

Sailing There are two watersports centres in the Isles of Scilly – **The Sailing Centre** (Porthmellon, St Mary's, T01720-422060, sailingscilly.com) and **Ravensporth Sailing Base** (Tresco, T01720-424919, Jul-Aug only). Windsurfing and dinghy sailing lessons cost from £30 per hour or you can hire windsurfers (£12-18/hr), sit-on kayaks (singles £10/hr, doubles £12/hr) and sailing dinghies (from £17.50/hr).

Snorkelling You can hire wetsuits, masks, fins and snorkels from **Island Sea Safaris, Ravensporth Sailing Base** and **The Sailing Centre** (see above). **St Martin's Dive School** (Higher Town, St Martin's, TR25 0QL, T01720-422848, scillydiving.com) organizes two-hour snorkelling safaris (£22, minimum age 8), snorkelling with seals (£36, minimum age 8) and introductory scuba dives (£45, minimum age 14) which descend to around 2 m off a sheltered beach.

Wildlife watching Will Wagstaff is your man. No one knows the bird life of the Scilly Isles better. Contact **Island Wildlife Tours** (Sally Port, St Mary's, TR21 0JE, T01720-422212, £5-10) for details of guided walks.

Contents

South Cornwall

The ferryman at Looe Harbour.

Park Head

Penrose

Tredinnick

St Ervan · Rumford

St Jidgey · Burlawn

Washaway · Helland

Bodmin Forest

A389 · Bodmin

St Eval

B3274

Trenance

Berryl's Point

Trevarrian

St Mawgan

Talskiddy

Rosenannon

Withiel

St Lawrence

Nanstallon

Watergate Bay

Tregurrian

B3276

Newquay

A39

St Wenn

Tregonetha

Lanivet

Trebyan

Towan Head · Fistral Bay

Newquay Bay

St Columb Minor

St Columb Major

A3059

Trebudannon

Belowda

Victoria

Lockengate

A391 · Bilberry

Sweethouse

Redmoor

Newquay

Kelsey Head

West Pentire

Pentire

Mountjoy

Trevarren

A30

Tregoss

Roche

Bugle

Lanlivery

Luxulyan

Penhale Point

Holywell

Crantock

Lane

A392

St Columb Road

Indian Queens

Trezaise

B3279

Stenalees

A390

Penpillick

Carines

Kestle Mill

Fraddon

St Dennis

Hensbarrow Downs

Whitemoor

Penwithick

Trethurgy

Eden Project

5 · St Blazey

St Tywardreath

A3

Cubert

Penhale Ligger Sands or Perran Bay

A3075

St Newlyn East

A3058

Summercourt

B3275

Treviscoe

Nanpean

China Clay Country Park

B3274

Par

Par Sands

Polk

Mount

Rejerrah

Mitchell

Trethosa

Foxhole

B3279

High Street

Trewoon

St Austell

Charlestown

Carlyon Bay

Menat

Perranporth

Goonhavern

Newlyn Downs

Carland Cross

Trelassick

A3058

St Stephen

Coombe

Hewas Water

Sticker

Polgooth

Porthpean

Shipwreck & Heritage Centre

Porthpean

St Austell Bay

7

Bolingey

Zelah

New Mills

St Mewan

Tortoise Garden

B3273

Trenarren

B3285

Trevellas

Mithian

A3075

Peranzabuloe

Callestick

Trispen

Ladock

Grampound

A390

Trewithen Gardens

Lost Gardens of Heligan

Pentewan

Pentewan Beach

Mevagissey Bay

Goonbell

B3284

A30

Shortlanesend

Probus

B3287

St Ewe

4

Kestle

3

Mevagissey Sealife Aquarium

Allet

Tresillian

Polmassick

Mevagissey Museum

Mevagissey

Portmellon

Three Burrows

Blackwater

Kenwyn

Royal Cornwall Museum

Truro

Merther

Tresawle

Tregony

Trevarrick

St Michael Caerhays

Boswinger

Gorran Churchtown

Chapel Point

Threemilestone

Truro Cathedral

St Clement

Malpas

Kea

Gorran Haven

A390

Baldhu

St Michael Penkevil

Treworga

Portholland

Penare

Vault Beach

B3298

Bissoe

Playing Place

Old Kea

A3078

East & West Portholland

Caerhays

St Day

Carharrack

Carnon Downs

King Harry Ferry

Philleigh

Veryan

Portloe

Veryan Bay

Hemmick Beach

Dodman Point

Gwennap

Trelissick

Treworlas

Trewithian

Carne

Perranarworthal

Penpol

Feock

Trelissick Gardens

Pendower Beach

Gerrans Bay

Nare Head

The Roseland

A39

Ponsanooth

Stithians

Burnthouse

Mylor Bridge

St Just in Roseland

Carrick Roads

Gerrans

Portscatho

A394

Penryn

Flushing

National Maritime Museum

2

Longdowns

Mabe Burnthouse

A39

Falmouth

St Mawes Castle

St Mawes

Greeb Point

Budock Water

1

Pendennis Castle

Bohortha

Penjerrick

Gyllyngvase · Swanpool

Falmouth Bay

St Anthony

Towan Beach

Constantine

Trebah Gardens

Mawnan Smith

Maenporth

Rosemullion Head

Helford Passage

Mawnan

Helford River

Helford

St Anthony-in-Meneage

Nare Point

Manaccan

Millpool
Colliford Lake
Maidenwell
Siblyback Lake
Minions
Golberdon
Kelly Bray
St Ann's Chapel
Callington
Tamar Valley Donkey Park
Cardinham
Pensilva
Kit Hill Country Park
Harrowbarrow
Warleggan
Commonmoor
Darite
Gang
Cotehele House & Quay
Calstock
Mount
St Neot
Tremar
A390
Newbridge
St Dominick
Ley
St Cleer
Merrymeet
St Ive
St Mellion
B3257
Bere Alston
A388
Dobwalls
Pengover Green
Pillaton
The Cornish Maize Maze
Weir Quay
Liskeard
Quethiock
West Taphouse
East Taphouse
Doublebois
Menheniot
Blunts
Hatt
Cargreen
Bere Ferrers
A38
St Pinnock
A38
Landulph
Braddock
Tideford Cross
Landrake
Botusfleming
Restormel Castle
Herodsfoot
St Keyne
B3252
Trematon
A38
ostwithiel
Lostwithiel Museum
Porfell Wildlife Park
B3251
Tideford
Saltash
Couch's Mill
B3254
Trewidland
Trerule Foot
B3249
St Erney
Bocaddon
Duloe
Hessenford
St Germans
Plymouth
Lerryn ⑧
Sandplace
B3253
Morval
Polbathic
Lanreath
Pelynt
The Monkey Sanctuary
Sheviock
St German's River
A374
Devonport
Golant
Penpoll
Looe
East Looe
Seaton
Crafthole
Torpoint
Fowey Estuary
Lanteglos Highway
Trenewan
③
Portwrinkle
National Marine Aquarium
Fowey Aquarium
Fowey Museum
Polperro Heritage Museum
West Looe
Porthallow
B3247
Freathy
Millbrook
Mount Edgcumbe Country Park ⑩
Bodinnick
Fowey
Polruan
Lansallos
Polperro
Talland Bay
St George's or Looe Island
Whitsand Bay
Kingsand
Cawsand
Readymoney Cove
Pencarrow Head
Lantic Bay
Rame
bin nd
B269
Lantivet Bay
Rame Head
Penlee Point

English Channel

You must

❶ Steer a course to the amazing National Maritime Museum.

❷ Find a beach all to yourself on the Roseland Peninsula.

❸ Catch a crab off the harbour wall in Mevagissey or Looe.

❹ Lose yourself in the beautiful Lost Gardens of Heligan.

❺ Explore the steamy tropics at the iconic Eden Project.

❻ Learn to sail or windsurf from the beach at Polkerris.

❼ Ride the ferry between Mevagissey and Fowey, keeping a lookout for dolphins.

❽ Paddle a kayak to lovely Lerryn on the Fowey Estuary.

❾ Marvel at the treasure house of Cotehele.

❿ Plan a picnic in Mount Edgcumbe Country Park .

2 km
2 miles

Main photo: Little nipper – another one for the bucket. Opposite: Digging at Talland Bay; the Sail Loft at Polperro.

Southeast Cornwall

A rolling landscape of dairy farms dimpled with market towns, where hills nuzzle wooded creeks and fishing villages huddle around narrow harbours, the southeast is the soft underbelly of Cornwall – a gentle contrast to the drama-queen north with its showy beaches, surf and adrenaline sports.

But there's nothing flabby about the southeast. It might have more than its fair share of cream tea shops, but you can easily burn off the calories by kayaking, cycling, hiking and even surfing when there's a southwesterly swell.

Lying at the hub of the region, the china clay mining centre of **St Austell** snags the A390 as it meanders across southern Cornwall, passing the county's ancient seat of power at **Lostwithiel** before reaching the present-day capital of **Truro**. Cornwall's only city has a fine cathedral and museum, but it's the **Eden Project** near St Austell that gets the vote for Cornwall's most popular attraction. Over one million people make the pilgrimage to Eden each year – a green giant among lesser, though no less fascinating, sites nearby, such as the Shipwreck & Heritage Centre at the historic port of **Charlestown**.

South of St Austell, **Mevagissey**'s harbour is gridlocked with colourful trawlers and stalked by hordes of excited crab-hunters. Seek refuge from the ankle nippers in the nearby **Lost Gardens of Heligan**, or explore sandy beaches north and south of Mevagissey at **Pentewan** and **Gorran Haven**.

The coastline becomes wilder as you venture west onto the unspoilt Roseland Peninsula, a rural backwater that has sleepy **St Mawes** within waving distance of funky **Falmouth** – haven to yachties and home of the **National Maritime Museum**.

East of St Austell, fashionable **Fowey** (pronounced 'Foy') is another place where people love messing about on the water: sailing, pottering around in motor boats or kayaking to peaceful hamlets on the Fowey Estuary like **Lerryn**. Cross the estuary from Fowey to **Polruan** and the coast takes a rugged turn: cliffs marching eastwards, with narrow clefts leading to cutesy **Polperro** and the more substantial harbour town of **Looe**. Beyond lies the surf-strafed sweep of **Whitsand Bay** and the 'forgotten corner' of the **Rame Peninsula**, where historic **Mount Edgcumbe** presides over the Tamar Estuary. Plymouth is just a ferry ride (or bridge crossing) away, but steer yourself northwards and you'll find the Cornish treasure of **Cotehele House**.

Here to there

The Southeast Cornwall chapter covers the south coast, west from the Rame Peninsula to Dodman Point, just beyond Gorran Haven. Points west of this are covered by sections on The Roseland (see pages 170-173) and Falmouth (see pages 174-177). The Southeast Cornwall chapter extends north to include highlights in the Lower Tamar Valley, such as Cotehele House. Lostwithiel, the Fowey Estuary and attractions near St Austell, like the Eden Project, are also covered. For Truro, see pages 178-179.

Rame Head – Gorran Haven

Out & about Southeast Cornwall

Linger in Looe

Cornwall's southeast coast reaps a bumper catch of quaint fishing villages, and Looe is one of the best for a family day out that will barely cost you a penny. Park in **West Looe** beside the harbour, then walk across the bridge (admiring the beautiful views up the estuary) into **East Looe**. Fore Street has a good baker, so now is the time to stock up on picnic supplies if you need to. Nip down a side street to the quay and find a quiet spot for some crabbing. With a bit of luck you might be able to watch fishermen unloading their catch from brightly painted trawlers. Keep an eye out for grey seals – Looe Harbour is one of the best places in Cornwall to see them. If it's low tide, there's a tiny shingle cove next to the slipway, but you're better off walking towards Banjo Pier where Looe's main sandy beach stretches along the seafront (see page 153). This is also where you will find the lifeboat station. When you've finished your beach session, backtrack to the quayside, where a passenger ferry (40p) will take you back across the harbour to West Looe. From here, walk along Marine Drive for superb views across the harbour, continuing around the

East Looe.

headland to find a rocky shore that's good for rock-pooling at low tide. Looming offshore, **Looe Island** can be visited on boat trips (see page 155).

Remember the Rame

Roam free in the magnificent 865-acre **Mount Edgcumbe Country Park** on the Rame Peninsula – Cornwall's so-called 'Forgotten Corner'. There's an admission charge for the historic house (see page 160), but the

Did you see that splash? The tranquil tidal creeks of the Fowey Estuary are home to otters and kingfishers, so keep alert for signs of movement along the riverbank.

Visit Mevagissey

Why? Because not only is the crabbing around the harbour some of the best in Cornwall, but there's also a free museum and aquarium. The Mevagissey Sealife Aquarium is in a small building on the right-hand side of the harbour. There's barely enough space inside to swing a batfish, and it will only take you ten minutes or so to peruse the half-dozen tanks, but it's a great opportunity to see local fish (accompanied, you may well find, by bracing classical music). See if you can spot the conger eel in its pipe, Shelley the UK's largest oyster, dogfish and their egg cases, mullet, gurnard, triggerfish and flatfish. The aquarium also claims to have the biggest lobster in Cornwall, but Dai the Claw at Padstow's National Lobster Hatchery (see page 49) might have something to say about that. On the left-hand side of the harbour is the fascinating little Mevagissey Museum. Even the building itself is interesting: it was once used as a repair shop for smugglers' ships. Inside, you'll find all sorts of historical artefacts, but perhaps the most eye-catching exhibits are the wonderful black-and-white photos depicting life in Mevagissey during the 19th century.

Contact Mevagissey Sealife Aquarium, New Pier, T01726-843305; Mevagissey Museum, East Wharf, T01726-843568, Easter-Oct 1100-1600.

park costs nothing to visit and is open year round, daily from 0800. Dating from the 1500s, it's the earliest landscaped park in Cornwall and features ancient ruins, a Coastwatch station, free-running deer, formal Italian gardens and views across the sound towards Plymouth.

Catch a crab

Fowey, Looe, Mevagissey, Polperro... the crabbing in these south Cornwall fishing villages is legendary. Crab lines and buckets are sold everywhere, or you could make your own crabbing kit for nothing (see page 29).

Tackle the Tamar

A lofty lump of granite rearing above the Tamar Valley near Callington, 334-m-high **Kit Hill** (cornwall.gov.uk) has stunning views towards Bodmin Moor and Dartmoor, south to Plymouth Sound and (on a clear day) north to Bude. Grab your kite and a picnic and set off on the two-mile circular walk. The area is rich in history, with 19th-century mining remains (including the summit chimney stack) and a Neolithic long barrow dating from 3000 BC. Your kite, meanwhile, will probably share air space with buzzards and kestrels. Adders enjoy basking on sunny slopes and furry moth caterpillars can be seen on the heather during summer months.

Top: Pebble tower– how high can you go? Above: Is this the perfect skimmer?

What? No sand?!

No sulks or tantrums please. There's nothing wrong with a pebbly beach. In fact, you can have just as much fun on one of Cornwall's stony coves (and there are several on the southeast coast) as you can on a golden-sand one. For starters, there's stone-skimming. You'll need smooth, flat pebbles that fit comfortably between thumb and forefinger – crouch down, let loose with a flick of the wrist and see how many times you can make them skip across the sea (anything above seven is impressive). Pebble towers are also fun – see how many stones you can stack on top of each other, or use it as target practice (in an empty corner of the beach). If you're feeling arty, collect pebbles that all have a white vein running through them and arrange them side-by-side to create a 'rivulet' of quartz flowing across the beach.

Out & about Southeast Cornwall

Best beaches

The beaches here are found west to east, from Dodman Point to the Rame Peninsula. For Roseland beaches, see page 172.

Gorran Haven

Sheltered by a harbour wall, this sandy beach has safe swimming and is popular with families. Get your shrimping nets, crab lines, bait and inflatable dolphins at the Beachcomber.

Pentewan

This half-mile strip of sand is kept spotless by staff from the Pentewan Sands Holiday Park (see page 165) that backs much of the beach. The swimming is good and you can hire kayaks from Pentewan Watersports (T01726-844777).

Porthpean

A popular sandy cove with rock pools at low tide.

Charlestown

The pebble cove near the harbour is a good place for kids to burn off energy after all the cabinet perusal in the shipwreck museum (see page 157).

Carlyon Bay

This long sandy beach is in the throes of a controversial development plan to build a £250 million resort. Get the latest news at carlyonbeach.com or carlyonbay.org.uk.

Par Sands

A dune-backed beach with lots of sand and shallow water at low tide, easy access and a nearby café, Par Sands is a favourite with young families.

Polkerris

A small crescent of sand, partly sheltered by a stone quay, Polkerris combines an idyllic Cornish cove with excellent watersports at the Polkerris Beach Company (see page 155).

Readymoney Cove

A 20-minute walk from Fowey, Readymoney is a shingle and sand beach surrounded by woody cliffs and overlooked by the ruins of St Catherine's Castle.

Lantic Bay

Hemmed in by the 122-m hulk of Pencarrow Head, Lantic Bay is reached by a steep climb down

Wild one – escape the crowds on Lantic Bay.

from the cliff tops. There are no facilities and swimming can be dangerous due to rip currents – but this is still a hidden gem for escaping the crowds, watching the waves whomp against the rocks, or combing the strandline.

Talland Bay

Talland Bay is a sheltered cove with low headlands of mauve rock. Sand and rock pools are exposed at low tide and you can park right behind the beach, next to the Talland Bay Beach Café (see page 169).

East Looe Beach

With facilities close by, East Looe's sandy seafront beach is always a safe bet for families. Boat trips operate from the harbour, while West Looe's Hannafore Point beach is good for picnics and rock-pooling.

Whitsand Bay

A fine, three-mile swathe of surf-fringed sand, Whitsand brings a touch of north Cornwall to this stretch of coast – just take heed of the signs warning of rip currents, steep access and the risk of being cut off at high tide. Lifeguards patrol the beaches, of which Tregonhawke and Tregantle are best for families.

Cawsand & Kingsand

These pretty twin villages on the Rame Peninsula have small beaches of sand and shingle. There are rock pools at Kingsand and boat hire (kayaks, dinghies and windsurfers) at Cawsands.

Out & about Southeast Cornwall

Action stations

Adrenalin activities
Adrenalin Quarry
Lower Clicker Rd, Menheniot, PL14 3PJ, T01579-308204, adrenalinquarry. co.uk. Easter-Sep daily 1000-1800; Oct-Easter, call for times. Zip wire £12.50, hovercraft £50.

The biggest thrill ride in Cornwall that doesn't involve surf, Adrenalin Quarry's zip wire accelerates you to 40 mph over a 490-m-long cable suspended over a lake. And, if that doesn't get your heart thumping, hop in a single-seat hovercraft where, after a training lesson, you'll be heading full throttle from land to lake, skimming beneath cliffs at speeds of up to 30 mph.

Boat trips
Fowey Marine Adventures
Fore St, Fowey, T01726-832300, fowey-marine-adventures.co.uk. Looe Island Exploration (3 hrs) £35; Heritage Cruise (1 hr) £20 adult, £14 child; Family Special (40 mins) £16 adult, £8 child.

Wildlife cruises with added 'oomph': the 12-seat, high-speed RIB *Kernow Explorer* whisks you out of Fowey in search of dolphins, seals, basking sharks, sunfish, seabirds and peregrine falcons. The Family Special nips over to Lantic Bay, stopping en route for rock-pooling and birdwatching, while the Heritage Cruise heads further out to sea where the best marine-life encounters are often to be had.

Fowey River & Sea Cruises
Town Quay, Fowey, T07891-516635, foweycruise.com. Apr-Oct daily.
Choose from trips to Polperro, Lerryn, Charlestown, Lostwithiel and around Fowey Harbour.

Fowey Town Quay Boat Hire
Fowey, T07989-991115, fowey-boat-hire.co.uk. Apr-Oct daily.
Explore the tidal creeks of the River Fowey. Self-drive boats take up to five passengers.

Wind in the Willows
The Ticket Shop, 5 South St, Fowey, PL23 1AR, T01726-833616, fowey. co.uk. Various dates May-Sep. £12.25 adult, £8 child.
Gentle cruise from Fowey up the river to Lerryn with time to enjoy

a cream tea in the creekside village. Learn about Kenneth Grahame and how the area gave him inspiration for his classic book.

Boat trips from **Looe** are chalked up on quayside boards and include mackerel fishing on the *Boscastle Lass* (T07887-875726), *Emma Louise* (T07770-267155) and *Marsalu* (T0787-944 1083), rides out to Looe Island in the ex-RNLI lifeboat *William Cantreel Ashley* (T01503-263110) and 45-minute cruises in a glass-bottom boat (£5 adult, £4 under-10s).

In **Mevagissey**, you can hire self-drive motorboats, book a cruise around Mevagissey Bay or join a mackerel-fishing trip. Check the boards on the harbourfront for times and fares.

Mevagissey-Fowey Ferry
Lighthouse Quay, Mevagissey, T07977-203394, mevagissey-ferries. co.uk. Apr-Oct daily from 1000. Return fares £12 adult, £6 child. Taking around 35 minutes to link two of Cornwall's most charismatic ports, the 50-seat *Bessie James* often has encounters with dolphins and basking sharks. Ask the crew for a free map with details of walks around Fowey (the ferry docks at Whitehouse Quay) or

---

2hr MACKEREL FISHING TRIPS

RODS & TACKLE SUPPLIED
KEEP YOUR CATCH

£12 Per Person

TO BOOK -
07973 957 550

---

the 45-minute walk to Heligan Gardens if you are going to Mevagissey.

Canoeing
See page 156.

Cycling
Pentewan Valley Cycle Hire
West End, Pentewan, PL26 6BX, T01726-844242, pentewanvalleycyclehire.co.uk. Daily 0900-1700. Adult bike £12/day, child's bike £8/day, tag-a-long £8/day. Pedal north from Pentewan on National Cycle Route 3 (mixture of traffic-free and on-road) to St Austell or branch off south to the Lost Gardens of Heligan and Mevagissey (all traffic-free). The Eden Project (see page 162) is also within reach.

Go-karting
Kartworld
Menheniot, PL14 3PJ, T01579-347229, kartworldcornwall.co.uk. Easter-Oct daily from 1000, Nov-Easter Sat-Sun from 1000. Racing tracks for all ages, including an infant circuit for children six and under (using 5-mph, coin-operated karts).

Horse riding
Polmartin Riding
Polmartin Farm, nr Herodsfoot, PL14 4RE, T01503-220428, polmartinfarm.com. Call for rates. BHS-approved riding school in beautiful countryside.

Multi-activity
The following operators offer a range of activities, such as canoeing, sailing and cycling.

Active 8
Liskeard, T01579-320848, activecornwall.co.uk.

Adventure Cornwall
Lombard Farm, nr Fowey, T01726-870844, adventurecornwall.co.uk. See also page 167.

Surfing
Discovery Surf School
Belle Vue Rise, Hooe, Plymouth, Devon, PL9 9QD, T07813-639622. Jul-Aug daily. £38/2-hr lesson. Surf lessons at Tregonhawke Beach and Tregantle Beach on Whitsand Bay.

Watersports
Fowey Maritime Centre
Fowey, PL23 1BE, T01726-833924, foweymaritimecentre.com. Full-blown, RYA-accredited sailing school with less intense dinghy sailing courses for kids.

Polkerris Beach Company
The Pilchard Store, Polkerris, PL24 2TL, T01726-813306, polkerrisbeach. com. Sailing and windsurfing lessons from £33, kayak hire £12/2 hrs. This small centre (with its great café and shop) is right on the beach and offers personalized tuition in windsurfing, sailing and stand-up paddle surfing. You can also rent sailing dinghies, windsurfers and kayaks.

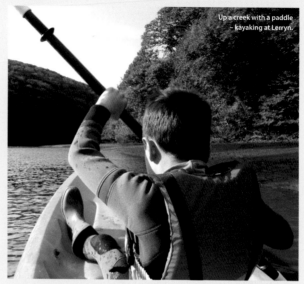
Up a creek with a paddle – kayaking at Lerryn.

Paddle power

Encounter Cornwall
Lerryn, PL22 0PY, T01208-871066, encountercornwall.com.
Kayaking taster and evening paddles £20 adult, £10 child; 3-hr river trips £25 adult, £12.50 child; half-day kayaking trips £30 adult, £15 child; Full-day kayaking trips £40 adult, £20 child; Single kayak hire £15/2hrs, £20/half day; double kayak hire £25/2hrs, £30/half day.
Children under 13 must be accompanied by an adult in a double kayak. Encounter Cornwall also offers walking and cycling trips.

Fowey Kayak Expeditions
Passage St, Fowey, PL23 1DE, T01726-833627, foweyexpeditions. co.uk, foweykayakhire.co.uk.
River Expeditions (May-Sep) £24 person (under-8s free); single kayak hire £8/hr, £18/half day, £22/day; double kayak hire £12/hr, £28/half day, £36/day.

'Believe me, my young friend, there is nothing – absolutely nothing – half so much worth doing as simply messing about in boats.' Of course, Ratty was spot on when he shared this nugget of wisdom with Mole in *The Wind in the Willows*. Moments later their boat struck the bank, but that didn't dent their enthusiasm for a jolly day out on the river.

Kenneth Grahame's children's classic was partly inspired by his holidays at Fowey, and now it's a simple matter to follow in the wake of Mole and Ratty by joining a canoeing trip on the river.

The antithesis to north Cornwall's surf scene, canoeing on the River Fowey is a relaxed affair – gentle paddling along sheltered creeks, water chuckling under your kayak's hull and picnics on the riverbank. It's also the best way to see the estuary's wildlife, which includes otters, egrets and kingfishers.

One of two canoeing operators on the river, Encounter Cornwall is based in the idyllic hamlet of Lerryn – an ideal place for novices to refine their paddling technique in stable open-cockpit or sit-on kayaks. Longer trips venture into the main Fowey Estuary, stopping perhaps for a look around the riverside settlements of Golant or St Winnow before nosing about in Woodgate Pill in search of kingfishers. With a whole day on the river (and some canoeing experience under your life vest), you could easily make it down to Fowey and Polruan, paddling in the shadow of huge ocean-going ships moored in the harbour. After lunch on a deserted beach, canoe back to Lerryn on a rising tide – a fantastic river adventure covering around 10 miles.

Fowey Kayak Expeditions offers guided five-hour canoeing trips upstream from Fowey, with about two and a half hours on the river and the rest of the time exploring Lerryn and Golant. If you're feeling independent and free-spirited, both operators also offer kayaks for hire – however, this is not recommended for beginners.

Out & about Southeast Cornwall

Charlestown Shipwreck & Heritage Centre

Charlestown, PL25 3NJ, T01726-69897, shipwreckcharlestown.com. Mar-Nov daily 1000-1700. £5.95 adult, £2.95 child (under 10s free). As close to a real-life treasure chest as you'll ever get, this wonderfully cluttered museum showcases artefacts from over 150 shipwrecks, including the *Titanic*, *Mary Rose* and *Lusitania*. You can also board the lifeboat *RNLB Amelia* and scurry through a tunnel (once used for transporting china clay) to a terrace overlooking Charlestown's docks where two square-rigged sailing ships are moored. Backtracking through the tunnel, you find yourself walking through a lifesize diorama of early 19th-century Charlestown buildings, including a harbour cottage,

blacksmith and cooper (barrel maker). This is followed by various maritime-themed displays – the old diving suits and diving bells will have children goggle-eyed, while the section charting the history of the RNLI is a must-see. There are a few hands-on gizmos, but nothing more high-tech than tapping out SOS on a morse code machine. The remainder of the museum is largely cabinets bursting with shipwreck paraphernalia. There's plenty of fascinating stuff here – but there's a lot of it, so be sure to equip children with I-Spy sheets (available at the entrance) to help buoy their enthusiasm levels.

Cotehele House & Quay

St Dominick, nr Saltash, PL12 6TA, T01579-351346, nationaltrust.org. uk. Garden daily from 1000; house and mill Mar-Nov Sat-Thu (mill daily) from 1100. £9.20 adult, £4.60 child (5-17), £23 family. Calstock ferry, T01822-833331.

Cotehele is a delightfully dingy Tudor manor, with grounds running down to an old quay on the River Tamar that can be reached by ferry from Calstock. A short walk downriver, the watermill has workshops featuring a blacksmith, carpenter, saddler and wheelwright. So, where to begin? If a family fun activity is running (usually Mondays, Tuesdays and Wednesdays during August), then make a beeline for the

Cotehele House.

Education Room. Otherwise, collect Tracker Packs or quiz sheets for the children and head for the manor house.

Little altered since its completion by the Edgcumbe family around 1539, Cotehele House is remarkably well preserved. The main hall is adorned with armour and weapons (and some whale jaw bones by the fireplace), while ancient tapestries festoon the walls of the dining room and bedrooms – infusing them with a perpetual, musty twilight, as if time really has stood still here for five centuries. Children will be kept busy trying to spot details in the tapestries for their quiz sheets. Ask one of the friendly and engaging National Trust volunteers if you need a clue – they'll also point out other features like the spy holes or 'squints' for peeping onto rooms below.

Outside, the formal gardens have views over the valley and conceal medieval treasures like the dovecote and stewpond (for keeping carp). It's a

steepish walk through beautiful woodland down to Cotehele Quay, where a discovery centre has scale models recreating the scene in the 19th century: coal, limestone and market produce being loaded onto barges for transport down the Tamar River. One of them – the *Shamrock* – is moored outside, but you can't go aboard. Instead, children will be happy exploring the Shipping Office, playing coits, practising knots and scribbling yarns at the craft desk. The quay is a lovely spot for a picnic and there's also a café selling ice creams.

The Lost Gardens of Heligan

Pentewan, PL26 6EN, T01726-845100, heligan.com. Apr-Sep daily 1000-1800; Oct-Mar, daily 1000-1700. £8.50 adult, £5 child (5-16), £23.50 family, free entry to shop and tearoom.

Any child who's read *The Secret Garden* will be intrigued by Heligan which seems to sprout straight from the pages of Frances Hodgson Burnett's classic novel about a hidden,

neglected garden nurtured back to life. Remember, though, that Heligan is now a large, working garden and conservation project – don't expect any fanciful forays into fairy-themed playgrounds or other children's attractions.

Instead, let your imagination run wild as you follow boardwalks through tunnels of banana palms and bamboo in the subtropical Jungle and discover natural sculptures on the Woodland Walk. See if you can spot the Giant's Head – montbretia sprouting in orange-tipped plumes from his head – or the mesmerising Mud Maiden, cloaked in ferns and ivy. Don't miss Horsemoor Hide which combines traditional wildlife-spotting (overlooking a bird feeding area, wildlife pond, meadow and woodland) with live CCTV footage of bats, birds and badgers. You can even use remote-controlled cameras to zoom in on whatever turns up. Nuthatches and woodpeckers often visit the nut feeders, while kingfishers occasionally stake out the pond.

Heligan's Northern Gardens are festooned with flowers, fruit and veg (including poo-powered pineapple) and there's an excellent tea room serving soups, roast lunches and snacks. At the entrance, Lobbs Farm Shop (see page 168) is the place to pick up local produce.

The *Shamrock* at Cotehele Quay.

Lost and found – Heligan's treasures include (from top left) a water cherub in the Italian Gardens, old-fashioned tools in the Vegetable Garden, a secret doorway in the Melon Yard, the Mud Maiden, Jungle Garden, Flower Garden and Giant's Head.

Out & about Southeast Cornwall

Amazing Cornish Maize Maze
Smeaton Farm, Pillaton, Saltash PL12 6RZ, T01579-351833, amazingcornishmaizemaze.co.uk. Jul-Sep daily 1030-1700. £5.50 adult, £4 child (3-16), £16 family. Frighteningly fiendish maze with a different theme each year, plus farm trail, play area and café.

China Clay Country Park
Wheal Martyn, Carthew, St Austell, PL26 8XG, T01726-850362, chinaclaycountry.co.uk. Year round daily from 1000. £7.50 adult, £4.50 child (6-16), £20 family. Ever wonder what those 'white mountains' are as you drive past St Austell? The story of china clay mining is revealed at this country park through historical trails, interactive displays and a platform overlooking a working pit. There's also a commando-style assault course for kids, a nature trail and café.

Fowey Aquarium
Town Hall, Fowey. May-Dec 1000-1700. £2 adult, £1.50 child (3-13). Built in 1950 by a local fishmonger, Fowey's dinky aquarium relies on fishermen and local anglers for stocking its tanks. You never know what the latest 'live catch' might be, but chances are you'll see conger eel, cuckoo wrasse, dogfish, mullet and lobster. A touch pool allows children to get to grips (gently) with crabs and starfish.

The Monkey Sanctuary
Murrayton, Looe, PL13 1NZ, T01503-262532, monkeysanctuary.org. Easter-Sep, Oct halfterm, call for opening times. £7.50 adult, £3.50 child (5-16), £20 family. Beating the drum for primate welfare, this inspired centre provides a stimulating home for capuchin and woolly monkeys – many of them confiscated as illegally kept pets. Keepers give talks and workshops throughout the day. You can help to make enrichment toys for the monkeys, explore a wildlife trail and bat cave, and tuck into award-winning vegetarian food at the Tree Top Café – proceeds of which go to the sanctuary's charity, Wild Futures (wildfutures.org).

Mount Edgcumbe
Cremyll, Torpoint, PL10 1HZ, T01752-822236, mountedgcumbe.gov.uk. Apr-Sep Sun-Thu 1100-1630. £6 adult, £5.50 child (5-15), £12.50 family; house and Tamar cruise tickets £9.50 adult, £5.70 child. The grand family home of the Edgcumbes, restored to its 18th-century splendour, is surrounded by formal gardens and the wider (free-to-enter) country park – see page 150.

Polperro Heritage Museum of Smuggling & Fishing
The Warren, Polperro, T01503-272423, polperro.org. Mar-Oct daily 1000-1800. £1.75 adult, £0.50 child. With its narrow lanes, wonky houses and higgledy-piggledy harbour, Polperro was always destined to become a tourist trap – but you can see a more gritty side to the village at this small museum with its 19th-century photos, ship models and artefacts. Walk or take a horse-and-cart or tram down to the village from the car park, passing Cornwall's Fairy Kingdom, the Chocolate Dream Company, model village and galleries, tea rooms and cafés galore. The museum is tucked away in the old pilchard factory by the harbour. See if you can also find the House on Props, then walk out to the harbour entrance, past the old Sail Loft, to see the lighthouse.

Porfell Wildlife Park
Trecangate, nr Lanreath, PL14 4RE, T01503-220211, porfellanimalland.co.uk. Apr-Nov daily 1000-1800 (plus weekends Feb-Apr). £8/adult, £5 child (3-13).

Polperro.

A peaceful, laid-back park with lemurs, meerkats, tamarins, zebras, capybaras, caracals and other furry favourites, plus a children's farm, woodland walks, café and picnic area.

Restormel Castle

Nr Lostwithiel, PL22 0EE, T01208-872687, english-heritage.org.uk. Apr-Nov daily from 1000. £3 adult, £1.50 child (5-15).

Battle imaginary dragons, rescue maidens in distress and strut your stuff, just like Edward the Black Prince did when he visited this splendid keep – now a ruined shell ripe for a picnic.

Tamar Valley Donkey Park

St Ann's Chapel, Gunnislake, PL18 9HW, T01822-834072, donkeypark. com. Apr-Sep, daily 1000-1700; call for winter opening. £6 person (under-2s free), £22 family.

Feed and pet donkeys, ponies, goats, sheep, pigs, rabbits and guinea pigs. You can also ride the donkeys or horse around in the play barn.

Trewithen Gardens

Grampound, nr Truro, TR2 4DD, T01726-883647, trewithengardens. co.uk. Mar-Sep Mon-Sat (plus Sun, Mar-May) 1000-1630. £7.50 adult, children under 12 free.

Renowned for its magnolias and camellias, this historic private estate has tranquil woodland walks, picnic areas and a tea room selling local produce.

Hit or miss?

**The Tortoise Garden
Topanga, Lower Sticker, St Austell, PL26 7JJ, T01726-65670, thetortoisegarden.co.uk. Easter-Sep daily 1000-1700. £2.50.**

The 150-odd tortoises here come in all shapes and sizes – from penny-sized hatchlings to lumbering 90-year-olds. And they've all got names and personalities – a guarantee of total fascination for most children. Just keep your fingers crossed that Zeus, an impressive seven-stone Sulcata tortoise from Africa, comes out of his shell to greet you; he was stolen from the sanctuary in 2009, but returned safely a few months later.

Rain check

Cinemas
White River Cinema
White River Place, St Austell, T0871-200 3304.

Vue
Barbican Leisure Park, Shapters Rd, Coxside, Plymouth, T08712-240240.

Indoor play & amusements
Kidzworld
Stadium Retail Park, Par Moor Rd, St Austell, PL25 3RP, T01726-815553, kidzworlduk.co.uk. Apr-Sep daily 1000-1900, Oct-Mar Wed-Sun 1000-1900. £1-2 adult, £3.50-5.95 child (2-12). Vast play zone with climbing towers, drop slides and assault courses; pirate-themed zone with shooting galleries and remote control ships; separate under-fives play area and tropical-themed restaurant.

Indoor swimming pools
Lux Park Leisure Centre
Coldstyle Rd, Liskeard, PL14 3HZ, T01579-342544, cornwall.gov.uk.
Polkyth Leisure Centre
Carlyon Rd, St Austell, PL25 4DB, T01726-223344, polkythleisure.co.uk.
Saltash Leisure Centre
Callington Rd, PL12 6DJ, T01752-840940, cornwall.gov.uk.

Museums & aquariums
Fowey Museum
Town Hall, Fowey. Easter-Oct Mon-Fri 1030-1700. £1 adult.
Lostwithiel Museum
Fore St, Lostwithiel. Easter-Sep daily 1030-1230, 1430-1630. Free.
National Marine Aquarium
Rope Walk, Coxside, Plymouth, PL4 0LF, T01752-600301, national-aquarium.co.uk. Year round daily from 1000. £11 adult, £6.50 child (5-16), £30 family, 4D cinema £2.
Just across the border in Devon, Plymouth's stunning aquarium is easy to reach from southeast Cornwall. Divided into six zones, the aquarium has huge tanks containing living reefs, sharks and a loggerhead turtle called Snorkel. The Shallow Zone showcases local marine life, while Explorocean has interactive exhibits on the technology behind ocean discoveries.

Don't miss The Eden Project

Bodelva, nr St Austell, PL24 2SG, T01726-811911, edenproject.com. Year round daily from 1000 (car parks open 0900 during summer school holidays). On the door entry £16 adult, £5 child (5-15), £38 family; online tickets £15 adult, £5 child (5-15), £36 family; reduced prices for walkers or cyclists £12 adult, £24 family, children free.

Bulging from an old china clay pit like a giant string of silvery frog spawn, Eden's vast biomes have become an icon, not just of British tourism, but of sustainability. Visiting this hallowed shrine to vegetation has almost become a rite of family holidays in Cornwall – a peat-free pilgrimage that's right up there with surfing and Stein's fish 'n' chips. And it's hardly surprising. Not only is the Eden Project immensely fun and educational for kids, but it also reconnects them with the environment, plunging them into an earthy succession of habitats, from jungle to global veggie patch.

Zig-zagging along paths below the visitor centre, most people make straight for the Rainforest and Mediterranean Biomes, but don't overlook the outdoor space – it's riddled with shortcuts, hideaways, stepping stones, spy-holes and sandpits. You might also bump into a Pollinator, one of Eden's resident interpreters who act as guides and impromptu storytellers. Everything you need for building a den can be found in the play area, while the Mechanical Theatre uses robots, puppets and film to bring plant stories to life. And, of course, everywhere you look you'll see real plants, growing, flowering, fruiting and generally giving your senses a thorough workout.

Brace yourself for the Rainforest Biome. Littl'uns might wilt in the hot and humid atmosphere, so take your time and make use of the water fountains scattered throughout this record-breaking greenhouse (240 m long, 110 m wide and 50 m high). As well as identifying tropical fruits and spices, you'll find out, through imaginative displays, how rubber, chewing gum and cola drinks are derived from rainforest plants. There's also a waterfall and jungle settlement to discover, while sharp-eyed explorers might spot a tree frog.

The Mediterranean Biome is just as mesmerising with its cork and citrus plantations, grape vines and perfume garden. There's a lot to see at the Eden Project, but try to leave a good hour or two for tinkering about with the interactive exhibits in The Core educational centre. The elaborate nut-cracking machine is addictive!

Seasonal events include summer den-making, Hallowe'en parties and a winter wonderland of ice skating, Christmas markets, music and storytelling.

Natural cycle

Cycle to the Eden Project and you not only fast-track through entrance queues and get a discount on admission tickets (see left), but you also help to reduce traffic congestion and feel really good about yourself. The **Clay Trails** cycle route (T0845-113 0065, sustrans.org.uk) links Bugle with the Eden Project along four miles of easy, mainly level gravel track (there's one moderate climb), passing woodland and a picnic shelter overlooking some lakes. A more challenging five-mile route between Wheal Martin and the Eden Project offers panoramic views of St Austell Bay and the clay mines. You can access both trails from National Cycle Network Route 3, which runs through Bodmin and St Austell. Really keen cyclists can follow a side trail to the China Clay Country Park (see page 160). If you need bikes, contact Pentewan Valley Cycle Hire (see page 155) or Jungle Cycle Hire (Bugle, T01726-852204).

Hot stuff – the luxuriant Rainforest Biome.
Above: lavender fields, a jungle settlement
and a big machine to crack a small nut.

Visiting this hallowed shrine to vegetation has almost become a rite
of family holidays in Cornwall – a peat-free pilgrimage that's right up
there with surfing and Stein's fish 'n' chips.

Sleeping Southeast Cornwall

Pick of the pitches

Bay View Farm

St Martins, Looe, PL13 1NZ, T01503-265922, looebaycaravans.co.uk. May-Sep. £10-23/pitch.

The name says it all – unzip your tent and you're gazing straight across Looe Bay from this wonderful coastal farm that's also home to seven shire horses.

Camping Caradon

Trelawne, Looe, PL13 2NA, T01503-272388. Apr-Oct. £10-20/pitch, plus £3 extra adult, £2 extra child.

Close to Looe, Polperro and Talland Bay, this family-run park has a games room, playground and club house.

Carlyon Bay Camping Park

Carlyon Bay, PL25 3RE, T01726-812735, carlyonbay.net. Apr-Sep, £12-27/pitch (2 adults), plus £5 extra adult, £4 extra child (3-15).

Just two miles from the Eden Project and a short walk to the beach, this spacious site has a heated swimming pool, playground and crazy golf.

Court Farm

St Stephen, nr St Austell, PL26 7LE, T01726-823684, courtfarmcornwall. co.uk. Apr-Sep. £9.50-27.50/pitch.

Perfect for starry-eyed campers, this small and very peaceful site, deep in the Cornish countryside, has an astronomy telescope.

East Crinnis Camping & Caravan Park

Lantyan, East Crinnis, PL24 2SQ, T01726-813023, crinniscamping. co.uk. Easter-Oct. £10-18/pitch.

A leafy, well-landscaped park with its own fishing pond, East Crinnis makes a good base for exploring south coast beaches, as well as the Eden Project and the fishing villages of Mevagissey and Fowey.

Heligan Park

St Ewe, Mevagissey, PL26 6EZ, T01726-842714, heliganpark.co.uk. Jan-Nov. £10.70-24.95/pitch (2 adults), plus £1.95-4.20 extra adult, £1.05-3.10 extra child.

Beautifully landscaped park next door to the Lost Gardens of Heligan, with 16 luxury holiday homes and 80 pitches for touring caravans and tents. Guests enjoy free use of the facilities (heated pool etc) at the sister site, Pentewan Sands.

Highertown Farm Campsite

Lansallos, PL13 2PX, T01208-265211, nationaltrust.org.uk. Easter-Oct. £4-5 adult, £2-2.50 child (2-12).

Quiet, rural and within easy walking distance of the beautiful beaches of Lantivet and Lantic Bay, this basic campsite has stunning coastal views.

Penmarlam Caravan & Camping Park

Bodinnick, nr Fowey, PL23 1LZ, T01726-870088, penmarlampark. co.uk. Apr-Oct. £6-9/pitch, £3.75-7.25 adult, £1.50-3.50 child (3-15).

Located on the east bank of the Fowey River, this tidy site has great views and easy access to Fowey on either the Bodinnick or Polruan ferry.

Pensagillas Farm

Grampound, TR2 4SR, T01872-530808, pensagillas-park.co.uk. £8-10/pitch, rental tents £25/night.

A short drive from Mevagissey and the Lost Gardens of Heligan, this rural site has a farm trail, fishing lakes and livery stables (should you choose to take your horse on holiday). For no-fuss camping, you can also rent ready-pitched tents, complete with beds and cooking gear.

Treveague Farm

Gorran, PL26 6NY, T01726-842295, treveaguefarm.co.uk. Apr-Oct. £6-18/pitch (2 adults), plus £2 extra person. Tipi £345-495/wk.

The perfect spot for wildlife lovers, Treveague Farm has a state-of-the-art hide with night vision cameras allowing you to watch the nocturnal antics of badgers and foxes. Everything from peregrine falcons to hummingbird hawk moths have been recorded at the farm; and there's a resident expert on hand to take you on nature walks. Treveague has wonderful coastal views, with footpaths leading to Gorran Haven, as well as the secluded Vault and Hemmick beaches. The farm's restaurant serves organic produce, and a storyteller visits during peak season to recount traditional folk tales.

The campsite at Treveague Farm, with views towards Gorran Haven.

Holiday parks

Killigarth Manor
Polperro, PL13 2JQ, T01503-272216, killigarth.co.uk.

Looe Bay Holiday Park
St Martins, PL13 1NX, T0871-641 0232, parkdeanengland.co.uk.

Meadow Lakes Holiday Park
Hewas Water, PL26 7JG, T01726-882540, surfbayholidays.co.uk.

Par Sands Holiday Park
St Austell Bay, PL24 2AS, T01726-812868, parsands.co.uk.

Pentewan Sands Holiday Park
Pentewan, PL26 6BT, T01726-843485, pentewansands.com.

River Valley Holiday Park
London Apprentice, St Austell, PL26 7AP, T01726-735533, cornwall-holidays.co.uk.

Tencreek Holiday Park
Looe, PL13 2JR, T01503-262447, dolphinholidays.co.uk.

Tregoad Park
St Martin, nr Looe, PL13 1PB, T01503-262718, tregoadpark.co.uk.

Trelawne Manor
Looe, PL13 2NA, T0844-847 1115, hoseasons.co.uk.

Seaview International
Boswinger, nr Gorran Haven, PL26 6LL, T01726-843425, seaviewinternational.com.

Sun Valley Holiday Park
Pentewan, PL26 6DJ, T01726-843266, sunvalleyholidays.co.uk.

Whitsand Bay Holiday Park
Millbrook, PL10 1JZ, T01752-822597, whitsandbayholidays.co.uk.

Sleeping Southeast Cornwall

Cottages

Bosinver Farm Cottages

Trelowth, nr St Austell, PL26 7DT,
T01726-72128, bosinver.co.uk.
£330-2660/wk.
Bosinver combines the rural
idyll of a farmstay (35 acres
of wildflower meadow, farm
animals wandering past your
doorstep etc) with the pick-and-
mix appeal of a self-catering
cottage agency and the facilities
of a holiday park. There is a
choice of no less than 19 highly
individual and stylishly furnished
cottages (sleeping 3-12)
scattered through this hidden
valley between St Austell and
Mevagissey. Local characters
include Lovejoy and Tinker

the Shire horses, and Chalky, a
tree-climbing Pygmy goat that's
fond of digestive biscuits. As
well as feeding the animals, kids
will love the play barn, games
room, adventure playground,
tennis court and outdoor pool.
Bikes are available for hire (the
Pentewan Valley Trail is nearby),
while groceries can be pre-
ordered from the local store.

Cornhill Farm Cottages

St Blazey, Par, PL24 2SP, T01726-
815700, cornhillfarmcottages.co.uk.
£360-650/wk.
Just a short walk from the Eden
Project, these converted stone
barns are on a small, family-run
farm with plenty of friendly
animals to become acquainted

with, from saddleback pigs to
miniature Shetland ponies.

Crylla Valley Cottages

Notter Bridge, nr Saltash, T01752-
851133, cryllacottages.co.uk.
£225-1431/wk.
The garden games, adventure
play area, wildlife walks and
complimentary baby equipment
are just one half of the deal
at Crylla Valley Cottages. Stay
here and you also get free
membership of a local country
club, with its indoor pool,
children's fun zone and sauna.

Fox Valley Cottages

Lanlawren Farm, Trenewan, PL13 2PZ,
T01726-870115, foxvalleycottages.
co.uk. £300-1165/wk.
Sitting pretty in seven acres
of unspoilt countryside, three
miles west of Polperro, this
group of 10 holiday cottages has
the added bonus of an indoor
swimming pool, spa and sauna.

Green Acres Cottages

Penpillick, Par, PL24 2RU, T01840-
213537, greenacrescottages.co.uk.
£500-1200/wk.
A luxurious development of 10

Childhood memories made here

award winning Cornish farm cottages, in the countryside, near the sea

Pat Smith, Bosinver Farm Cottages, St Mewan, St Austell PL26 7DT

bosinver
farm cottages
award winning self catering in cornwall

T01726272128
www.bosinver.co.uk

stone cottages with stunning countryside views, Green Acres has an indoor pool, sauna and small 'garden' farm.

Tredethick Farm Cottages
Tredethick, Lostwithiel, PL22 0LE, T01208-873618, tredethick.co.uk. Call for rates and availability.
The owners of these nine traditional cottages (mostly clustered around a courtyard) have stopped at nothing to make this a rural paradise for children. Feeding the animals is almost a daily routine – and it's followed by pony riding on Monday and Wednesday mornings. The play barn has practically its own beach with 10 tons of sand: enough to satisfy the most stringent of sandcastle connoisseurs. There's also a wendy house, slide, giant trampoline, ride-on tractors and a football pitch. The farm trail, meanwhile, is your ticket to exploring fields and woods, or joining a footpath leading to the riverside hamlet of St Winnow. Then there's the farm shop with local treats like organic ice cream, Cornish fudge, elderflower pressé and – music to most parents' ears – readymade meals. You see, it's not just kids that are made a fuss of at Tredethick Farm. Grownups also get their fair share of goodies – from the well-equipped cottages to the comfy sofas, fresh-ground coffee and magazines in the soft play area.

Best of the rest

Adventure Cornwall
Lombard Farm, nr Fowey, PL23 1NA, T01726-870844, adventurecornwall.co.uk. Houses Feb-Oct, £420-1680/wk; yurt May-Oct, £310-780/wk.
Proof that the action isn't always confined to Cornwall's north coast, Adventure Cornwall runs canoeing trips on the River Fowey and rock climbing on Bodmin Moor from its base at Lombard Farm. As well as two contemporary cottages (both sleeping six), there's a five-berth yurt with wood burner and hot tub, plus a large tipi for overnight camps. Fowey is within easy walking distance, while a more adventurous 50-minute hike will take you to rarely crowded Lantic Bay.

Deer Park
Forest Holidays, see page 16.

Also recommended
Honicombe Manor Resort
St Ann's Chapel, PL17 8JW, T01822-832583, honicombemanor.co.uk.

Mount Brioni
Looe Hill, PL11 3JN, T01503-250251, cornwall-self-catering-holidays.com.

Notter Mill
Notter Bridge, Saltash, PL12 4RW, T01752-843694, nottermill.co.uk.

Valleybrook
Lansallos, PL13 2QE, T01503-220493, valleybrookholidays.com.

Splashing out

Fowey Hall Hotel
Fowey, PL23 1ET, T01726-833866, foweyhallhotel.co.uk. Nightly B&B rates £140-270/double room, £185-395/suite, £265-540/interconnecting rooms.
Going posh with kids only works when you find a luxurious hotel devoid of pretentiousness, where staff are able to engage with life forms lower than navel height and where the term 'child friendly' doesn't in fact mean 'child friendly but we'd really rather not, thank you awfully.' Does such a place exist? Yes. In fact, there's a whole chain of them called Luxury Family Hotels and one of them sits proud above Fowey Estuary with views across to Polruan and the open sea. A 19th-century mansion that was thought to be the inspiration for Toad Hall in *The Wind in the Willows*, Fowey Hall is set in five acres of gardens and is just a short stroll from Readymoney Cove and the town of Fowey itself. Facilities include an OFSTED-registered Den for children under eight, a playroom for older kids and an indoor pool. Rooms are large and indulgent (although you'll need a suite if you have two children) with everything on hand – from DVDs to baby equipment – to make your stay hassle-free. Fine food and a brand new Aquae Sulis Retreat add the finishing touches.

Eating Southeast Cornwall

Cornish Orchards Farm Shop
Westnorth Manor Farm, Duloe,
PL14 4PW, T01503-269007,
cornishorchards.co.uk. Easter-Nov.
Mon-Fri 1000-1700, Sat 0930-1230.
Cider, apple juice, elderflower
pressé, honey and preserves.

Lobbs Farm Shop
Heligan, St Ewe, PL26 6EN, T01726-
844411, lobbsfarmshop.com. Year-
round Mon-Fri 0930-1730 (1700 in
winter), Sat-Sun 1030-1630.
This fabulous farm shop at
Heligan Gardens (see page 158)

Lobbs Farm Shop.

Market days
Callington Farmers' Market
Town Hall, Friday 0900-1300.

Grampound Produce Market
Village Hall, Saturday 1000-1300.

Liskeard Farmers' Market
Moorswater Industrial Estate,
every other Friday 0900-1100.

Lostwithiel Farmers' Market
Community Ctr, Friday 1000-1400.

Mevagissey Farmers' Market
West Wharf, Sunday 0900-1300.

Truro Farmers' Market
Lemon Quay, Saturday 0900-1600.

has meat and cheese counters,
fruit, vegetables, dairy products,
bread, jams, chutneys, biscuits,
ice cream, smoked fish and
other local produce – much of it
sourced from the owner's Kestle
Farm (30-minute tours available
during spring and summer). The
farmhouse kitchen produces
freshly cooked quiches, pork
pies and seasonal salads, while
the adjacent Countryside Barn
has displays on farming.

Purely Cornish Farm Shop
St Martins, nr Looe, PL13 1NX,
T01503-262680, purelycornish.co.uk.
Stock up on cheese, clotted
cream, pasties and other local
produce and enjoy a light meal,
organic coffee or smoothie
at the Chillout Bar. The Purely
Cornish Deli in East Looe,
meanwhile, is the place to go
for pick-and-mix hampers.

Taste of the Westcountry
Fore St, St Cleer, Liskeard,
PL14 5DA, T01579-345985,
tasteofthewestcountry.co.uk.
Year round, daily 0900-1800.
Local seasonal fruit and
vegetables, sausages and
burgers for the barbecue,
pasties, bread, cakes, cheeses,
ice cream, jams and chutneys.

Ice cream
East Looe is the home of **Treleavens**
luxury hand-made Cornish ice cream
and sorbet. There are shops on Fore
Street, East Looe, and Lansallos
Street, Polperro (treleavens.co.uk).

Crooked Inn
Saltash, PL12 4RZ, T01752-848177,
crooked-inn.co.uk.
Traditional pub with family
dining room, children's play area
and farmyard pets.

House on the Props
Polperro, PL13 2RE, T01503-272310,
houseontheprops.co.uk.
Propped up on timbers from
the *Maverine*, wrecked nearby
around 1700, this teetering tea
room serves breakfasts, lunches
and afternoon teas. Try the
scrummy home-baked cakes.

Lerryn River Stores
Lerryn, T01208-872375.
Cream teas, sandwiches, ice
cream and anything else you
might need for a picnic on the
green overlooking the creek.

Louis' Tea Rooms
Kit Hill Country Park, Callington,
PL17 8AX, T01579-389223.
Treat yourself to a scone after
hiking up Kit Hill (see page 151).

Muffins Tea Room
Fore St, Lostwithiel, PL22 0BN,
T01208-872278, muffinsdeli.co.uk.
Tue-Sat 1000-1700.
Delicious cakes, cream teas and
light meals made with fresh,
local ingredients. Try the tasting
plate (£6.95) for a selection of
meat, fish and cheeses from
local suppliers, served with
bread, olives and chutney.

Pinky Murphy's Café

North St, Fowey, PL23 1DB, T01726-832512, pinkymurphys.com. Mon-Sat 0900-1700, Sun 0930-1600.
Colourful, cool and quirky, Pinky Murphy's serves a legendary FatBoy hot chocolate (£2.95), plus some great soups, meat and veggie platters, ciabattas, paninis and baguettes.

Rashleigh Inn

Polkerris, PL24 2TL, T01726-813991, rashleighinnpolkerris.co.uk. Daily, meals served 1200-1400, 1800-2100.
Eat inside or out at this 300-year-old boathouse right on the beach. Fresh seafood a speciality.

Sams

Fore St, Fowey, PL23 1AQ, T01726-832273, samsfowey.co.uk.
The kids' menu at this lively, fun eatery really hits the spot, with home-made burgers, lasagne, calamari, fish, mussels, shell-on prawns, chicken and a wicked pudding just £6.95 for two courses. Sams also has a beach café (T01726-812255) in the old lifeboat station at Polkerris, serving fresh pizzas and seafood.

Talland Bay Beach Café

Talland Bay, PL13 2JA, T01503-272088, tallandbaybeachcafe.co.uk. Easter-Oct daily.
This chirpy little café sits right above the beach at Talland Bay – a pretty perfect spot for a cream tea, pasty or fresh crab sandwich (£4.95). You can also buy beach gear here.

Talland Bay Beach Café.

The Wheelhouse Restaurant

West Quay, Mevagissey PL26 6UJ, T01726-843404, wheelhouse.me.uk.
Formerly a net loft, this harbourside restaurant has a well-deserved reputation for sublime seafood. The all-day menu features tasty starters like hot crab pot with avocado and parmesan (£5.95), while mains (£7.50-9.50) include old favourites like Cornish fishcakes, cod and chips and Fowey River mussels. Starters on the evening à la carte menu range from panfried calamari (£4.95) to seared St Austell Bay scallops (£6.95). For a main course, push the boat out with a Seafood Medley of mussels, scallops, prawns and calamari (£17.95).

Also recommended
Wreckers

Charlestown Harbour, PL25 3NJ, T01726-879053.
More of the same from the owners of the Wheelhouse Restaurant (see above).

Fish & chips

A quality chippie, **The Other Place** (Fore St, Fowey) is hard to beat. **Trebonney** (Fore St, Roche, St Austell) also has an excellent reputation. In Mevagissey, try the **The Big 'Un** (Olivers Quay).

Posh nosh

Q @ The Old Quay House

Fore St, Fowey, PL23 1AQ, T01726-833302, theoldquayhouse.com.
Lunch daily May-Sep and weekends Oct-Apr; dinner daily.
Relaxed yet stylish, Q spills out onto a terrace overlooking the Fowey Estuary. Local ingredients from land and sea are given a Mediterranean zing with lunchtime dishes such as a mussel and crab linguine (£16). The dinner menu (£27.50 for two courses or £30 for three courses) is likely to include equally sumptuous dishes, like grilled sardines with a pine nut and celery salad or grilled bream with ginger butter.

Trawlers

The Quay, East Looe, PL13 1AH, T01503-263593, trawlersrestaurant.co.uk. Tue-Sat from 1830.
Fine dining with a view of the harbour, Trawlers is predominantly a fish restaurant and has a daily changing menu. Expect to pay around £25 for a two-course meal, which might well include culinary delights like roasted monkfish wrapped in pancetta with caramelized butternut squash and creamed leeks or crispy-skin sea bass with a lobster thermidor sauce.

Also recommended
Austell's

Beach Road, Carlyon Bay, PL25 3PH, T01726-813888, austells.net.

The Roseland

Where exactly this Area of Outstanding Natural Beauty begins and ends is a little hazy but, for the purposes of this book, it's the stretch of coast between Dodman Point and St Mawes. You'll know you've reached the Roseland Peninsula when hedgerows start to press in on either side, grass sprouts along the middle of the road like a green mohican and the lane fizzles out in a sleepy fishing village or deserted cove.

Get your bearings

Dangling like a loose thread from the A390 between Truro and St Austell, the A3078 is the only main road into the Roseland. It's just one of the ways, however, of reaching St Mawes, the peninsula's harbour town on the estuary opposite Falmouth. Joining two ends of the B3289, the car- and passenger-carrying **King Harry Ferry** (T01872-862312, kingharryscornwall.co.uk) takes 10 minutes to rattle across a narrow neck of the Fal – and in doing so saves you a 27-mile loop via

Walk this way

If you or your children get a sense of déjà vu at St Anthony, it's probaby because the lighthouse here featured in the animated television series *Fraggle Rock*. Guiding ships into Falmouth Harbour (and away from the Manacles reef), the lighthouse is not open to the public, but there are still some fascinating walks at this westernmost tip of the Roseland Peninsula. Just beyond the car park and holiday cottages are the remains of fortifications where big guns once swept the approach to the Carrick Roads. During the Second World War, a Battery Observation Point was built to monitor the position of enemy ships. You can find it by following the rock-cut ditch path where gun-control officers and signallers once scurried to their posts. Duck inside the concrete bunker and peep through the narrow slit. The views are amazing, stretching from St Mawes Castle across the estuary to Pendennis Castle and beyond to Gyllyngvase beach, Maenporth beach and the Helford rivermouth. Look carefully and you should just make out the Goonhilly satellite dishes pimpling the Lizard. Of course, most children will be more interested in sighting a Nazi U-boat sneaking into the harbour or a full-blown Spanish Armada. In reality, you're more likely to see container ships, oil tankers, yachts, fishing boats and perhaps a Royal Navy Fleet Auxillary ship or destroyer. A short stroll beyond the Observation Point is a bird hide overlooking cliffs above an inaccessible shingle beach. By now your spying skills should be so well-honed that fulmars and even peregrine falcons may fall within your sights.

St Anthony Head
T01872-862945, nationaltrust.org.uk. Year round daily. Free admission.

the A390 and A3078. If travelling by foot, the **St Mawes Ferry** (T01326-313201) plies the Carrick Roads, linking Falmouth and St Mawes in just 20 minutes. Once in St Mawes, head to the **Roseland Visitor Centre** (The Square, TR2 5AG, T01326-270440, stmawesandtheroseland.co.uk) for ferry times, walk leaflets and other information.

Dawdling along the waterfront at St Mawes is pleasant enough – the quayside bakery serves proper pasties or children can fritter some pocket money on the stoneware sculptures of seals and puffins in the Waterside Gallery. The main attraction here, though, is **St Mawes Castle** (see page 172) – a short walk along the seafront. Don't forget shrimping nets as there are some good rock pools along this stretch of coast at low tide. You could also try crabbing off the harbour wall (crab lines are for sale in the post office stores).

You'll know you've reached the Roseland Peninsula when hedgerows start to press in on either side, grass sprouts along the middle of the road like a green mohican and the lane fizzles out in a sleepy fishing village or deserted cove.

When the tide turns, Towan Beach is ripe for rock-pooling.

Off the beaten track The Roseland

Castles & kayaks

Sharing guard duties with Pendennis Castle (see page 176) across the estuary, **St Mawes Castle** (T01326-270526, english-heritage.org. uk, Apr-Nov Sun-Fri from 1000, Nov-Mar Fri-Mon from 1000, £4.20 adult, £2.10 child) is one of the best preserved and most elaborately decorated of Henry VIII's coastal fortresses. A quiz sheet is available to help children appreciate the castle's strategic role in defending the crucial anchorage of the Carrick Roads from French and Spanish fleets. Rather embarrassingly, the castle – though virtually impregnable from the sea – was hopelessly prepared for a land attack during the Civil War. The castle's Royalist commander took one look at the advancing Parliamentarians, ducked briefly as a warning cannon ball whistled overhead, then promptly surrendered.

One of the best ways to admire St Mawes Castle is from the sea and, although the Falmouth ferry passes beneath its ramparts, you can take a more leisurely look by hiring a sea kayak. **St Mawes Sit-on Kayaks** (The Quay, St Mawes, TR2 5DG, T07971-846786, stmaweskayaks.co.uk, Easter-Sep daily 0900-1700) has easy-to-paddle double kayaks (children under 16 must be accompanied by an adult) for £15 for up to two hours, £25 for a four-hour session or £35 for a whole day. Try to hire one of the Peekaboo kayaks (same rates), which have a clear panel built into the hull, allowing you to gaze at the fishes as you paddle. Although sit-on kayaks are extremely stable, you should only venture around St Anthony Head in calm sea conditions. Otherwise, stick to the sheltered Percuil River (separating St Anthony Head from St Mawes) or head up the Carrick Roads to St Just in Roseland, stopping at beaches as you go.

Hit the beach

The nearest good beach to St Mawes is **Towan** – an easily overlooked cove reached by a short walk across fields from the National Trust car park at Porth Farm (on the road between St Anthony and Portscatho). A mixture of coarse sand and pebbles, it is fringed by the sheltered, turquoise-dappled waters of Gerrans Bay and has rock pools at low tide.

Further west, **Pendower** (or Carne) is a mile-long sandy beach overlooked by the exquisite **Nare Hotel** (T01872-501111, narehotel.co.uk), where you might prefer to pop in for a seafood lunch or afternoon tea at the Quarterdeck Restaurant rather than splash the kids' inheritance on an overnight stay (suites cost up to £350 per person per night).

A stunning two-mile cliff walk around Nare Head leads to the tiny fishing hamlet of **Portloe** (also reached by narrow lanes). There's a small shingle cove here at low tide.

Next along the coast are the hidden twin-beauties of **East** and **West Portholland**. You can park at either, but East Portholland has the bigger sandy beach (only exposed as the tide ebbs) and the delightful Journey's End Café, which serves snacks and drinks from the back door of a cottage on the seafront.

Nearby, **Caerhays** (Porthluney Cove) has a beach shop and café, plenty of sand at low tide and a grassy area for retreating to at high tide. Tucked away behind the bay, the castellated mansion of **Caerhays Castle** (T01872-501310, caerhays.co.uk) has lovely gardens to explore.

From Caerhays, it's a squeeze to get down the lanes leading to **Hemmick Beach** – you're better off parking at Penare and walking to this idyllic sandy cove nestled in the lee of Dodman Point.

Canvas & cottages

A short walk from sandy coves, **Trewince Farm** (Portscatho, TR2 5ET, T01872-580430, trewincefarm.co.uk, May-Sep, £10-16) has just 25 pitches – most with sea views. For an equally splendid location, but with holiday park facilities, try **Seaview International** (Boswinger, PL26 6LL, T01726-843425, seaviewinternational.com, Apr-Oct, camping pitches £10-58, static caravans

£245-1034/wk).

A haven for wildlife and a paradise for children, **Pollaughan Cottages** (Portscatho, TR2 5EH, T01872-580150, pollaughan.co.uk, year round, £360-1650/wk) sit pretty on a 22-acre farm. Dragonflies and moorhens make a beeline for the wildlife pond, while kids make a fuss of the two donkeys, four pygmy goats and assorted chickens, ducks and sheep. There's also a soppy black labrador called Bryher, a trampoline, tennis court, safely fenced nature pond and a pick-your-own veggie patch. Porthcurnick Beach, meanwhile, is just a 20-minute stroll away. Choose one of three well-equipped, open plan cottages (sleeping up to six) or opt for the three-bedroom wing of the Victorian farmhouse.

For other self-catering cottages on the Roseland, try **Roseland Holiday Cottages** (T01872-580480, roselandholidaycottages.co.uk).

Splashing out

Designed with families in mind, the **Rosevine** (Portscatho, TR2 5EW, T01872-580206, rosevine. co.uk, £950-2350/wk) is a classy coastal retreat consisting of a Georgian house divided into 12 apartments and suites – each with one or two bedrooms, a sitting and dining area and small kitchen. You can eat 'downstairs', self-cater or do a bit of both. There's even a deli service providing breakfast boxes, packed lunches and freshly prepared supper dishes that you can heat up for a quiet meal in. Rosevine also hits the spot with its excellent facilities: a children's den, indoor pool and wooden play area to name a few. The hotel overlooks Gerrans Bay and has a sandy beach just 140 m from its garden gate.

Grab a bite

Hidden away in the old pilchard fishing village of Portscatho, **Ralph's** (T01872-580702, daily 0700-1900) does a roaring trade in pasties and also stocks a good range of locally caught seafood and other Cornish produce.

From top: St Mawes Ferry; fishing nets and flip-flops; pygmy goat at Pollaughan Farm; digging at Towan; view across Hemmick beach.

The working water mill at **Melinsey** (nr Veryan, T01872-501049) is a peaceful spot for a light lunch or cream tea. There are willow crafts on display and a lovely walk alongside the mill pond.

In St Mawes, stock up on picnic supplies or indulge in a lunch platter or cream tea at **Café Chandlers** (The Quay, T01326-270998, cafechandlers.co.uk). For traditional pub fare, try the **Victory Inn** (T01326-270324, victory-inn.co.uk).

Falmouth

A shipshape mix of historic port, working harbour and Victorian seaside resort, Falmouth makes a great day out – no matter what the shipping forecast. Rainy days might send you scuttling for the brilliant National Maritime Museum, while fair weather raises all kinds of possibilities, from ferry trips along the Fal Estuary to landlubbing on Falmouth's string of sandy town beaches. In fact, once you begin uncovering the wealth of attractions in and around this mighty deepwater refuge (Cornwall's very own Sydney Harbour), you might well be tempted to drop anchor and base yourself here for extended shore leave.

Get your bearings

Ditch the car. It's more fun (and kinder on Falmouth's congested roads) to arrive by ferry. Flying the flag for car-free travel throughout the Fal Estuary, **Fal River Links** (falriverlinks.co.uk, see also pages 176 and 181) represents several ferry operators shuttling back and forth between Falmouth and St Mawes, Flushing, Mylor Yacht Harbour, Trelissick Garden and Truro. One of the most innovative services is the **Falmouth Park & Float** (May-Sep Mon-Fri, first boat 1000, last boat 1740). Leave your car at Ponsharden (just off the A39 as you approach Falmouth), then hop on a ferry that will whisk you straight to **Custom House Quay**, a short swagger from the National Maritime Museum. All-day Float Passes cost £15 for one car and up to seven passengers. Falmouth's other main ferry dock is the nearby **Prince of Wales Pier** where the **tourist information centre** (T01326-312300, discoverfalmouth.co.uk) can be found.

Wise up to the sea

National Maritime Museum
Discovery Quay, Falmouth, TR11 3QY,
T01326-313388, nmmc.co.uk. Daily 1000-1700.
£8.75 adult, £6 child (6-15), £24 family.
The next best thing to messing about in boats on
the sea, this outstanding museum is awash with
nautical nuggets. Start your voyage of discovery in
the **Main Hall** where an airborne flotilla (suspended
on wires from the ceiling) includes three Olympic-
gold-winning yachts. The 1866 steam launch *Waterlily*
sits sedately beneath them, while the **Survival Zone**
stirs things up with epic tales of endurance at sea
– don't miss the *Edna Maïr*, a tiny dinghy in which the
Robertson family survived for 38 days in the Pacific
after their yacht sank. The **Nav Station** gallery has
plenty of interactive gizmos for mini-skippers (steer a
boat against the tide and make for the safe harbour);
the **Quarterdeck** explores how the design of boats
has been adapted for hunting, fishing or sport; the
Cornwall Galleries are full of yarns about smugglers,
shipwrecks and pilchard fishing, while **The Hold** has
a different exhibition most years (in 2010 the theme
is 'Lighthouses: Life on the Rocks'). Don't forget to
climb to the **Look Out** with its panoramic views over
Falmouth Harbour, or to immerse yourself in the **Tidal
Zone**, which provides a mesmerizing window on the
harbour's marine life, from mullet to barnacles (stand
there long enough and you'll see the tide rise and
fall). To prevent certain mutiny be sure to take plenty
of 50p coins – you'll need them at the **Waterfront**,
where radio-controlled yachts can be steered
across an indoor pool that's ingeniously strafed by
an artificial breeze. For a breath of real sea air, step
outside onto the **Museum Pontoon** to see which
historic boats have called into port. The museum also
has a waterside café and a gift shop overflowing with
books, model boats and other maritime nicknacks.

*Witchcraft – model boats
'fly' through the National
Maritime Museum as if by magic.
Right: the museum's Tidal Zone.*

Let's go to... Falmouth

Fine art & fortresses

Largest and most intact of Cornwall's castles, **Pendennis Castle** (Castle Dr, TR11 4LP, T01326-316594, english-heritage.org.uk, year round daily from 1000, £6 adult, £3 child (5-15), £15 family) squats on a headland just to the east of Falmouth Docks and offers superb views across the estuary to its partner castle at St Mawes (see page 172). Originally built by Henry VIII to guard the harbour against the threat of French and Spanish warships, the fort is now a military time capsule with Tudor guns, First World War guard house and Second World War tunnels. It's an exciting place to explore, with activity sheets, workshops and events for children during the summer holidays.

Equally family-friendly, the **Falmouth Art Gallery** (The Moor, TR11 2RT, T01326-313863, falmouthartgallery.com, year round Mon-Sat 1000-1700, free admission) has been a recipient of the *Guardian* newspaper's Kids in Museums award. There's nothing hushed or stuffy about this place. Noise is positively welcomed and there are activities for children of all ages, including babies.

Hit the beach

Closest to the town centre, **Castle Beach** is overlooked by Pendennis Castle and is a good spot for rock pools and a picnic. Next door is **Gyllyngvase**, Falmouth's most popular beach with a Blue Flag Award, safe swimming and lots of facilities, including toilets, lifeguard, deckchair hire, lost child centre and the Gylly Beach Café (see opposite). The sand here is just the right consistency for satisfying sandcastles. Follow the coast path west over the headland and you will find **Swanpool Beach**, a sheltered sand and pebble cove with crazy golf and a café. Just inland

Gyllyngvase Beach.

is Swanpool Nature Reserve where you can see ducks, swans and the occasional kingfisher on a brackish lagoon. A mile south of Falmouth, **Maenporth** is a sandy beach sheltered from the wind by low cliffs and offering watersports such as sea kayaking and windsurfing.

Falmouth Harbour.

Take to the water

Orca Sea Safaris (Discovery Quay, TR11 3QY, T01326-214928, orcaseasafaris.co.uk, daily, minimum age 6) runs wildlife cruises from Falmouth in its fast, 12-seat RIB. The one-hour Bay Discovery (£24 adult, £16 child, £75 family) zips across Falmouth Bay in search of seals and seabirds. The two-hour Coastal Explorer (£39.50 adult, £28 child, £125 family) ventures further afield, giving you a better chance of dolphin and basking shark sightings, while the half-day Kids' Education Experience (£40 person) combines a two-hour cruise with two hours of expert-guided rock-pooling.

Offering summer boat trips from Customs House Quay, **Newmans Cruises** (T01872-580309, newmanscruises.co.uk, May-Sep Mon-Sat departures at 1100, 1300 and 1500, return fares £9 adult, £4.50 child) head upriver to the wooded wonderland of Trelissick Gardens – see page 178 for details of cruises from Truro to the gardens, and page 181 for other Fal River Link services.

To take control of the helm yourself, make your way to Mylor Yacht Harbour where **Mylor Boat Hire** (Mylor, TR11 5UF, T01326-377745, mylorboathire.co.uk) has a veritable armada for hire, from family motorboats and traditional sailing yawls to zippy RIBs. Expect to pay around £17 per hour or £70 per day for a four-person motor boat.

Further up the estuary, **Loe Beach Boat Hire** (Feock, TR3 6SH, T01872-864295, loebeach.

co.uk) can kit you out with various sail-, paddle- and motor-powered craft, and also has an RYA Watersports Centre.

Cornish Diving (Bar Rd, Falmouth, TR11 4BN, T01326-313178, cornishdiving.co.uk) offers pool-based Bubblemaker courses for small fry as young as eight, while the **Falmouth Surf School** (Woodlane Close, Falmouth, TR11 4QU, T01326-212144, falmouthsurfschool.co.uk) takes board riders in search of Cornwall's best waves. A half-day course (£25) will get you up and standing, while full-day tuition (£40) will perfect your jump-up. At just £15, the school holiday Grommet Course for nine- to 13-year-olds is excellent value.

If your grommets are also into raft building, coasteering, kayaking, sailing and windsurfing, sign them up for the Kids' Club at **Elemental UK** (Swanpool Beach, T01326-318771 or 07795 480474, elementaluk.com, Sat-Sun during school holidays, £15/half day, £28/full day).

Check in
Falmouth Beach Resort Hotel (Gyllyngvase Beach, T01326-310500, bw-falmouthbeachhotel. co.uk, B&B £69-77 adult, £17-19 child (5-10), £34-38 child (11-15); cottage and apartments £478-999/ wk) offers versatile accommodation, including family suites, two self-catering apartments and a three-bed cottage. Facilities include babysitting, early mealtimes for children and a swimming pool.

For holiday cottages in and around Falmouth, check out the selection at **Falmouth Holiday Cottages** (falmouthholidaycottages.net).

Grab a bite
A crisp, battered crust above the rest, **Harbour Lights Fish & Chips** (Arwenack St, T01326-316934, harbourlights.co.uk) has a takeaway and sit-down restaurant with great views of the harbour. Also enjoying a prime waterfront location, **Pizza Express** (Maritime House, T01326-318841, pizzaexpress.com) overlooks Discovery Quay near the National Maritime Museum. For Falmouth's ultimate seaview meal, however, the **Gylly Beach Café** (Cliff Rd, T01326-312884, gyllybeach. com) is right on Gyllyngvase Beach. The Gylly's clean, minimalist style makes it feel like there's nothing between you, the beach and the ocean. Watch the waves, the ships moored offshore and the distant lighthouse on St Anthony's Head, while you tuck into a varied menu that includes breakfast treats like waffles with berry compote, honey and yoghurt (£5.95), lunch snacks such as salmon and dill fish cakes (£7.95) and dinner mains (from £10) such as crab and crayfish linguine. For more upmarket dining, try **The Three Mackerel** (T01326-311886, thethreemackerel.com) at Swanpool Beach.

Falmouth Beach Resort Hotel.

Let's go to...

Truro

Let's face it. The vast majority of families on holiday in Cornwall are unlikely to put Truro on their 'must do' list. The capital of the Duchy of Cornwall just seems to get in the way, particularly if you're trying to drive to Falmouth or the Lizard on the A39 and get snarled up in traffic on its outskirts. Don't be too hasty, however, in wanting to bypass Cornwall's only city. Not only does Truro have a magnificent cathedral and the county's best museum, but it can also be the staging post for adventures downriver.

Get your bearings

It can be a nightmare trying to park in Truro, so leave your car at the park-and-ride (Langarth Park on the A390 at Threemilestone). Buses stop at the Royal Cornwall Museum and Victoria Square, from where it's a short walk along St Nicholas Street and Boscawen Street to reach the **tourist information centre** (T01872-274555). Cut through Cathedral Lane to reach Truro's fine Gothic pile, or head down Lemon Street to the local produce and Fairtrade market or **Plaza Cinema** (T01872-272894). Leading from Lemon Street, Back Quay provides access to the theatre, **Hall for Cornwall** (T01872-262466, hallforcornwall.co.uk).

City highlights

Free to enter, the **Royal Cornwall Museum** (River St, TR1 2SJ, T01872-272205, royalcornwallmuseum. org.uk, Mon-Sat 1000-1645) has a busy schedule of family events, including treasure trails, craft activities and storytelling. You can also pick up Explorer Backpacks (£1) to help kids interpret the exhibits in the main gallery where 5000 years of Cornish history are revealed. The Bonython Gallery has displays on Cornish habitats and wildlife with a special discovery area for families, while the Rashleigh Gallery is all-a-glitter with minerals and gems. Upstairs, there's a small gallery with a quirky collection of Egyptian artefacts, including the 2500-year-old mummy of Ast Tayef Nakht. The River Street Café in the museum's lobby has a good selection of sandwiches and paninis, as well as soup, home-made cakes, fresh fruit juices, smoothies and Roskilly's ice cream.

You can't miss **Truro Cathedral** (St Mary's St, T01872-276782, trurocathedral.org.uk, Mon-Sat from 0730, Sun from 0900, free admission). The Neo-Gothic landmark (built from Cornish granite between 1880 and 1910) has a spire rising 76 m above the street. Inside, there are spectacular vaulted arches and stained glass windows.

City escapes

Departing from Truro's Town Quay, **Enterprise Boats** (T01326-374241, enterprise-boats.co.uk, call for family rates) provides a seasonal ferry link between the city and Falmouth (or St Mawes), stopping en route at **Trelissick Gardens** (Feock, TR3 6QL, T01872-862090, nationaltrust.org.uk, year round daily from 1030, £7 adult, £3.50 child, £17.50 family). With woodland spilling down to the estuary shore, this tranquil garden has two circular walks. Neither takes more than about 45 minutes, so you've got plenty of time for a stroll before hopping on the next Falmouth-bound ferry.

Above: Barbed message – the Royal Cornwall Museum bristles with intriguing exhibits, including this Stone Age arrowhead.

Neo-Gothic marvel –
Truro Cathedral.

Grown-ups' stuff Cornwall

Inroads

Getting there

By car Reach the end of the M5 near Exeter, then it's decision time – either take the **A30**, looping north of Dartmoor, and enter Cornwall just before Launceston (your best option if you're heading for the north coast or far west), or take the **A38**, dipping below Dartmoor and crossing the Tamar Bridge (£1 toll eastbound only) into South Cornwall. If you fancy a detour through North Devon, you could also reach Cornwall by taking either the A361 or A377 to Barnstaple before picking up the **A39** Atlantic Highway (breezing into Cornwall just north of Bude). You can also join the A39 at junction 27 of the M5.

The A30 shoulders the heaviest load of traffic, but it is dual carriageway most of the way to Penzance, with single-carriageway sections at Temple, near Bodmin, and also between Carland Cross (where the A39 goes south to Truro) and the Three Burrows roundabout (where you can head south on the A390 to Truro or north on the A3075 to Newquay). Peak-time delays are likely at these locations – try to avoid travelling on Fridays (1500-1800) or Saturdays (1000-1700).

By coach Falmouth, Newquay, Penzance, St Austell, St Ives, Truro and most other main centres in Cornwall are served by **National Express** (T08717-818178, nationalexpress.com), with connecting services from Bristol, Birmingham and London.

By ferry Chain ferries shuttle back and forth across the Tamar between Devonport and Torpoint every 10 minutes at peak times. The fare – only payable eastbound – is the same as using the toll bridge (see left). Contact **Tamar Crossings** (tamarcrossings.org. uk) for more details.

By plane Several airlines serve **Newquay Cornwall Airport** (newquaycornwallairport.com),

Click ahead
Useful travel planning websites include: theaa.com, nationalrail. co.uk, rac.co.uk, seat61.com and traveline.info.

including the county's very own budget airline, **Air Southwest** (T0870-241 8202, airsouthwest. com), which has flights from Bristol, Cork, Dublin, Glasgow, Leeds, London City, London Gatwick, Manchester and Newcastle from £29, including taxes. Car hire with Avis can also be booked through the airline.

Other services to Newquay Airport are offered by **BMI Baby** (T0871-224 0224, bmibaby. com) from Manchester and Birmingham; **Flybe** (T0871-700 2000, flybe.com) from London Gatwick, Edinburgh and the Isle of Man; **Jet2.com** (T0871-226 1737, jet2.com) from Belfast and Leeds, and **Ryanair** (T0871-246 0000, ryanair.com) from London Stansted.

By train Operated by **First Great Western** (T08457-000 125, firstgreatwestern.co.uk), the direct London Paddington to Penzance service takes between five and six hours, calling at Liskeard, Bodmin, Par, St Austell, Truro, Redruth, Camborne, Hayle and St Erth (see page 182 for branchline connections). Expect to pay around £80 for an adult return fare, £40 for a child (5-15), but check online for special offers.

A30 pit stops

A386 junction Fuel (north- and southbound).
B3257 junction Fuel and Subway (southbound only).
B3274 junction Fuel (north- and southbound).
B3275 junction Fuel, Premier Inn and McDonalds (northbound only).
A39 junction Fuel (accessible north- and southbound).
A390/3075 junction Fuel and Starbucks (north- and southbound).
A3074/3301 junction Fuel, Travelodge, McDonalds, Boots Midnight Pharmacy, M&S, Next, Costa Coffee (north- and southbound).
Penzance outskirts Morrisons, McDonalds, 24-hour Tesco (including fuel).

Isle be bound (getting to the Scillies)

British International Helicopters (T01736-363871, islesofscillyhelicopter.com) flies from Penzance Heliport to St Mary's and Tresco in around 20 minutes, daily except Sundays. Day trip return fares are £96 for adults, £60 for children (under 15) and £20 for infants (under 2); period returns cost from £145, £90 and £50 respectively. **Isles of Scilly Travel** (T0845-710 5555, ios-travel.co.uk) operates Skybus services to the islands, Monday-Saturday, from Bristol, Exeter, Land's End, Newquay and Southampton, using Twin Otter and Islander aircraft capable of carrying up to 19 people. As a guide, expect to pay around £145 for an adult saver return and £82 for a child (2-15), departing from Land's End Airport. The *Scillonian III* (book through Isles of Scilly Travel) sails throughout the summer (Mon-Sat, plus occasional Sun departures) leaving Penzance at 0915 and arrives at St Mary's around 1200. Expect to pay around £80 for an adult saver return, £40 for a child (2-15). Day trip returns are £35 and £17.50 respectively.

Getting around

Public transport timetables can be downloaded from cornwallpublictransport.info.

By bicycle Cornwall has several excellent cycling trails, including the **Camel Trail** (see page 38), the **Coast to Coast Trail** (page 70) and the newly extended **Mineral Tramways Mining Trails** (page 70) centred around Camborne and Redruth – all of which are ideal for families.

By bus All operators offer free travel for under-fives. **First Group** (T0845-600 1420, firstgroup.com) has a FirstDay Cornwall ticket (£6.50 adult, £4.30 child, £15.50 family) allowing unlimited travel throughout Cornwall. For unlimited travel on **Western Greyhound** (T01637-871871, westerngreyhound.com) choose the Day Explorer (£7 adult, £4.50 child, £14 family)

Truro's park and ride

(T01872-279270, parkfortruro.org.uk) operates from Langarth Park, Threemilestone (A390), Monday-Saturday 0700-1900.

The **Ride Cornwall** one-day travel pass is valid on CrossCountry and First Great Western trains and all First and Western Greyhound bus services for £10 adult, £7.50 child, £24 family and also gives you 10% off ferry fares between Falmouth, St Mawes and Truro.

By car Car hire is available from **Avis** (Newquay Airport and Truro, T08445-446109; avis.co.uk), **Cornwall Car Hire** (Newquay, T01637-850971, cornwallcarhire.co.uk), **Enterprise** (Penryn T01326-373355, enterprise.co.uk), **Europcar** (Newquay Airport, T01637-860337, europcar.co.uk), **Hertz** (Newquay Airport, T01637-860869, hertz.co.uk) and **St Ives Car Hire** (T0845-057

⊜ Scenic bus rides

Scenic bus rides on First buses:
35 Falmouth–Mawnan Smith–Helford Passage–Glendurgan and Trebah–Constantine–Gweek–Flambards–RNAS Culdrose–Helston.
81B Plymouth–Torpoint Ferry–Sheviock–Crafthole–Seaton–Hessenford–East Looe–Polperro.
300 Penzance–Newlyn–Porthcurno–Land's End–Sennen Cove–St Just–Botallack–Geevor Tin Mine–Zennor–St Ives–Carbis Bay–Marazion–Penzance (route operates clockwise and anti-clockwise).

Scenic bus rides on Western Greyhound buses:
501 Newquay–Perran Sands–St Agnes–Porthtowan–Portreath–Godrevy–Hayle Towans–St Ives.
556 Newquay–Porth–Watergate Bay–Tregurrian–Newquay Airport–Mawgan Porth–Porthcothan–Constantine Bay–St Merryn–Harlyn Bay–Padstow.
584 Wadebridge–Rock–Polzeath–Port Isaac–Camelford
594 Wadebridge–Camelford–Tintagel–Boscastle.
595 Boscastle–Crackington Haven–Widemouth Bay–Bude.

9373, stivescarhire.co.uk). For ultimate surf chic (or just a great family touring holiday), hire a VW campervan from **Cornwall Campers** (T01872-571988, cornwallcampers.co.uk). Weekly rates start at around £500.

By ferry There are 16 ferry services in Cornwall. A network of ferries, boats, buses and trains, **Fal River Links** (T01872-861914, falriverlinks.co.uk, see also pages 170, 174 and 176) is a one-stop shop for car-free travel in the Falmouth area. Services include: **Enterprise Boats** (T01326-374241, enterprise-boats.co.uk) linking Truro, Falmouth, St Mawes and Trelissick Gardens; **Falmouth Park & Float** (see page 174), **King Harry Ferry** (T01872-862312, kingharryscornwall. co.uk, see page 170) saving 27 miles on the road trip between St Mawes and Falmouth, and **St Mawes Ferry** (T01872-861910, kingharryscornwall.co.uk) crossing the Fal between St Mawes and Falmouth.

Other fun (and useful) ferry routes to try include Calstock–Cotehele Quay (page 157), Mevagissey–Fowey (page 155) and Padstow–Rock (page 48).

By foot You can plan short forays on the 630-mile **South West Coast Path** by logging onto the official website, southwestcoastpath.com.

By plane Scenic flights over the Penwith Peninsula and to the Isles of Scilly (see page 181) are available at **Land's End Airport** (T01736-788771, landsendairport.co.uk).

😊 Kids' gear

Stock up on family travel essentials at the following websites: lioninthesun.com, minicontego.com, muddypuddles.com, nomadtravel. co.uk, simplypicnic.co.uk, sun-togs. co.uk and youngexplorers.co.uk.

By train Scenic branch lines (greatscenicrailways.com) include **St Erth–St Ives**, following the shores of the Hayle Estuary and St Ives Bay with stops at Lelant and Carbis Bay (see page 111); **Truro–Falmouth**, a half-hourly service linking Perranwell and Penryn; **Par–Newquay**, a route joining the north and south coasts, and **Liskeard–Looe**, an hourly service through the Looe Valley. Buses run to the Eden Project from St Austell station and Helston from Redruth station.

Family holiday operators
Encounter Cornwall (T01208-871066, encountercornwall.com, see also page 156) offers cycling and walking and multi-activity breaks. A three-day cycling tour combining the traffic-free Camel Trail and Clay Trails with the quiet back lanes of the Cornish Way costs from around £235 per person, including bike hire, B&B and luggage transfer. **Footsteps of Discovery** (T07899-928131, footstepsofdiscovery.co.uk) runs family survival weekends in a Cornish wood where you learn all the basics – from fire lighting to building a shelter (that you

MINERAL TRAMWAYS

Mining Trails
walk • cycle • ride

www.cornwall.gov.uk/mineral-tramways
www.cornishmining.org.uk
E&HAdmin@cornwall.gov.uk
Tel: 0300 1234 202

CORNISH MINING
WORLD HERITAGE

Online resources

Cornwall Tourist Board
visitcornwall.com

Regional tourist information
Bodmin
bodminlive.com

Boscastle & Tintagel
visitboscastleandtintagel.com

Bude
visitbude.info

Camelford
visitcamelford.co.uk

Falmouth
discoverfalmouth.co.uk

Fowey
fowey.co.uk

Isles of Scilly
simplyscilly.co.uk

Launceston
visitlaunceston.co.uk

Liskeard
liskeard.gov.uk

Looe
visit-southeastcornwall.co.uk

Newquay
visitnewquay.org

Padstow
padstowlive.com

Penzance, St Ives & St Just
visit-westcornwall.com

Redruth
cornwall.gov.uk/cornwallcentre

St Austell
cornish-riviera.co.uk

St Mawes
roselandinfo.com

Truro
truro.gov.uk

Further information
BBC Cornwall
bbc.co.uk/cornwall

British Surfing Association
britsurf.co.uk

Cornwall Tourist Attractions
cata.co.uk

Cornwall County Council
cornwall.gov.uk

Cornish Food & Drink
foodfromcornwall.co.uk

Cornish Mining World Heritage Site
cornish-mining.org.uk

English Heritage
english-heritage.org.uk

Forestry Commission
forestry.gov.uk

Gardens of Cornwall
gardensofcornwall.com

National Trust
nationaltrust.org.uk

Royal National Lifeboat Institution
rnli.org.uk/beachsafety

South West Coast Path
nationaltrail.co.uk

South West Lakes Trust
swlakestrust.org.uk

Sustrans
sustrans.org.uk

Surf forecast
magicseaweed.com

Tide charts
bbc.co.uk/weather/coast/tides/

Environmental groups
Blue Flag beaches
blueflag.org

Cornwall Sustainable Tourism
cstn.org.uk

Cornwall Wildlife Trust
cornwallwildlifetrust.org.uk

Duchy of Cornwall
duchyofcornwall.org

Environment Agency
environment-agency.gov.uk

Isles of Scilly Wildlife Trust
ios-wildlifetrust.org.uk

Marine Conservation Society
mcsuk.org

Natural England
naturalengland.org.uk

RSPB
rspb.org.uk

Surfers against Sewage
sas.org.uk

spend your second night in).
Outdoor Adventure (T01288-362900, outdooradventure.co.uk, see page 36) operates a residential outdoor centre overlooking Widemouth Bay, near Bude. Family holidays are available here during July and August and cost £676 per week for adults and £558 per week for children (eight to14) all inclusive. You just need to decide what activities to do.

Which map?

Ordnance Survey (ordnancesurvey.co.uk) produces a general touring map of Cornwall (Tour 1). For more detail, choose a Landranger map; for walking and other activites go for an Explorer map.
Landranger maps:
190 Bude & Clovelly
200 Newquay & Bodmin
201 Plymouth & Launceston
203 Land's End & Isles of Scilly
204 Truro & Falmouth

Explorer maps:
101 Isles of Scilly
102 Land's End
103 The Lizard
104 Redruth & St Agnes
105 Falmouth & Mevagissey
106 Newquay & Padstow
107 St Austell & Liskeard
108 Lower Tamar Valley & Plymouth
109 Bodmin Moor
111 Bude, Boscastle & Tintagel
112 Launceston & Holsworthy

Grown-ups' stuff Cornwall

Tots to teens

There's something for all ages in Cornwall, from nappy-bound beach blobs shovelling sand into their mouths, to strutting surf-dude teens trying to stay cool after being dumped by a wave.

Babies (0-18 months)

Renting a cottage or holiday caravan gives you the flexibility and independence to maintain those all-important baby-care routines. Look for properties that provide baby gear to save you having to pack cots, sterilisers etc. For a spot of adult relaxation, several family-friendly hotels offer crèches or baby-listening services. **Baby Friendly Boltholes** (babyfriendlyboltholes.co.uk) is a good place to start.

Weever fish.

🔴 **This** hurts

Cornwall is generally very safe. Most serious accidents happen when people ignore warnings from beach lifeguards (see page 5) or stray too near cliff edges. You should also be wary of weever fish, buried in sand at the low-water mark on North Cornwall beaches with just five poisonous spines protruding from their backs. The sting can be excruciating. Submersion in very hot water is the best treatment. Better still, wear wetsuit boots when in the sea at low tide.

Toddlers/pre-school (18 months-4 years)

Make sure your cottage or holiday park is as toddler-proof as possible with enclosed gardens, fenced-off pools, stair gates etc. Days on the beach demand vigilance with this age group, but they can also burn off energy in more carefree situations, such as one of Cornwall's farm parks – many of which have soft play areas.

Kids/school age (4-12 years)

These are probably the best years to take kids on a camping holiday – it's still an adventure for them and they can help out with basic chores, like fetching water. Cornwall has stunning campsites – some a barefoot stroll from the beach. King Arthur and his knights often storm onto junior school curriculums, so a visit to Tintagel is a must. You can also exercise young minds at historic properties owned by the National Trust and English Heritage, or at one of Cornwall's science centres, zoos or aquariums. A great way to enforce beach safety, surf lessons usually have a minimum age of eight.

Teenagers (13 years+)

Cornwall can be very cool. Teens will thrive at north coast surf resorts like Bude and Newquay with their non-stop beach sports, trendy beach cafés and designer shops, while quieter locations like Fowey will suit active types passionate about learning to sail. Some holiday parks and hotels

Child's play – Praa Sands.

have special clubs and activities for teenagers (far more preferable to Newquay's nightlife). Renting a large property which you can share with friends who also have teenagers is often a good way to keep teen strops at bay.

Single-parent families

Check with attractions to see if they offer single-parent family admission (cheaper than the normal family rate based on two adults and two children). With their organized activities and onsite entertainment, holiday parks are a good way to meet up with other families. **Single Parent Fun** (singleparentfun. com) has plenty of suggestions for days out and things to do, while **Cornwall Council** (cornwall. gov.uk) organizes Father and Son

🔘 **Shop** ahead

Before you leave home, order fresh, local Cornish produce and other food essentials online at food4myholiday.com and it will be delivered direct to your holiday cottage (and even put in the fridge) ready for your arrival.

★ **Holiday** heaven

Offering the UK's widest choice of self-catering holidays, **Hoseasons** (hoseasons.co.uk) has nearly 50 lodges and parks to choose from in Cornwall, from lively Holywell Bay to laid-back Sea Acres, plus a great range of country cottages.

Weekends at its four outdoor education centres (see below).

Special needs

Several holiday operators, such as Gwel an Mor near Portreath and Pollaughan Farm on the Roseland Peninsula have accommodation specially designed for wheelchair users. The **Cornwall Access Awareness Partnership** (cstn. org.uk) promotes accessible local services, while **Disability Now** (disabilitynow.org.uk) lists accessible hotels, cottages and B&Bs. **Disability Cornwall** (disabilitycornwall.org.uk) is also a good source of information.

Dog owners

Cornwall Tourism (see page 189) produces a leaflet detailing dog-friendly beaches and attractions.

⚙ **Active** tykes

Holiday activities – from sailing to survival courses – are available at outdoor education centres (cornwall.gov.uk) at Carnyorth (nr St Just, T01736-786344), Delaware (nr Gunnislake, T01822-833885), Porthpean (nr St Austell, T01726-72901) and St Just in Roseland (T01326-270885).

✚ **Beach** safety

Beach lifeguards patrol popular beaches during the main season. **Red and yellow flags** show lifeguarded areas – the safest place to swim, bodyboard and use inflatables. **Black and white chequered flags** show areas for surfboards and other non-powered craft – never swim or bodyboard here. **Orange windsocks** show offshore winds, so never use an inflatable when the sock is flying. **Red flags** mean danger! Never go in the water when the red flag is flying under any circumstances. See also page 5.

Cottages & holiday parks

Cottage agents
Cornwall wide – see individual chapters for local agents.

Blue Chip Vacations
T0844-561 2001,
bluechipvacations.com

Child Friendly Cottages
childfriendlycottages.co.uk

Classic Cottages
T01326-555555
classic.co.uk

Cornish Cottage Holidays
T01326-573808
cornishcottageholidays.co.uk

Cornish Cottages
T01326-240333
cornishcottagesonline.com

Cornish Gems
cornishgems.com

Cornish Traditional Cottages
T01208-821666
corncott.com

Cornwalls Cottages
T01872-264441
cornwallscottages.co.uk

Duchy Holidays
T01872-572971
duchyholidays.co.uk

English Country Cottages
T0845-268 0785
english-country-cottages.co.uk

Helpful Holidays
T01647-433593
helpfulholidays.com

Hideaways
T01747-828170
hideaways.co.uk

National Trust Holiday Cottages
T0844-800 2070
nationaltrustcottages.co.uk

Powells Cottage Holidays
T01834-812791
powells.co.uk

Premier Cottages
T0114-275 1477
premiercottages.co.uk

Southwest Holiday Cottages
T01752-260711
southwestholidaycottages.com

Toad Hall Cottages
T01503-272303
toadhallcottages.co.uk

Welcome Cottages
welcomecottages.com

West Country Cottages
T01803-814000
westcountrycottages.co.uk

Holiday park companies
See individual chapters for listings of parks.

Haven
T0871-230 1930
haven.com

Hoseasons
T0844-847 1103
hoseasons.co.uk

John Fowler Holiday Parks
T01271-866766
johnfowlerholidays.com

Parkdean
T0844-335 3623
parkdean.com

Family websites

all4kidsuk.com
askamum.co.uk
childfriendly.co.uk
family-travel.co.uk
mumsnet.com
takethefamily.com
travellingwithchildren.co.uk
babygoes2.com

Parkdean

We've got the **biggest** choice of award winning parks in Cornwall

Whether you're looking for a fun-filled family holiday by the beach or a relaxing stay in the glorious Cornish countryside, we have a park for you.

Located in beautiful Cornish spots by Newquay, The Lizard, Looe and Rock, our family parks have superb caravan and lodge accommodation with fantastic indoor and outdoor facilities to keep the kids happy all day long!

- Kids' clubs from tots to teens
- Swimming pools, play areas, mini ten pin bowling and mini golf
- Sports courts, archery, laser combat plus agility and assault courses
- Surf & dive schools and Blue Flag beaches nearby
- Live family evening entertainment
- Choice of bars and restaurants
- Excellent touring & camping facilities

To find out more about each park's facilities or to order a brochure call us now on **0844 335 3623** or click parkdean.com

Information correct at time of going to print. Some activities may be restricted to school holiday periods. Only selected parks offer touring & camping facilities.

Grown-ups' stuff Cornwall

Essentials

Baby supplies
Truro Mothercare, Pydar St.

Camping supplies
Penzance Millets, Market Jew St.
St Agnes Aztec Leisure, Trevellas.

Doctors & medical centres
Bude The Stratton Medical Centre, Hospital Rd, Stratton, EX23 9BP, T01288-352133.
Falmouth Trescobeas Surgery, Trescobeas Rd, TR11 2UN, T01326-315615.
Helston Helston Medical Centre, Trelawney Rd, TR13 8AU, T01326-572637.
Mevagissey Mevagissey Surgery, River St, PL26 6UE, T01726-843701.
Newquay The Health Centre, St Thomas Rd, TR7 1RU, T01637-872956.
Penzance Bellair Clinic, Alverton Rd, TR18 4TA, T01736-575500.
Redruth Manor Surgery, Forth Noweth, TR15 1AU, T01209-313313.
St Austell The Park Medical Centre, Bridge Rd, PL25 5HE, T01726-73083.
St Ives The Old Stennack School, Stennack, T01736-796413.
St Just Cape Cornwall Surgery, Market St, TR19 7HX, T01736-788306.
Tintagel Tintagel Medical Centre, Bossiney Rd, PL34 0AE, T01840-770214.
Truro Tregony Surgery, Well St, Tregony, TR2 5RT, T01872-530483.

Hospitals
The following hospitals have A&E departments:
Bodmin Bodmin Hospital, Boundary Rd, PL31 2QT, T01208-251300.
Bude Stratton Hospital, Hospital Rd, Stratton, EX23 9BP, T01288-287700.
Falmouth Falmouth Hospital, Trescobeas Rd, TR11 2JA, T01326-434700.
Fowey Fowey Community Hospital, Green Lane, PL23 1DU, T01726-832241 (minor injuries).
Launceston Launceston General Hospital, Link Rd, PL15 9JD, T01566-765650 (minor injuries).
Newquay Newquay Hospital, St Thomas Rd, TR7 1RQ, T01637-893600 (minor injuries unit only).
Penzance West Cornwall Hospital, St Clare St, TR18 2PF, T01736-874000.
Redruth Cambourne Redruth Community Hospital, Longreach House, Barncoose Terrace, TR15 3ER, T01209-881688.
St Austell Penrice Hospital, Porthpean Rd, PL26 6AA, T01726-291100.
Truro Royal Cornwall Hospital Trust, Treliske, TR1 3LJ, T01872-250000.

Pharmacies
Bodmin Day Lewis, Fore St.
Bude Boots, Belle Vue.
Camelford Alliance, Market Sq.
Falmouth Boots, Market St.
Fowey Boots, Fore St.
Hayle Alliance, Fore St.
Helston Steven Hall, Meneage.
Launceston Boots, Broad St.
Looe Looe Pharmacy, Fore St.
Mevagissey Alliance, Fore St.
Newquay Boots, Bank St; Drury's, St Thomas Rd.
Padstow Alliance, Market St.
Penzance Boots, Market Jew St.
Redruth Boots, Fore St.
St Agnes Alliance, Vicarage Rd.
St Austell Alliance, Victoria Place; Boots, Fore St.
St Ives Boots, High St.
St Just Ramsay Pharmacy, Fore St.
St Mawes St Mawes Pharmacy, Kings Rd.
Saltash Lloyds, Fore St.
Tintagel Alliance, Fore St.
Torpoint Alliance, Fore St.
Truro Alliance, Lemon St; Boots, Pydar St.
Wadebridge Day Lewis, Regency Arcade, Molesworth St.

Surf supplies
Fraddon Cornwall Surf Centre, Kingsley Village.
Newquay Ann's Cottage, Fistral Beach.

Supermarkets
Bodmin ASDA, Launceston Rd; Co-operative, St Mary's Rd; Morrisons, Priory Rd; Sainsbury's, Dennison Rd.
Bude Co-operative, Lansdowne Rd; Co-operative, Burn View Rd; Morrisons, Stucley Rd.
Camborne Lidl, North Roskear Rd; Tesco, Wesley St.
Camelford Co-operative, High St.
East Looe Co-operative, Fore St; Spar, Bayview Rd.
Falmouth ASDA, Jennings Rd; Co-

operative, Ponsharden Industrial Estate; Lidl, Falmouth Rd; Tesco, Killigrew St.
Hayle Lidl, Loggans Mill.
Helston Lidl, Penzance Rd; Somerfield, The Parade; Tesco, Clodgey Lane.
Launceston Co-operative, Western Rd; Co-operative, Newport Industrial Estate; Lidl, Hurdon Rd; Tesco, Tailstocks Rd.
Liskeard Morrisons, Plymouth Rd.
Lostwithiel Co-operative, Quay St.
Newlyn Co-operative, The Strand.
Newquay Co-operative, Oakleigh Terrace; Lidl, Treloggan Rd; Morrisons, Treloggan Rd; Sainsbury's, Fore St; Somerfield, Fore St.
Padstow Tesco, Sarah's Lane.
Penzance Lidl, Western Promenade; Morrisons, Eastern Way; Tesco, Branwell Lane.
Perranporth Co-operative, Station Rd.
Port Isaac Co-operative, New Rd.
Redruth Morrisons, Agar Road, Pool; Tesco, Tolgus Hill.
St Austell ASDA, Cromwell Rd; Lidl, East Hill; Tesco, Daniel Lane.
St Ives Co-operative, The Stennack; Tesco, St Ives Rd.
St Just Co-operative, Market Sq.
Saltash Waitrose, Tamar View.
Truro Marks & Spencer, Lemon Quay; Sainsbury's, Treyew Rd; Somerfield, Victoria Sq; Tesco, Garras Wharf.
Wadebridge Co-operative, Jubilee Rd; Lidl, Eddystone Rd; Tesco, West Hill.
West Looe Spar, Princes Sq.

Cornwall Tourist Board
VisitCornwall, Pydar House, Pydar Street, Truro, TR1 1EA.
T 01872-322900
F 01872-322895
Email: enquiries@visitcornwall.com
visitcornwall.com.

Tourist information centres
Bodmin Shire Hall, Mount Folly, PL31 2DQ, T 01208-76616.
Boscastle The Harbour, PL35 0HD, T 01840-250010, visitboscastleandtintagel.com.
Bude Crescent Car Park, EX23 8LE, T 01288-354240, visitbude.info.
Camelford North Cornwall Museum, The Cleave, PL32 9PL, T 01840-212954.
Falmouth 11 Market Strand, Prince of Wales Pier, TR11 3DF, T 01326-312300, acornishriver.co.uk.
Fowey South St, PL23 1AR, T 01726-833616, fowey.co.uk.
Hayle Hayle Library, Commercial Rd, TR27 4DE, T 01736-754399.
Isles of Scilly Hugh Town, St Mary's, T 01720-422536, simplyscilly.co.uk.
Launceston Market House Arcade, Market St, PL15 8EP, T 01566-772321, visitlaunceston.co.uk.
Liskeard Forester's Hall, Pike St, PL14 3JE, T 01579-349148, liskeard.gov.uk.
Looe The Guildhall, Fore St, East Looe, PL13 1AA, T 01503-262072.
Lostwithiel Community Centre, Liddicoat Rd, PL22 0HE, T 01208-872207.
Mevagissey St Georges Sq, PL26 6UB, T 01726-844857.

Newquay Marcus Hill, T 01872-322900, visitnewquay.org.
Padstow Red Brick Building, North Quay, PL28 8AF, T 01841-533449, padstowlive.com.
Penzance Station Approach, TR18 2NF, T 01736-362207, visit-westcornwall.com.
Perranporth Tywarnhayle Sq, TR6 0ER, T 01872-575254.
Redruth Cornwall Centre, Alma Place, TR15 2AT, T 01209-219048, cornwall.gov.uk/cornwallcentre.
St Agnes Churchtown, TR5 0QW, T 01872-554150.
St Austell Bypass Service Station, Southbourne Rd, PL25 4RS, T 01726-879500, visitthecornishriviera.co.uk.
St Just Library, Market St, TR19 7HX, T 01736-788165.
St Ives Guildhall, Street an Pol, TR26 2DS, T 01736-796297.
St Mawes Roseland Visitor Centre, Millennium Rooms, The Square, TR2 5AG, T 01326-270440, roselandinfo.com.
Tintagel Bossiney Rd, PL34 0AJ, T 01840-779084, visitboscastleandtintagel.com.
Truro Boscawen St, TR1 2NE, T 01872-274555, truro.gov.uk.

Toys & beach gear
Bude Wonder Years, Queen St.
Falmouth Toymaster, Arwenack St.
Mullion Cornish Kites, Meaver Rd.
Newquay Venus, Tolcarne Beach.
Padstow Dukeswood Toys & Craft, Duke St.
Port Isaac The Gullery, Fore St.
Watergate Bay Venus, Watergate Bay Beach.

Index

credits

Footprint credits

Project Editor: Jo Williams
Text Editor: William Gray
Picture Editor: William Gray
Proofreader: Sophie Jones
Layout & production: William Gray
Maps: Kevin Feeney

Managing Director: Andy Riddle
Commercial Director: Patrick Dawson
Publisher: Alan Murphy
Publishing managers: Felicity Laughton,
Jo Williams
Digital Editor: Alice Jell
Design: Mytton Williams
Marketing: Liz Harper, Hannah Bonnell
Sales: Jeremy Parr
Advertising: Renu Sibal
Finance & administration: Elizabeth Taylor

Print

Manufactured in India by Nutech.

Footprint Feedback

We try as hard as we can to make each Footprint guide as up to date as possible but, of course, things always change. If you want to let us know about your experiences – good, bad or ugly – then don't delay, go to footprinttravelguides. com and send in your comments.

Photography credits

All photographs by William Gray, except:
p107 (pasty) and p113 (Porthmeor Beach)
Stephen Aaron Rees/Shutterstock.
p116 (helicopter) Bjorn Heller/Shutterstock.

Publishing information

Footprint Cornwall with Kids, 1st edition
© Footprint Handbooks Ltd, April 2010

ISBN 978-1-906098-96-4
CIP DATA: A catalogue record for this book is available from the British Library

* Footprint Handbooks and the Footprint mark are a registered trademark of Footprint Handbooks Ltd

Published by Footprint

6 Riverside Court
Lower Bristol Road
Bath BA2 3DZ, UK
T +44 (0)1225 469141
F +44 (0)1225 469461
discover@footprinttravelguides.com
footprinttravelguides.com

Distributed in North America by

Globe Pequot Press, Guilford, Connecticut

Ordnance Survey This product includes mapping data licensed from Ordnance Survey® with the permission of the Controller of Her Majesty's Stationery Office. © Crown Copyright. All rights reserved. Licence No. 100027877.

Acknowledgements

A family effort, this book would not have been possible (nor nearly as much fun to research) without the huge support, enthusiasm, beach critiques, ice-cream tasting and tent-pitching skills of Joseph and Eleanor Gray, and their mother, Sally. The author would also like to offer special thanks to Julia Cox at VisitCornwall for her valuable advice and support.